# GRIDIRON GENIUS

# GRIDIRON GENIUS

## A MASTER CLASS IN WINNING CHAMPIONSHIPS
## AND BUILDING DYNASTIES IN THE NFL

### MICHAEL LOMBARDI

**CROWN
ARCHETYPE**
NEW YORK

Crown Archetype and colophon is a registered trademark
of Penguin Random House LLC.

Library of Congress Cataloging-in-Publication Data
Names: Lombardi, Michael, 1959– author.
Title: Gridiron genius : a master class in winning championships and building
    dynasties in the NFL / Michael Lombardi.
Description: First edition. | New York : Crown Archetype, 2018.
Identifiers: LCCN 2018012339 | ISBN 9780525573814 (hardback) | ISBN
    9780525573838 (ebk)
Subjects: LCSH: National Football League—Management. | BISAC: SPORTS &
    RECREATION / Football. | BIOGRAPHY & AUTOBIOGRAPHY / Sports. |
    SPORTS & RECREATION / Coaching / Football.
Classification: LCC GV955.5.N35 L66 2018 | DDC 796.332/64—dc23
LC record available at https://lccn.loc.gov/2018012339

ISBN 978-0-525-57381-4
Ebook ISBN 978-0-525-57383-8

PRINTED IN THE UNITED STATES OF AMERICA

Book design by Andrea Lau
Jacket design by Elena Giavaldi
Jacket photograph: Boston Globe/Getty Images

10 9 8 7 6 5 4 3 2 1

First Edition

*For Millie,*
*My Summer Wind, without whom nothing else matters.*

# CONTENTS

FOREWORD BY BILL BELICHICK      ix

## INTRODUCTION
JUMPING THE ROUTE      1

## 1 THE ORGANIZATION
CULTURE BEATS EVERYTHING      9

## 2 THE COACH
A STUDY IN LEADERSHIP      27

WHAT TO ASK AN NFL HEAD COACH CANDIDATE      51

## 3 TEAM BUILDING
IN SEARCH OF PROGRAM GUYS      63

## 4 SPECIAL TEAMS

THE MEANING OF ALL-IN                    94

## 5 OFFENSE

FINDING THE SEAMS                    111

## 6 DEFENSE

WHERE SIMPLICITY IS COMPLEX                    138

## 7 GAME PLANNING

PREPARING TO IMPROVISE                    167

## 8 WHILE I HAVE YOU

MY BIGGEST PET PEEVES                    202

## 9 WWBD

WHAT WOULD BELICHICK DO?                    225

## 10 FEARLESS FORECAST

THE FUTURE OF FOOTBALL                    241

ACKNOWLEDGMENTS                    260

INDEX                    267

# BILL BELICHICK

A lot of people write books about football. But only a few of them have Mike Lombardi's credentials.

In 1991, when I became the head coach of the Cleveland Browns, one of the first things that I addressed was our scouting system, and for that I turned to Mike Lombardi. Mike and I worked together on building a grading scale and value system for college scouting that would be consistent with our pro scale. Mike directed Dom Anile, our director of college scouting, and Jim Schwartz, a college scouting assistant, to refine, cross-check, and re-cross-check that system until they had created something that still works today.

Mike was brilliant. The value system and scouting manual he developed were unique, because each player's skill evaluation incorporated the priorities of our coaches (including Nick Saban, defense; Ozzie Newsome, offense; Scott O'Brien, special teams; Pat Hill and Kirk Ferentz, offensive line; and Jim Bates, defensive line). In each of the next three years, Mike and I read through literally every player in the NFL, as well as every player on our draft board, to make sure he was valued properly and might fit into our schemes. Our grades, which were closely monitored by Jim Schwartz, deviated from other systems, which graded players as starters and backups. Mike and Jim categorized nonstarters into roles, and three-down players were valued more highly than first- and second-down "starters." Also, special teams players had real value in this system. It was and is no coincidence that our special teams units in Cleveland and New England have consistently ranked near the top of the league.

A decade later, when I became the head coach of the Patriots, I replaced the existing personnel system with the one Mike developed. Ernie Adams and Scott Pioli made some adjustments to it that reflected the changes in the NFL, in personnel and schemes, over the previous 10 years. But Mike's system never lost its usefulness. I have had the great fortune to have an outstanding staff of coaches and personnel people throughout my coaching career. Many have moved to other programs, in the NCAA as well as the NFL, and took the fundamentals of Mike's system with them. The roots of that system have been replanted so many times that it is all over the game today.

Another of Mike's many strengths is his ability to dig up undervalued players. He was relentless in the pursuit of talent. In Cleveland, we had an outstanding offensive line made up of players that Mike had identified in college—Tony Jones, Wally Williams, Orlando Brown—long before they became some of the highest-paid players at their position. Mike also signed defensive tackle Bob Dahl, with the idea of converting him to the offense. He was soon starting at guard.

In 2014, I hired Mike to assist me in New England. His knowledge and experience proved again to be invaluable, as he helped me, Nick Caserio, and our staff assemble our Super Bowl XLIX championship team. His recommendation to sign running back

Dion Lewis and his successful pursuit of free agent center David Andrews are just two examples of his many contributions to that team.

Mike is one of the smartest people I have worked with. He has a thorough understanding not only of personnel but of coaching, team building, and the salary cap, too. His work ethic, attention to detail, and near-photographic memory made him both valuable and versatile to me at the two organizations at which we worked together. This is my chance to thank him for his contributions.

—BILL BELICHICK

# INTRODUCTION

## JUMPING THE ROUTE

*Something just did not look right.*

—BILL BELICHICK

With 26 seconds left in Super Bowl XLIX, the Seattle Seahawks had the ball at the 1-yard line with three chances to advance the 36 inches Pete Carroll's team needed to defeat Bill Belichick's New England Patriots. Although the rest of the world believed the game was all but over, I knew the truth.

Belichick had the Seahawks right where he wanted them.

I had rejoined Belichick's staff about a year earlier, in February 2014. It was the culmination of three decades of my bearing witness to a handful of brilliant, driven men as they revolutionized America's real national pastime. My education began in 1984, when I was lucky enough to join Bill Walsh's staff as a scouting assistant at the beginning of the San Francisco 49ers dynasty, and I have been taking notes ever since.

After four years with Walsh, for whom I worked my way up to an area scout position, I moved on to Cleveland. By the time I left nine years later, I was the Browns' director of pro personnel. But more important, along the way I swapped one legendary mentor for another as Belichick arrived in 1991 to begin honing his head coaching skills. Then it was on to Oakland, where I spent a decade with the National Football League's last true maverick, Al Davis, as a senior assistant, the kind of vague title Davis handed out when he didn't want anyone to know what exactly was going on behind the curtain in Raiderland. After a return to Cleveland, this time to be general manager, I found myself back with Belichick, this time in New England. My title with the Patriots—coaching assistant—did not begin to define my role. I was there to prepare the team for the college draft and free agency and to contribute to game planning. It was a mix of scouting and coaching, with a little organizational health maintenance thrown in.

By then, Belichick had been ensconced in New England for 14 years and was gaining traction as the greatest coach ever—of any sport, in any era. I was thrilled to be back in the fold.

And then I showed up for my first day of work.

It was a miserable winter day in Foxborough and an equally miserable setting. The predawn staff meeting convened in a tiny, windowless subterranean bunker that was serving as Belichick's office while the stadium was being remodeled. Each time the famous coach brought up his team's horrendous goal-line defense—the one that gave up 13 touchdowns and 2 field goals in 15 "goal-to-go" situations the previous season—his mood increasingly matched his surroundings: dark, cold, and ominous. All the men in the room were terrified, myself included, but to be completely honest, I was also curious to watch the master at work again. The problem that had his full attention was one of modern football's most challenging: how to evolve the goal-line defense in an era of spread passing attacks.

Here's the dilemma in a nutshell: The traditional goal-line defense is known as a 6-2 for the six defensive linemen and the two linebackers who back them up in a large-body attempt to clog an inside run game. The other three defenders are defensive backs, typically two fleet-footed corners and one hard-hitting safety, tasked with pass coverage. This scheme worked for decades because around the goal line NFL offenses generally relied on a dense power formation that replaced some receivers with blocking tight ends to bolster the short-yardage run game and typically left some defensive backs with no one to cover. In the endless chess game that is NFL strategy, however, teams had begun to take more and more chances through the air in goal-line situations, employing a spread formation that featured at least three receivers and forced the defense to cover the entire width of the field. Most significantly, a three-wide-receiver formation resulted in a very exploitable mismatch against a secondary with only one safety.

"We need a traditional goal-line defense that can also cover three receivers," Belichick told us, his mind churning through a thousand different possibilities like a gridiron computer.

The only way to do that was to replace the safety in the 6-2 with a third corner who would be a better matchup for a speedy wide receiver. Doing that, however, would take one of New England's best players, safety Devin McCourty, off the field. Belichick weighed the risks and decided he was willing to take the chance. It wouldn't be easy. Often, taking away one element of the offense makes the defense vulnerable in other ways. I call it the "Curly in the Boat Problem." You know the one: The Three Stooges are in a rowboat that springs a leak, and Curly has the bright idea to punch another hole in the hull to let the water out, creating, of course, a much bigger problem. That wasn't going to happen in New England. Belichick is a lot of things, but he's definitely not a stooge.

Nor is he reckless. Indeed, as much of an iconoclast as Belichick can be—as much of a rule breaker and gambler—he is also a traditionalist, the son of a football coach who believes that although practice doesn't make perfect, it gets you closer to perfection each time you do it. He is a five-tool leader, adept at *strategy, tactics, preparation, execution,* and what you might call *situational intuition,* the rare ability to know which among the first four is required and when.

We worked over the next months, throughout the entire off-season and preseason, implementing and perfecting Bill's ingeniously simple goal-line solution. Once the season started, though, we never encountered a situation that called for the three-corner goal-line formation—a 62 Nickel, you might call it. Not one time. The same thing held true in the postseason against the Baltimore Ravens and the Indianapolis Colts: no cause to debut our goal-line gamble. Seven months, hundreds of practices, thousands of man-hours, and almost two dozen preseason and regular-season games had gone by. All the time and energy invested in perfecting Belichick's goal-line wrinkle was looking very much like an utter waste.

Until the Seahawks had the ball on our doorstep with 26 seconds left in Super Bowl XLIX.

On that warm Arizona night, everybody could practically feel the time, the game, and some small part of Belichick's legacy slipping away. Well, everybody except Belichick, who wasn't worried about any of it. He wasn't about to drill a second hole in his rowboat. Instead, Bill was focused intently on the Seattle sideline. From his vantage point across the field at the University of Phoenix Stadium, he sensed confusion and indecision in his opponent. "Something just did not look right," he told me later. Instead of calling a time-out, an eerily calm Belichick just stared straight ahead, a predator stalking his prey.

Suddenly, he burst into action, becoming the aggressor. Shouting into his headset, Belichick commanded: "Just play goal line."

Except he didn't mean our traditional 6-2 goal line. Instead, our safeties coach, Brian Flores, yelled, "Malcolm, go!" and undrafted rookie Malcolm Butler entered the game as the third corner.

Everyone had expected Belichick to take a time-out to preserve precious seconds for his team if they got the ball back after the Seahawks inevitably took the lead—everyone including Seattle's coach, Pete Carroll. When no time-out came, I suspect it might have thrown him just a little. Whatever the case, Carroll looked to the field, saw the six Patriots defensive linemen there, and yelled into his own headset, "They're in goal line!" His countercall, sending in three receivers, was intended to spread the field. Instead, it played right into Belichick's trap.

I've studied the NFL's smartest men my whole career, and it's never anything less than breathtaking when you realize they are operating on a different level than their peers. Believing they had speed and horizontal space on their side, Seattle stacked two receivers on the right. At the snap, though, Butler, a cornerback skilled in man coverage—as opposed to the safety who ordinarily would have been in that spot—expertly read the play. He exploded toward wideout Ricardo Lockette, beating him to the ball and securing the most critical interception in Super Bowl history, not to mention yet another Lombardi Trophy for Belichick and the Patriots.

Someone wise once said: "The world gets out of the way for people who know where they are going." He might as well have been describing my 13-year-old self in the summer of 1972, when I discovered Strat-O-Matic baseball with my two best friends, Michael Sannino and Danny Reynolds. From the moment I opened the box of that early sports-simulation game, I knew my calling.

The weather along the Jersey Shore made famous by Bruce Springsteen was hot and humid and the beach was just a two-minute walk away, but the three of us pretty much stayed in my mother's air conditioner–less kitchen from sunrise to sunset. The game—a precursor to fantasy that consisted of cards with outcomes informed by the actual stats of real Major League Baseball players and activated by dice throws—unleashed a passion in each of us. We made our own rules, insisting on a two-to-one vote for any changes. We gave each player card a grade that was based on our own statistical analyses. We held leaguewide drafts rather than accepting the teams as they were packaged. Each of us was fully committed to the dual roles of GM and coach for his team. (To paraphrase the Hall of Fame football coach Bill Parcells, we not only shopped for the groceries, we cooked, too.)

In other words, we were obsessed, except that the obsession extended far beyond childhood for me. Strat-O-Matic, as I think back, gets most of the credit for my love of scouting and team building. Later that decade I transferred my obsession to the NFL draft. It wasn't anything like it is today: a significant event in a carefully scripted year-round NFL calendar that attracts millions of fans from all over the world. There was no television coverage for any of the rounds—that started in 1980—let alone all of them, and so if you wanted to follow in real time (as I most certainly did), you had to make your way to the host hotel in New York City. Seats were limited, which meant, for me, taking an early Long Island Rail Road train from Hofstra University in Hempstead, New York, to make sure I got one. The palpable current of excitement and potential on draft day assured me that this was what I wanted to do for my life's work.

Strat-O-Matic aside, my first love was football since the moment in the late 1960s when I saw a man on our family's little black-and-white television who had the same last name as mine (and who looked like one of my uncles). That man, Vince Lombardi, legendary Green Bay Packers coach, didn't have to be related to me to become my role model.

Like most boys, I dreamed of one day suiting up in the NFL.

Man, I wanted to play. And so I did: on Pop Warner teams; in high school in Ocean City, New Jersey; and then in boarding school at Valley Forge Military Academy in Pennsylvania, which I attended in part to learn discipline but also to stay on the field while I got my grades up so that I could attend a good college. By then I knew an NFL career was not in the cards—I was already a good enough scout to evaluate my own athletic gifts as lacking—but I decided to go to a school somewhere that would allow me to prolong my career a bit longer as I figured out how to get a job on an NFL side-line or in a front office. College let me stay in the game, but it also let me learn the game. I often spent weekends attending coaching clinics throughout the Northeast. Frat parties were not my thing; football was the dream, and I chased it hard.

In some ways I'm still chasing. I often think about the legend-ary baseball executive Branch Rickey, who, after being fired at age 74 as general manager of the Pittsburgh Pirates, was asked to name his most significant accomplishment. Rickey—who, among other achievements, orchestrated Jackie Robinson's breaking of the Major League Baseball color barrier and invented the game's farm system—quietly replied, "It hasn't happened yet."

Although this book is drawn from a lifetime spent in football front offices, it's not a life story as most are written. I won't bore you with tales of inspiring childhood coaches (though I certainly had them) or highlights from my own playing career (I had a few of those, too). I will leave the teaching of technique and fundamen-tals to better instructors; there will be no extended treatises about the hand placement of the nose tackle or the footwork of the tight end. Although such nuances are the bones and ligaments of the game, I'm more interested in the entire body, with an emphasis on the brain: not only strategy and tactics that make a difference on the field but philosophy and theory that matter off it. Football is ultimately a business, and as in any successful business the most important ingredients are a sound culture, a realistic plan, strong leadership, and a talented workforce.

Rather than a detailed recounting of my life and career—I save that for my kids—this book is meant to be an accounting of the lessons I've learned along the way, lessons that I hope will be of interest to serious fans but also to anyone who wants to know about what makes a great organizational thinker in any field: football or the Fortune 500. I will focus on the lessons I've learned from the men who, collectively, are largely responsible for the modern game of professional football: Davis, the Hall of Fame Oakland Raiders owner/coach who was the beating heart of the pass-happy American Football League, which merged with and forever changed the stodgy NFL; Walsh, the Hall of Fame inventor of the West Coast offense, which continues to dominate the game today; and Belichick, who may understand more about what happens on a gridiron than anyone else in history.

Each of these men has contributed to my Ph.D. in advanced football. It's a degree that was 35 years in the making as I worked for, coached alongside, and managed men who have won 11 of those Lombardi Trophies, many of those wins the result of the kind of foresight, ingenuity, and sheer force of will displayed by Belichick during that goal-line stand in Arizona. The story behind that now-legendary play is just one of many that I have collected over my career, and if you have listened to my podcast work or read my pieces for The Ringer and elsewhere, you may recognize some of what I have to say here. But much more of it will be new. I could argue that no one has had as much direct access as I have to the men most responsible for transforming pro football into the game it is today. And I would argue that no one is better suited to highlight and explain the brilliant lessons and revelatory insights of these masters.

If you want to learn lifetime lessons, there's no better teacher than a lifetime student.

Class begins now.

# 1

# THE ORGANIZATION

## CULTURE BEATS EVERYTHING

*Champions behave like champions before they're champions.*

—BILL WALSH

ill Walsh drove a Porsche. Well, he owned a Porsche, I should say, since I was the one who drove it. I was 25 in 1984 when I left a recruiting coordinator position at the University of Nevada–Las Vegas to join Walsh's staff with the San Francisco 49ers. The best part of my new job as a scout was to drive Walsh wherever he needed to go. As with most things in Walsh's world, there was no set pattern or agenda. Some days I just dropped him at home. Other days I took him to the airport or to a speaking engagement across the state. For me, the longer the ride, the better. I could hardly believe my incredible good fortune.

The assignment, considered by most to be grunt work suitable for only the youngest members of a staff, was nothing less than the beginning of my formal education in the game of professional football. What could be better? Me behind the wheel of a slick sports car as I listened to the running commentary of Bill Walsh: commentary on world events or Villanova's NCAA tournament upset of Georgetown or military history or—his favorite subject above all others—the blueprint he was building for an advanced, all-encompassing philosophy that would transform the 49ers into the envy of and model for every other organization in sports.

By the time I arrived, Walsh was well on his way to genius status. As a longtime assistant coach in Cincinnati under the legendary Paul Brown, Walsh first changed the course of NFL history with his invention of the West Coast offense. His intricate evolution of the passing game was built around precise timing and movement. It attacked the defense by stretching the field horizontally with short passes that served almost like handoffs, getting the ball to playmakers just as they reached top speed in open spaces. After a falling-out with Brown, Walsh left the Bengals in 1975 and, after a brief stop in San Diego, spent two years as the head coach at Stanford, where he led the football team to back-to-back bowl game wins. Since he was comfortable in the school's academic environment, the last place anyone ever expected Walsh to jump to next was the 49ers.

Most football fans today think of San Francisco as the NFL's dynasty of the 1980s, but few remember that before Walsh showed up in 1979 the team was widely regarded as the worst in the league and quite possibly the most dysfunctional franchise in all of pro sports. The previous general manager, Joe Thomas, had gutted the organization from top to bottom. Thomas fired three head coaches in less than 12 months, including one, East Coast native Pete McCulley, who insisted that everything run on his time; that meant that the usual 7 A.M. team meetings began at 4 A.M. Thomas also cut talented players such as quarterback Jim

Plunkett, who went on to win two Super Bowls with the Oakland Raiders. Worst of all, Thomas had traded away five of the 49ers' top picks in upcoming drafts for a washed-up, wobbly-kneed O. J. Simpson. The game-day losses were so definitive and the weekday atmosphere so poisonous during a 2–14 season in 1978 that a disgusted 49ers assistant left the sideline on one embarrassing Sunday to sit with his wife in the stands.

In short, Walsh took over a team with no high draft picks, no quarterback, and no hope. Three years later, that team won the Super Bowl.

It got there by following Walsh's formula, what he called his Standard of Performance: an exacting plan for constructing and maintaining the culture and organizational DNA behind the perfect football franchise. Let's face it, the word *perfect* and the very idea of "building the perfect organization" are either clichés or fantasies to most coaches. Not to Walsh. Perfection drove him endlessly and, sometimes to those around him, maddeningly.

His obsession with perfection meant he constantly pushed his people, regardless of experience or position in the organization, to learn more. He was naturally curious, always searching for ways to fix his team or just better accomplish the simplest task, and he demanded the same thing of his staff. He never wanted us to follow familiar paths to knowledge. He was trying to build a lasting, self-perpetuating culture to counter the groupthink that was then pervasive in the NFL and still is today.

Walsh, in other words, was trying to "disrupt" football long before anyone thought to use that term in business, let alone sports.

From his lectern in the passenger seat, Walsh told me, "If we are all thinking alike, no one is thinking." He was a master communicator, deftly asking questions he already knew the answer to as a lead-in to another lesson. "Have you heard of Tom Peters?" he once asked me. My first thought was, *Is he that punter in the draft?* When it quickly became clear that I had no clue who Peters was, Walsh began an impromptu dissertation on the merits of *In Search of Excellence,* the book that Peters, a famed management consultant, wrote with Bob Waterman. Walsh loved the book and urged me to head to the store immediately to buy a copy. (There was no Amazon back then.) Which, of course, I did. And reading Peters spurred in me a lifelong love of his management philosophy, as Walsh knew it would.

In the book, Peters and Waterman offer a list of eight attributes that drive organizations to become excellent. The similarities to Walsh's Standard of Performance were no coincidence. Walsh himself said, "Running a football franchise is not unlike running any other business: You start first with a structural format and underlying philosophy, then find people who can implement it." But if football was his business, building the finest organization was his goal.

The best way I can describe Walsh's philosophy is that he thought of a football team as being like a brand-new automobile, believing that the finished product could be only as good as the assembly line that created it, all the way down to the tiniest bolt and the smallest detail performed by the seemingly most insignificant worker. Everything needed to mesh on and off the field. No part could survive without the others. It was a process Walsh was constantly thinking and rethinking as he built his culture of success.

His meticulousness was evident everywhere, from his spotless sneakers to his impeccable office. Once, as I was walking down the hall in the team facility, I heard him yell to me, "Are you just going to ignore that photo?" Unable to discern the offending picture, I asked him which one he meant. "The one that's tilted sideways" was his straightforward reply. To this day, if there is a picture hanging out of line, I am compelled to straighten it. Walsh was extremely demanding in a quiet way. You never wanted to be the source of that disappointed look on his face. He was a boxer in his younger days and a military buff as a grown-up. At the same time, he could have stepped into an economics class at Stanford and held forth quite proficiently. His was, in short, a unique and powerful presence wherever he went, particularly inside that Porsche, and his voice remains loud and clear in my ear today.

Walsh's dedication to his Standard of Performance was a way of life for him; his intention was always to use it to influence more than the game on the field. I truly believe that's why he left the comfort of Stanford for the challenge of the downtrodden 49ers. He wanted to test his theories in the worst possible circumstances, at the highest level of the game. The fact that those theories passed that test with honors is a surprise to no one who knew the man in almost any capacity or context.

Walsh left his legacy of greatness in players, coaches, and support staff alike. He was as concerned with how the receptionists answered the phones at team headquarters as he was with Joe Montana's throwing motion. Once, during a preseason game at the 49ers' home field, Candlestick Park, I was in the coaches' box, waiting for the team to return to the sideline after halftime. Suddenly, Walsh was screaming into my headset. When I asked what he needed, he said bluntly, "Remind me to fire the PA announcer. He is horrible." That was classic Walsh, tuned in to all things 49ers, not just the action on the field.

No detail was too small, not even the location of his parking spot at the team's facility inside the sprawling Red Morton Park recreational complex in Redwood City. He reserved the first space, closest to and aligned perfectly with the entrance, for his Porsche. That was fine with me. Each time the call came to my desk from his assistant declaring that "Coach needs a ride" I'd get excited. My understanding of the 49ers' unique culture was about to be expanded again.

Ever seen *The Late Late Show*'s signature segment, "Carpool Karaoke"? Host James Corden chauffeurs around a music star, a pop culture icon, or even a first lady as they sing along with the radio. But he also takes it as an opportunity to get them chatting about life. There's something about a car's interior, private yet informal—not to mention the dueting—that allows Corden to get an intimate glimpse into the thoughts of even the most guarded stars. Driving Walsh around in his Porsche was my version of Carpool Karaoke (without the warbling; neither of us wanted to hear the other sing).

I've worked with some of the greatest minds in football, and believe it or not, one common thread that bound them was a rather odd "game show" way they had of interacting with their staff. Starting in 1997, I spent almost a decade in Oakland working alongside the iconic owner of the Raiders, Al Davis, and he treated most of our interactions as if we were on *Jeopardy!* Davis, in the Alex Trebek role, required that I instantly furnish fully formed questions that were based on answers he threw my way. And Davis was nowhere as patient as Trebek. As soon as his secretary got me on the phone, he'd break in with some version of this greeting: "I have three things for you." (The number varied, but nothing else did.) I never replied, instead just waited for answer number one. "You know that guy from Utah who missed a season with a knee injury?" Davis might say. My answer: You mean offensive lineman Barry Sims? (Technically, I guess I should have said, Who is offensive lineman Barry Sims?) "Yes, Sims," Davis would reply. "How big are his hands?" If I wasn't able to provide the exact measurement off the top of my head, I would be banned from Final Raider Jeopardy. The one thing you could never say to Al(ex) was "I'm not sure; let me look it up." That drove him nuts. "Aw, fuck, Lombardi, I could look it up myself," he'd snap. That was my daily interaction with Davis for most of a decade.

Bookended around my time with Davis, I worked with Bill Belichick in Cleveland and then again in New England. His game was closer to *20 Questions*. Detroit Lions general manager Bob Quinn worked on Belichick's staff for 16 years, and he recently described Bill's quiz show interrogation better than anyone: It's 6:45 A.M., and you're still half asleep. As you wait in line at the omelet station inside the Patriots' practice facility, Belichick shuffles up and asks you a dozen questions about the seventh player on the practice squad. Those who weren't ready to engage in a half-hour in-depth conversation on the spot found themselves in the worst place in the NFL: Bill's doghouse.

Walsh's concert was Carpool Karaoke. He liked to doodle, and in the same way that President Kennedy drew sailboats he day-dreamed about building someday, Walsh drew up football plays from every era. If he caught me glancing over as he sketched, he would delight in giving me the play's background and origin. Walsh's mind never turned off, and writing things down seemed to be the best method he had to catalog his thoughts. He used 3-by-5 index cards and short sharp pencils like the ones golfers keep score with, and when he wasn't doodling, he made lists of things that needed to get done in an elegant left-handed hand-writing that was part cursive, part print.

Honestly, I think Walsh cherished those pencils more than the Porsche. In 1981 he signed veteran linebacker Jack "Hacksaw" Reynolds—who became the heart and soul of a 49ers defense that won two Super Bowls—in part, I'm sure, because Reynolds brought a full box of sharpened pencils to every team meeting, as if he were the world's toughest CPA about to meet with a client. Walsh, by the way, liked to say that whereas Hall of Fame defensive back Ronnie Lott *had* character, Hacksaw *was* a character. And he was right. Hacksaw got his nickname as a senior at the University of Tennessee when, after a frustrating loss to Mississippi, he went to a Kmart, purchased 13 hacksaw blades, and proceeded to cut through his 1953 Chevy.

Anyway, with all that time to think and talk inside the Porsche, Walsh honed his Standard of Performance, writing down its 17 principles with those beloved pencils. (Walsh loved to teach more than anything, but a close second for him was making lists like this one.) These tenets would inform the creation and mainte-nance of a football dynasty:

1. Exhibit a ferocious and intelligently applied work ethic directed at continual improvement.
2. Demonstrate respect for each person in the organization.
3. Be deeply committed to learning and teaching.
4. Be fair.
5. Demonstrate character.
6. Honor the direct connection between details and improvement; relentlessly seek the latter.
7. Show self-control, especially under pressure.
8. Demonstrate and prize loyalty.
9. Use positive language and have a positive attitude.
10. Take pride in my effort as an entity separate from the result of that effort.
11. Be willing to go the extra distance for the organization.
12. Deal appropriately with victory and defeat, adulation and humiliation.
13. Promote internal communication that is both open and substantive.
14. Seek poise in myself and those I lead.
15. Put the team's welfare and priorities ahead of my own.
16. Maintain an ongoing level of concentration and focus that is abnormally high.
17. Make sacrifice and commitment the organization's trademark.

The Standard of Performance was Walsh's attempt to instill a winning attitude in every member of his organization. In fact, as he admitted in his book *The Score Takes Care of Itself,* he was far more focused on the process of creating a culture, of establishing a foundation for sustainable success, than in drawing up the perfect game plan. His Standard of Performance wasn't a way to define his genius; it *was* his genius. It was the compass that guided everything he oversaw—coaching, scouting, management—allowing him to transform the 49ers from a laughingstock to a powerhouse in fewer than 1,000 days. By accomplishing that feat, Walsh essentially used football to prove the famous dictum of another management expert, Peter Drucker: "Culture can eat strategy for lunch." That's why, for people inside the NFL, people in the know, Walsh's Standard of Performance is as much a part of his lasting impact as his West Coast offense. Maybe even more.

Because the Thomas era had been so destructive, Walsh had to rebuild every aspect of the organization—from the talent on and off the field, to the quality of the workplace, to the practice fields. No detail was too small for Walsh to consider because, to his assembly-line way of thinking, only the sum of them all could produce the organization he wanted. As he was fond of saying, if he managed to perfect the culture, the wins would take care of themselves.

And so he went about teaching the team not just what to do but how to think. The team facility was Walsh's classroom, and before long he had schooled everyone. He called meetings with each department, opened his notebook, and started to lecture on the essence of every job, how to act while doing each job, and, most important, how to improve the way the job was done. When he lectured on "culture" and the way champions behave, he got locked in, never looking at his watch or wondering where he needed to be next. It was a rare and refreshing change from the way every other NFL team was run, with every minute scheduled, bathroom breaks included.

Walsh's first student and possibly his most important was Eddie DeBartolo Jr., and the lesson he imparted was how to be an owner. DeBartolo knew he had made a mistake when he hired Thomas, giving so much authority to a man who wasn't the coach. Upon hiring Walsh, DeBartolo let everyone know that the coach was the boss and made it clear that as the owner he would never undercut Walsh's decision making. That authority was the key to Walsh's system because it created a hierarchy that avoided the common organizational fissures between front office and coaches. Walsh knew that most teams in the NFL endure their share of internal strife, or as he often referred to it, "the Civil War." Walsh, both head coach and GM, eliminated a major source of headaches and inefficiency with a single job description. There would be no infighting or backstabbing or favoritism because he was the only voice talking to DeBartolo about the overall direction of the franchise.

Walsh turned next to the members of the scouting department. He preached to us every day about the importance of learning the whole game, of being more than typical college scouts, whom he belittled as "former bad coaches telling good coaches what to do." Of course, this required that we go above and beyond anything we had done before. It was, however, in accordance with the first rule of his Standard of Performance: *Exhibit a ferocious and intelligently applied work ethic.* Work smarter, he said, not longer. He wanted us to see players not as a collection of data and stats but in the context of the schemes they ran. To Walsh, grading a player without understanding the role coaches were asking him to fill was not only scouting blindly, it was just plain lazy. We needed to scout "inside out, not outside in"; that is, our analysis had to be informed by a detailed understanding of each position on the field as defined by each particular organization and scheme. He demanded nuance from his scouts—and that was not typical.

The best illustration of Walsh's impact on the 49ers' scouting department was the lead-up to the 1986 draft. After the retirement of Fred Dean, one of the most relentless pass rushers in NFL history and an eventual Hall of Famer, the team struggled to create any pressure on the quarterback whatsoever. Walsh wanted to find someone in the draft to replace Dean, someone who could bring constant pressure, not just sack the quarterback once in a while.

Walsh called me into his office to discuss what he was looking for. Out came one of his famous lists. Scratching away on those

3-by-5 cards with those tiny golf pencils, Walsh had once compiled 30 specific details he believed made a great offensive lineman. Now in his hands was a list of criteria for the next great 49ers pass rusher: 6'4" with long arms, great feet, and an explosiveness off the ball. Truth be told, Walsh was not all that concerned with how this particular player defended the run or if he even had enough heft to hold up in the trenches. He had done the math—recalculated the physics, timing, and geometry of pass protection, especially in light of the wide, sluggish offensive tackles who were populating most huddles—and realized the key was leverage, reach, and quickness.

Having received my orders, I headed down to my "office" in the team meeting room and began to comb through scouting reports our staff had filed from the field. I eliminated players because they were too short or too slow or because their arms didn't stack up, which is to say just about every single player available. When I was done, just two collegiate footballers remained. The first was Romel Andrews, a defensive end from the University of Tennessee at Martin. The other was an outside linebacker who had been converted to inside linebacker at tiny James Madison University. Some guy named Charles Haley.

I called both schools to have the players' film (we used actual 16-millimeter reels and projectors back then) sent to our offices. When they arrived, I called in Walsh to watch with me. The lights dimmed, the projector flickered to life, and there was the 6'5", 255-pound Haley, a former high school basketball player with an explosive first move to match. Haley was also a tight end in high school, so he had giant strong hands, which he pistoned into defenders to create separation. His reach and his stride were so long that after two steps upfield and a dip of his inside shoulder, he had the quarterback in a bear hug. On the first play we watched, Georgia Southern's excellent running quarterback Tracy Ham began an option play toward the side of the field away from Haley, leaving Haley several yards behind the ball right after the snap.

At that point most defenders give up, saving their energy for another down. Instead, we watched in slack-jawed awe as Haley raced toward Ham, somehow closing the gap on one of the quickest QBs in college. Just as Ham felt Haley on his back, though, he pitched the ball to the running back. Again, in normal circumstances, a trailing outside linebacker would be left in the dust. Haley quickly and instinctively slingshotted himself off Ham, engulfing the running back in his long arms for a four-yard loss.

Walsh reached over, turned off the projector, and asked, "Do we need to see any more?" He had his guy. We took Haley in the fourth round—our patience reflecting a certainty that no other team understood Haley's value the way we did—and he registered 12 sacks as a rookie. (Haley, though, was only one highlight of that 1986 draft, but more on that in Chapter 3.) Until Tom Brady, he was the only player in NFL history to win five Super Bowls—two with the 49ers, three in Dallas—and he finished his career with 100 sacks and a bust in the Hall of Fame.

The year before we drafted Haley, some of us traveled to the first-ever NFL Scouting Combine in Tempe, Arizona, to watch potential draft prospects work out in front of representatives of all the teams. On the practice field of Arizona State University, a long hot day extended deep into the night. An exhausted Walsh had no desire to sit through more, and so he summoned me to get the car to drive him back to our hotel. Once we were on the road, I could sense Walsh wasn't at all happy—he was neither doodling nor making a list—so I casually asked him what was wrong. Honestly, noting his mood, I figured my question would be ignored. To my surprise, he went on a tirade about our quarterbacks coach Paul Hackett, who was thinking of leaving.

Walsh used the same incredible feel that found game-changing players such as Haley to build his coaching staff. But just because he put such an emphasis on loyalty, growth, and, above all, obedience to his standard, it didn't mean that everyone else in his mercenary profession did. Unfortunately, Walsh took what others might consider normal job movement personally. In this case, it went beyond the prospect of losing a vital conduit of our West Coast offense. Walsh considered Hackett's solicitation of another job to be disloyal, and that was far more damaging to team culture than any setback in strategy. Hackett had always claimed that his lifelong ambition was to learn at the right hand of Walsh. Was that all a lie? Had Walsh fallen short of his expectations? What about the standards he'd set? Walsh was furious, and for the 20 miles back to the hotel, I heard all about it.

Hackett ended up staying one more season before heading to Dallas in 1986 to become the offensive coordinator and heir apparent to Cowboys head coach Tom Landry. After he left, we began to look for two men to replace him. One would coach the quarterbacks, and the other would handle tight ends and wide receivers. Once again, Walsh gave me a specific list of criteria for what he wanted in potential candidates.

I headed downstairs to where the 49ers stored all the college media guides. This was an era of college football in which the run-heavy option was the preferred offense, but Walsh needed someone who was comfortable throwing the ball. My task was simple: I had to find bios of the few top passing offensive coordinators in the NCAA, cut them out, and glue them onto a piece of paper. The work was important, but it was not glamorous, and it wasn't long before I realized it wasn't so simple, either. In many cases the college offensive coordinator was actually not the guy most responsible for the air attack. Brigham Young University, for example, was one of the best passing schools at the time, but its coordinator by title was actually the offensive line coach, Roger French. I knew he would hold no interest for Walsh. I clipped French's bio just in case, but I also clipped the quarterback coach, Mike Holmgren.

Holmgren looked promising: He was a San Francisco native, a former college quarterback at the University of Southern California, and an eighth-round pick of the St. Louis Cardinals in the 1970 draft. After his pro career fizzled, he spent a year as the offensive coordinator and quarterback coach at San Francisco State before moving to BYU. Under the direction of head coach LaVell Edwards, the school overcame its small size to become a dominant force by breaking with the game's norms, throwing the ball all over the field. This was the kind of thinking Walsh loved. And just as had happened when we scouted Haley, Walsh took one look at Holmgren's bio and knew he had found his next right-hand man. I picked up Holmgren at the San Francisco airport twice: once for his interview and again to bring him to his new house after he took the job.

Holmgren and I became good friends. He called me "Scooper" because I was so tuned in to what was going on around the NFL. Once in a while, though, I still remind him that with one slice of my scissors, Roger French could have been working for the 49ers instead.

The thing is, hiring coaches like Holmgren was a convoluted path to building a staff. It required Walsh to spend lots of time and energy coaching his coaches. But he lived for that kind of challenge. That was why he hired guys who were intelligent before they were anything else, guys who were not typical products of the football industry. His special teams coach Fred von Appen may still be the only coach in NFL history who read Sylvia Plath every day before heading out to the practice field. (Maybe the violence of her poetry helped prepare him for the carnage of kickoff coverage.)

Whether they came from a Mormon university or were fans of morbid imagery, Walsh wanted men he could mold and develop. He firmly believed that coaches with too much experience in other systems would have a hard time clearing their heads of old ideas to make room for new ones. Over time philosophies become rigid. Methods and styles take root in one's DNA, making it harder to change direction or adapt to another way. Walsh was constructing something different in San Francisco, something revolutionary even, and he knew it would be very unlikely that a fully indoctrinated coach would be able to contribute to the new 49ers culture. Therefore, Walsh opted for less experienced men who shared his curiosity and displayed a willingness to learn his system and methods.

I still didn't quite understand this when, several weeks after Holmgren came on board, I asked Walsh during another Carpool Karaoke session why he hadn't hired an experienced pro coach. In particular, I knew that our vice president of player personnel, John McVay, had pushed for Lindy Infante, a veteran NFL assistant who had been the head coach of the upstart United States Football League's Jacksonville Bulls until that league folded. Infante interviewed with us, and though he seemed to have all the qualifications, he left Walsh unimpressed. "My system of offense is in place," Walsh said to me. "I'm not interested in other ideas outside the boundaries of this offense. I'd rather teach someone my system, then let their creativity take over."

This sounded familiar, and I soon realized why. Walsh was a big believer in the business and leadership philosophies of Dee Hock, the founder of Visa, whom the author Tom Peters often referenced in his speeches. "The problem is never how to get new, innovative thoughts into your mind," Hock said. "But how to get old ones out."

Walsh's ideas about hiring and culture were so far ahead of their time that even decades later the best minds in the business still struggle mightily to implement their own version of the Standard of Performance. Many have tried to copycat Walsh's offense by hiring his former assistants and associates or anyone else who could lay claim to the West Coast lineage, believing that simply employing someone to run the scheme is enough to create the kind of success Walsh had with it. But the reason there are so many failed Walsh disciples—Ray Rhodes in Philadelphia and Green

Bay, Marty Mornhinweg in Detroit, Mike White in Oakland, and George Seifert in Carolina, to name a few—is that Walsh installed way more than an offense.

Seifert's career is the most explicit example of this misunderstanding. After taking over for Walsh in San Francisco, Seifert was 98–30 in eight seasons, winning two more Super Bowls for the 49ers. Clearly, though, Seifert benefited greatly from the culture already etched in stone by Walsh. The further away the team moved from Walsh's leadership, the less success it had. Since losing their connection to Walsh, the 49ers, with only one Super Bowl appearance in the last two-plus decades, have not been the same. Neither was Seifert.

Seifert resigned from the Niners after the 1996 season. He went 16–32 as the Panthers head coach and was fired after a disastrous 1–15 record in 2001. Seifert, you might say, knew Walsh's recipes—he had a complete understanding of the West Coast offense—he just didn't understand the most important ingredient: culture.

Another example: Before University of Alabama head coach Nick Saban could become one of the greatest coaches in college football history, he had to learn the same lesson. After grinding away in the profession for almost 20 years, he got his first big break in 1991, when he was named defensive coordinator of the Browns under Bill Belichick, himself an indirect Walsh disciple. When Saban moved on to head coaching stops of his own at Michigan State and LSU, he implemented the program made famous by Walsh and Belichick. You could see it in the way he scouted players, coached his coaches, and developed the talents of each employee. And what worked for Walsh and Belichick worked for Saban.

Saban failed only once, after returning to the NFL to coach the Miami Dolphins in 2005. The Dolphins at that time were still very much Don Shula's franchise. And why not? Sure, Don Shula had been retired for a decade, but the team had been one of the best in the NFL for a generation under his rule. As a result, though,

Saban met with internal resistance as he tried to embed his own culture. There was zero buy-in to the new system, with players and executives alike balking at what they perceived to be a radical transformation. The final straw for Saban was the situation surrounding free agent quarterback Drew Brees. Saban knew the potential of the former Charger, but he was not allowed to sign Brees and his surgically reconstructed throwing shoulder. Brees signed with New Orleans instead, where that shoulder has thrown more than 58,000 yards. After missing out on Brees, Saban understood that he would never be able to get the Dolphins to do things his way, and after going 6–10 in 2006, still his only losing season as a head coach, Saban jumped to Alabama. There he had the freedom to build the organization from the ground up. All he's done is win five national championships in less than a decade. (The man he took over for in Tuscaloosa? Don's son Mike.)

One of Walsh's frequently repeated decrees was "Don't be a copycat." It made him crazy when opposing coaches would attend clinics on the West Coast offense just so they could steal his play designs, mostly because it implied that pass routes were the key to the 49ers' success. They missed the fundamental point, the true genius of it all, and that angered Walsh no end.

The inevitable failures of those wannabes—and the particular cautionary tale of George Seifert, for that matter—led me to formulate a little theory of my own: "The Emeril Lagasse Theory." Lagasse, you may know, is a longtime New Orleans restaurateur and bestselling cookbook author who was a television personality in the first wave of celebrity chefs. His food is delicious and his recipes are easy to follow, yet he never feared that another aspiring cook would usurp his work and put him out of business. He knew that being able to follow a recipe is a very different thing from duplicating a particular and personal culinary ethos. It is the creator alone who understands just what the dish is trying to accomplish, and so he's the only one who knows just how to make the ingredients work together. Lagasse also knows that, as with an assembly line or a football franchise, the smallest deviation from the process upends the final product (especially if it's andouille gumbo). That's why there is no need to worry about knockoff restaurants. If copycatting were a useful shortcut to success, there would be Lagasse-style restaurants in every city and San Francisco 49er clones in every football stadium.

Or, today, New England Patriots clones. The now-famous Patriot Way, the unique and uniquely powerful culture Belichick has honed over the last decade and a half, is a living tribute to Walsh's Standard of Performance and his revolutionary organizational philosophies. And like Walsh, many of Belichick's disciples, most prominently Charlie Weis and Josh McDaniels, have failed as head coaches after—to keep the cooking metaphor going—stepping out of the frying pan and into the fire. They knew all their mentor's recipes; they just didn't know how to cook them. Few grasp what was behind the dynasty in San Francisco then or in New England now: the details, the mind-set, the superhuman sacrifices made every second of every day to establish and maintain an utter commitment to the culture.

Every NFL owner wants his team to be the next Patriots, the next link in the Walsh chain, until, realizing how challenging the task is, they all lose their appetite to see an overhaul through to the end. You can't cook up a success unless you have created the right culture. It doesn't work.

Just ask Emeril.

# 2

# THE COACH

## A STUDY IN LEADERSHIP

*Flying by the seat of his pants always suggests to me a leader
who hasn't prepared properly and whose pants may soon fall down.*

—BILL WALSH

In *The Godfather: Part II*, Michael Corleone asks Frank Pentangeli
to make peace with the Rosato brothers. Pentangeli hates the
idea. He knows that neither side has an interest in settling and
that any meeting will be a waste of his time.

In 1996 I had my own *Godfather* moment. John Shaw, then
president of the St. Louis Rams, asked me to meet with his vice
president of football operations, Steve Ortmayer. The team had no
openings in its personnel department; Shaw just wanted to gauge
if Ortmayer was open to some outside assistance. Like Pentangeli,
I knew Ortmayer would be against the idea—strongly. He was

going to guard his turf. I expected that the trip to Macomb, Illinois, new summer home of the recently relocated Rams, was going to be like a meeting with the Rosato brothers: a total waste of time.

Instead, my Frankie Five Angels meeting with the Rams was the beginning of a bizarre but fascinating and insightful summer I spent navigating the secret (and sometimes highly dysfunctional) subculture of the NFL's highest executive levels. And although this adventure didn't lead to any great job offers, it did bring me something even more valuable—a deeper understanding of, and improved procedures for, the most challenging and important transaction in sports: hiring a head coach.

After spending the 1995 season in Cleveland as director of player personnel, I was offered a chance to stay in another role but chose to move on. I had two years remaining on my contract, but my phone was ringing off the hook for meetings and special assignments, in part because potential employers figured they could get me on the cheap. In the NFL, no one is allowed to get paid twice, to double dip. Every contract has an offset clause that essentially says that a team is only responsible to make up the difference if a former employee's new job pays less than his old deal. This language is often enforceable even if a person takes a job in television. Any job connected to football activates an offset.

That was all fine with me, though. It gave me an opportunity to fulfill a career goal.

When I was a scouting assistant in San Francisco in the 1980s, Bill Walsh told me that Al Davis had taught him more about football than anyone else, and ever since I had dreamed of working for the Raiders. While I waited for that moment, I read everything I could about what Davis thought and how he behaved, anything that helped me understand what made him so successful. Inevitably, our paths crossed—at the Scouting Combine in Indianapolis—and we became friends. Not surprisingly, our friendship centered on football. Before long, he was calling my home, usually late at night, to talk about the draft, or a coach, or some player who had caught his eye. Once, in 1992, my mother, Jane, was over, watching our kids while my wife, Millie, and I were out celebrating the end of draft season. Davis called while we were out, and my mother, who had no earthly idea who he was, had a 10-minute conversation with him about the jazz singer Billy Eckstine. Davis was a charmer when he wanted to be. When Millie and I returned home, my mother said: "Michael, this nice man Al called. You better hurry up and call him back."

When he called in the summer of 1996, it was about a job as a senior assistant. Of course, I accepted, not realizing that I had just stepped into the cross fire of one of the NFL's longest-running feuds between two of its highest-profile (and stubbornest) owners. In one corner, Browns owner Art Modell—a buttoned-down, league-first company man. In the other, Davis—one of the game's great renegades. My summer in NFL exile was just getting started.

Davis was prepared to hire me at a reduced rate knowing (gleefully, perhaps) that Modell would have to make up the difference. But when I told Modell about the deal and his tab, he was not pleased. In fact, he made it perfectly clear that there was no way in hell he'd pick up Davis's bill. His stance was not about the money or me; it was about who was on the other side of the transaction. Modell went so far as to tell me he'd pay my whole salary just to prevent me from helping that "son of a bitch" in Oakland.

I knew then there was no way Modell would let me out of my contract to work for Davis. Blocked from my dream job by my old boss, I began to look elsewhere. I spent one lovely day in the desert with Arizona Cardinals owner Bill Bidwill. I had heard that in the 1970s Don Coryell got the head coaching job with the Cardinals after writing a note to the Bidwills that impressed them. So I had done the same thing, knowing that the team wasn't happy with its front-office situation. But because the guy whose job I wanted was still under contract, we had to be a little secretive.

Bidwill picked me up at the airport himself and drove me to his house, where we talked all day in his pool cabana. He must have enjoyed the conversation as much as I did because as we headed back to the airport, he blurted out, "I don't care if anyone knows we're meeting; let's stop by the office. I want to show you our facility." (It was a late Friday afternoon in June, though, so really there was little risk of anyone being around to spot us.)

Once Bidwill brought me to the office, I figured I was in. Now, you might think it wrong to interview for a job that isn't open, but morality and NFL management have a dicey relationship. Campaigning for someone else's job is just part of the landscape. We've all had it done to us, and we've all done it to someone else. Whenever you hear a front-office guy talk about transparency or trust, make sure to take it with a grain of salt. First, if I declined the interview, Modell most certainly would have argued that I was violating my contract by not actively looking for work. Second, how was I to know what Bidwill told anyone about our meeting? That was on him. You just cannot say no to an owner who wants to meet. As it turned out, Bidwill never offered me a job or made changes to his front office, but I didn't regret the trip one bit.

A few months later the Rams called, and I found myself jetting off to the Midwest for my Frankie Five Angels meeting. Well, not exactly jetting. The view out the window of the small prop plane— basically, cornfields and more cornfields—might have appealed to some but not to a guy who left a New Jersey beach town on a way-too-early flight. Upon landing at the General Wayne A. Downing Peoria International Airport, I was greeted by a familiar face: David Razzano, a West Coast area Rams scout whose dad gave me my NFL start in San Francisco. Over the next 90 minutes, heading south along Highway 24, we traded "remember when"s as Razzano made it rather clear that the Rams were pretty much devoid of every positive organizational quality we'd experienced with the Niners.

For starters, Shaw, who had orchestrated the team's move with Ortmayer from Los Angeles after the 1994 season, was still running things remotely. Like the Wizard behind his curtain in Oz, Shaw controlled everything in St. Louis from his office 2,000 miles west on Pico Boulevard. From my initial conversation with him, it was also clear that he already was thinking of making a coaching change if he didn't see dramatic improvement in 1996.

Razzano and I were used to one man running the show. In San Francisco there never was any confusion about who set the direction and made the decisions: Walsh. But in St. Louis, the GM, Ortmayer, had little authority over roster moves. When it came to college prospects Shaw listened only to John Becker, vice president of player personnel, and on the subject of free agents and other pro prospects, Shaw relied on the Giddings scouting service. Teams pay a lot of money to companies such as Giddings to help evaluate their own roster and players around the league, and in the car headed to my meeting, Razzano indicated that this service was Shaw's bible. All of which left Ortmayer with little power—or juice—in the Rams hierarchy.

The previous season had been the Rams' first in St Louis. Despite the move from LA and a first-year NFL head coach, Rich Brooks, the Rams finished 7–9—and that was after losing their final three games, all at home, while giving up 121 points in the process. Seven wins under those circumstances should have created optimism in the Rams' camp, but by the time Razzano turned into the Western Illinois University parking lot, I had a pretty good sense that no one was happy with Brooks. The rest of the front office, I was about to learn, already had gone to the dogs.

Having just spent five years with Bill Belichick in Cleveland, three as director of pro personnel and two as player personnel director, essentially fulfilling the duties of a general manager, I knew I could help this team. But when I sat down for my meeting, Ortmayer's assistant was busy training her puppy in the team office, and it was clear from the get-go that the Rams GM was way more interested in the pet than in discussing what I could offer.

Ortmayer used every yelp the pup made to avoid engaging with me. I mean, I like dogs as much as the next guy, but if he asked how the "little fella" was doing one more time, we were going to have a different kind of *Godfather* moment on our hands. Belichick, by the way, is a real dog lover, too, but I promise you he never wasted one minute of one day playing with a mutt in the office. I thought I was being punked by Ortmayer, I really did.

It was just another reminder of what a professional, well-run workplace Belichick had created in Cleveland and just how rare that kind of an atmosphere is in the NFL. After three long, odd, and totally wasted hours, I was on my way back to the Peoria airport with Razzano, and even though Ortmayer promised to call in a few days, I knew a full-time job with the Rams was a longer shot than that puppy getting properly housebroken.

With my job search going nowhere, I had no choice but to head to my summer home in New Jersey to wait and see how things might shake out. Luckily, I live within driving distance of NFL Films' headquarters. Steve Sabol, keeper of the archive there, was kind enough to give me access to the latest game tapes. Two things happen when you are between NFL jobs. The first is that you fall behind on league trends. The second and more important is that you quickly lose touch with the incoming draft class. Before you know it, you've become obsolete. I was determined to avoid those pitfalls, and so each day I commuted 100 miles to stand in front of one of Sabol's tape machines. Sabol was a real retro guy—a lover of the 1950s, old music, and old-school diners. He loved the history of the game most of all, and that was displayed in the archival photos that lined the walls in his office and every other wall in the building. Visiting NFL Films is like walking around the Hall of Fame in Canton, Ohio.

But the nostalgia and independent study distracted me for only so long. The truth was that in a matter of months I had gone from watching games in a cushy chair on my own big screen at the

Browns facility, to coming tantalizingly close to breaking down film in Oakland with Al Davis, to manning a five-by-eight monitor with no remote and no chair, crammed in a corner of a warehouse in South Jersey. But hey, if you love the game, you make do.

Meanwhile, the Rams started the 1996 season 1–5, reinforcing Shaw's lack of faith in his leaders. Not that anyone in St. Louis had any clue what he was thinking. Because he remained in LA and worked for an absentee owner, Shaw was free to operate in the shadows, making moves and wielding all the power without being seen or sharing his thoughts with the people doing the work on the ground in St. Louis. Shaw's way of doing business might seem mysterious and less than ideal, but it's a pretty good example of why so many coaches hate front-office types.

Walsh always believed that general managers of losing organizations survived because they were "firmly in the owner's comfort zone," commanding quite a salary while doing very little. He loved to speculate about what a dinner would look like with an owner, a GM, and a personnel man of a losing team. Over martinis, the GM says, "Look, we have the best facilities and administration and exhibition schedule. We set up everything just right to get the job done." Over appetizers the personnel man says, "Well, we had a great draft; I know because I read it in the papers." By the time dessert arrives, the owner would have been convinced that his team had everything it needed to win a Super Bowl. Except they'd be wrong, because they wouldn't have the most important thing: a decent coach.

Give him credit; that's exactly what Shaw was thinking when he called me later to arrange a second meeting in St. Louis. For that one, Shaw also invited his first lieutenant, executive vice president Jay Zygmunt. Hailing a cab from the airport, I headed to Shaw's apartment in downtown Clayton, Missouri, a weekend retreat that was both office and residence for him when he was forced to come east for games or organizational get-togethers.

Because of the tight travel turnaround his assistant had scheduled for me, I knew Shaw was going to get right to the point. There would be no puppies this time.

When I arrived, Shaw was sitting at the far end of a long banquet table, where he announced that he was not happy with the direction of the team—which was a little weird considering that he was its main architect. What he wanted me to do was spend the next two months researching the qualities of successful NFL head coaches and then create a list of candidates who fit those parameters. He was emphatic about me being thorough in my research so that he would have the unimpeachable data necessary to dump Brooks at the end of the season.

As I cabbed back to the airport, a thousand ideas ricocheted around my head, and I was excited and grateful to get out of the NFL Films basement and into an actual assignment. I just wasn't at all sure how or where to begin such a monumental task. I've always been fascinated with the careers of great coaches. My last name is Lombardi, after all; I already knew everything there is to know about the Green Bay legend. That would be good groundwork for my portfolio of great-head-coach characteristics. I also had extensive firsthand knowledge of both Walsh and the young Bill Belichick.

Lombardi. Walsh. Belichick. What traits did those men share, and how could I assess them accurately for Shaw? My head swam the whole way home. Quickly, though, I mapped out a plan. Over the next month, I evaluated every head coach who had led his team to a Super Bowl since 1984, the year I entered the NFL. I devoured all I could on all of them—their beginnings, influences, career trajectories—trying to uncover common threads. I didn't care if they had gotten their start on the offensive or defensive side of the ball; winners come from both. Nor did I care what positions they might have coached early on. If the Steelers had listened to those who said offensive line coaches don't make great head coaches, they never would have won four Super Bowls under Chuck Noll.

Plus, having just spent three seasons in Cleveland with another tremendous offensive line coach, Kirk Ferentz, I knew they could definitely be head coaching material. (Ferentz eventually got his dream job and proved me right with 143 career wins and counting at the University of Iowa.) But the deeper I dug—the more data I accumulated—the further it took me from a conclusion. Before I knew it, I had dozens of amazing, highly successful coaches with a wide range of backgrounds and experiences on my list.

But what was I missing? Why couldn't I connect the dots?

Then, one day, sitting in a makeshift home office with my five-year-old son, Matthew, and *SportsCenter* playing on a loop in the background, it clicked. As I studied former Kansas City Chiefs and Buffalo Bills head coach Marv Levy, I had my *Jerry Maguire* epiphany: Coaches are first and foremost great leaders. Good coaches may be clever play callers or demanding drill sergeants or organized middle managers. But in the ultimate team sport, real success doesn't depend on tactics or discipline or order. It always comes down to how well a coach leads. I substituted the word *leader* for *coach,* and my research was transformed. I needed to define what made a great leader.

I immediately turned to the works of Tom Peters and Warren Bennis, the management gurus we studied during my days with the 49ers. They had established a handful of standard leadership qualities that I could apply, supplemented by my own hard-learned insight, to just about any coaching candidate throughout history and into the future. Those qualities were as follows.

## COMMAND OF THE ROOM

Followers need something to commit to. Great leaders know how to grab a team's attention and then show them what they're all fighting for. As Belichick says, "Unless commitment is made, there are only promises and hopes but no plans." You can't buy into a plan unless one is laid out clearly and plainly for the entire franchise. On the first day of preparation for Super Bowl XLIX, Belichick stood in front of his Patriots in the team meeting room and told them, "We have to understand how to play this game in order to win." Then, once he had their attention, he carefully explained how he intended to win the game. He never raised his voice, never made dramatic gestures. His voice barely wavered from his usual monotone. But when I looked around the room as he spoke, everyone was taking notes. He wasn't interested in what happened the week before. He spent no time reminiscing about what got them to that moment or what the outside world was saying about the burgeoning "Deflategate." He cared only about what was ahead and how to move forward with a collective blueprint that gave them the best chance of victory.

But this kind of alpha-dog magnetism goes only so far. No one can command a room better than Jon Gruden. Gruden, back now for his second shift with the Raiders after going 95–81 with Oakland and the Tampa Bay Buccaneers between 1998 and 2008, has incredible communication skills, but his words sometimes work against him. To hear him tell it, Gruden never has enough offensive talent for the schemes he has devised. Without fail, the last team he coached was more talented than his current one. How do I know this? I was with him in Philadelphia when he was the offensive coordinator and I was the pro personnel director. He would walk around the office complaining, "Can you believe I have to play these guys?" before rattling off names such as Ricky Watters, Charlie Garner, and Irving Fryar. By all accounts, those guys were at the very least competent pros or, I could argue, far better than that. But to Gruden's eyes, there was always something wrong with each of them.

When I moved on to Oakland, he was there, too—and, believe it or not, giving the exact same speech, though with a twist. This time he let it be known that the talent he coached in Philadelphia was far superior to what he was currently saddled with. I heard

Gruden being interviewed once by a TV production crew as background for a Raiders' nationally televised game, and as usual he was complaining about his lack of offensive talent. Finally, a member of the announcing team called him out: "Jon, you do realize that your quarterback [Rich Gannon] is having an MVP season?"

That was when I realized that Gruden told this no-talent story as motivation—for himself. None of it was about his team; he was pushing himself to work harder and smarter. Problem is, it's not exactly the best way to develop trust and respect in your players, and eventually it will backfire. If he were better at this part of the job—better at coping than complaining—he could still be one of the greats. But if he hasn't learned from his first tour, he'll end up flaming out again, just as he did after winning a Super Bowl in Tampa Bay.

## COMMAND OF THE MESSAGE

What good is a plan if you can't articulate it? Part of what made Hall of Fame coach Bill Parcells an exceptional leader was his brilliant communication skills. Watch clips of him as he addresses his team and listen to the simple metaphors he uses to help players understand. If he wanted better teamwork, he might say: "We're not playing solitaire out here." Short and sweet, it drives home the point and isn't going to be misunderstood. Parcells was a master at using humor and metaphor. Belichick, in contrast, is better at using video to detail exactly what might happen if players don't follow the plan. His bluntness is a beacon. "Look at this idiot, operating on his own, not doing what he should do," he might say, pointing to the screen, with the object of his ridicule as likely to be a Pro Bowler as a third-string fill-in.

Whether you use metaphors or game film, delivery isn't as important as meaning. Players can't accomplish anything unless they can visualize the path.

## COMMAND OF SELF

Personal accountability is the ultimate sign of strength. When a leader admits mistakes, it shows the team that he expects as much from himself as he does from his players. When a coach cuts a high draft pick or an expensive free agent, it may look bad in the media, but it has a big impact in the locker room. No one ever complains about the long hours in New England because Belichick's car is always the last to leave the team parking lot. He never asks players or staff to do more than he's willing to do.

In his play *Antigone,* Sophocles sums it up best: "All men make mistakes, but a good man yields when he knows his course is wrong and repairs the evil. The only crime is pride." Ego is the leading cause of unemployment in the coaching world. Those who thrive in this profession don't place their needs ahead of the team's. Of course, some ego is essential. It becomes a problem when it gets in the way of your decision making. The right kind of ego demands perfection, not praise.

Walsh most definitely had an ego; he did not deny the "genius" label that others gave him. He loved attention, but it never clouded his vision for the franchise. Likewise, few in football have ever managed their egos the way Belichick has. He is not worried about where an idea comes from; he cares only about whether it makes the team better. He knows that as the man running the organization he's going to get the credit by default, so he makes sure to spread it around. That's a rare thing in the NFL.

Rarer still are coaches who can admit when they're wrong. The NFL is full of insecure coaches who won't admit a mistake or share credit; in fact, they may even steal an idea or two. By contrast, you will constantly hear Belichick proclaim to his staff and players, "I screwed that up" or "That's on me." Command of self means sharing the blame and the credit alike, and this offers the advantage of allowing Belichick to step in at crunch time and say, "We did it your way, and it didn't work—now we're going to do it my way."

Being honest with oneself is the first step and one that coaches often are reluctant to try, especially someone new to the profession. Take Jim Harbaugh as an example. When I was in Philadelphia in 1997, Ray Rhodes, the head coach, asked me to find a special teams coach. I went through my research and recommended two guys: Rich Bisaccia from Clemson University and John Harbaugh from Indiana. We offered the job to Bisaccia, but when he chose to stay where he was, we happily hired Harbaugh. Four years later, when I was working in Oakland, Al Davis asked me to find a former NFL quarterback who might make a good coach. Because of the friendship I had built through John with the Harbaugh family, I brought up his brother Jim, who had just ended his playing career. We made him an assistant.

Jim was amazing from the start. He was one ex-player who really did have a great understanding of the game. What he needed work in was the other facets that define a great head coach. Computers and analytics were just coming online, and Jim, like a lot of us back then, had no idea how to use them. More troubling, though, was that he couldn't quite organize his thoughts into a coherent plan or message. It's one thing to know the game, quite another to be able to teach it. Jim worked hard to become the kind of clearheaded communicator the position demanded. The competitiveness and work ethic he had as a player may have even increased when he became a coach. That's unusual; more often than not, it's the other way around.

One late night, working alone at his makeshift desk in a room he shared with another Raiders assistant, John Morton, Harbaugh fell asleep on top of his keyboard. His nose landed on the M key, and when he woke up after several hours, there were pages upon pages of Ms on the screen.

I guess even back then he knew he would end up back in Ann Arbor.

## COMMAND OF OPPORTUNITY

As I formulated the pillars of leadership that would inform my coaching evaluations, I began to pick out the current men who fit them. It didn't take long to confirm that Belichick was one. After helping Parcells and the Giants win a pair of Super Bowls, he was considered one of the best defensive coordinators in the game, but his 36–44 record as a head coach in Cleveland included only a single playoff win. Few football people considered Belichick worthy of one of the most precious gifts in life: a second chance.

If my recommendation to Shaw was going to be Belichick, I needed more support to prove my case. So I went back to digging, this time for instances in which a second-chance hire proved to be the best choice. More often than not, looking for a coach in the NFL is a long walk down the statistical path of least resistance—that is, straight down Win-Loss Avenue. Just looking at records, though, without considering how they were amassed is a pretty shallow and lazy way to find your most important employee. Belichick, for example, took over an aging team in Cleveland that needed to be rebuilt. Making matters worse, he had to overcome a declining quarterback (Bernie Kosar) with a huge new contract and the power that comes from the owner calling him "the most important man in the organization." On top of that, it was the first year of the salary cap, a confusing and game-changing paradigm shift in the economics of the NFL. Within that context, the staff and culture Belichick was able to build in five seasons was a monumental achievement, not the failure implied by an overall record that was eight games under .500.

To this day, people ask me what the difference is between the Cleveland Belichick and the New England Belichick. My answer is always the same: very little. Okay, so he inherited a better team in New England and picked a Hall of Fame quarterback in the sixth round of the draft. (Some might say Tom Brady fell into his lap; nonetheless, he made the pick that everyone else had the chance to make, too.) But Belichick as a leader and the core beliefs he instilled were the same in both places. The difference people perceive is not with Belichick but with the owner. In New England, Robert Kraft approved of, even demanded, a culture change and gave Belichick nearly total control of football operations to achieve it. In Cleveland, Modell was both a meddler and a steadfast proponent of the status quo. If Belichick seemed bellicose with the Browns, well, you would be, too. It's one thing to lose because you failed as a leader, quite another to watch your lifelong dream go up in smoke because of restrictions assigned by outside forces. The biggest lesson Belichick learned in Cleveland was that he would take another head coaching job only if the right owner offered it.

The more I thought about Belichick's circumstances, the more I found myself circling back to Marv Levy, another example of a coach who overcame failure to grow and improve as a leader. A Harvard graduate, Levy had a quiet, professorial way about him, but his background in special teams had honed his ability to command and motivate. He was clearly a leader first; in fact, he may never have called a single play. But he was a successful head coach in the Canadian Football League and was on his way to becoming a successful NFL coach with the Kansas City Chiefs until the 1982 players' strike got in the way. Levy had been on an impressive upward curve in Kansas City—4–12, 7–9, 8–8, and 9–7 in his first four seasons—but the Chiefs' locker room was full of hardcore advocates for players' rights, and that adversely affected the team's chemistry once the strike ended. They went 3–6 during the strike year, and he was let go. No one expected to hear from Levy again. He had had his shot at the big time, and it didn't work out. End of story. But four years later, when Bill Polian became the Buffalo Bills' general manager, he looked past Levy's one bad year and hired his old friend (from their days in the USFL with the Chicago Blitz) at midseason. Four Super Bowl appearances and 112 regular-season wins later, Levy is firmly ensconced in Canton and serves as a patron saint for second acts in the coaching profession.

I was sure Belichick—who was back with Parcells, assisting him in New England—would thrive the way Levy had if he was given the opportunity. You see, becoming an NFL head coach is a process. You learn on the fly. It's a lot like the advice the late, great Glenn Frey, front man for the Eagles, once got about songwriting from Bob Seger. The veteran Detroit rocker told Frey that to make it in the music business he would have to write his own songs.

"What if they're bad?" Frey asked.

"Oh, of course they're bad; just keep writing until they're good," Seger told him.

That's what being a first-time NFL head coach is like. It is more than likely you're going to be bad at it. You just have to keep working at it until you get good and pray that you don't end up a one-hit wonder.

Essentially, Modell already had paid for Belichick's head coaching apprenticeship, and in my mind at least that should have been enough to vault him to the top of Shaw's list. But coaches are a bit like cars: Once they've been used, their value goes down because buyers (GMs and owners) are looking for that new coach smell. A team that needs a coach usually needs to win back its fan base. Though my research showed that there's a ton of hidden value in second-chance coaches, most owners and fans see them only as retreads.

## COMMAND OF THE PROCESS

None of the other pillars matter if a leader is not fair and consistent. When Jim Mora was the head coach of the Atlanta Falcons, his best player, DeAngelo Hall, bought a Bentley that was delivered to training camp on the night of a team bowling event. Mora had told the Falcons to ride to the event together on the bus, but Hall balked. He wanted to take his new wheels for a spin. Instead of sending a message that no one is above the team, not even when it comes to an off-season social event, Mora chose to appease his star. Making matters worse, he chose to ride shotgun. Wrong call. Playing favorites poisoned the Falcons' locker room, and bending the rules eroded Mora's authority. Six months later he was out of a job.

That situation might not seem like a big deal, but every move a leader makes is analyzed by the team, and any one of them can have far-reaching consequences. If the team bus rule can be broken, what about curfew? Or red zone assignments? That's why Brady never gets a pass on Belichick's rules. When the Patriots play at home, the quarterback stays in the same hotel, in the same kind of bed, as the rookie free agent who just made the team even though the superstar's big house and supermodel wife are less than 15 miles away.

When rules don't apply to everyone, the ensuing chaos collapses whatever foundation a leader has tried so hard to build.

've always loved the movie *Patton*, with George C. Scott in the title role as the hard-charging, ivory-handled-pistol-carrying commander of the Third Army in World War II. In the opening scene, as the general addresses the troops before the D-Day invasion, he quickly demonstrates all five areas of leadership. He commands his troop's attention and communicates his message. His perfectly balanced humility and pride show a clear command of self, he has bounced back from numerous setbacks, and he has an unwavering commitment to the process, in this case the battle plan. "No bastard ever won a war by dying for his country," Patton shouts on the screen. "You win it by making the other poor dumb bastard die for his country."

Having settled on my pillars of coaching leadership, I was on to phase two of my search for the Rams' next general: finding potential candidates. Each of the winning coaches I examined usually had three or four of the five leadership traits I was looking for. Losing coaches or those who couldn't sustain excellence over time rarely had more than two. Most NFL coaches have a plan and the communication skills to teach and implement it. What separates good coaches from great ones is often trust and accountability, and so that was what I focused on over the next few months as I prepared my report for Shaw.

On a Friday in December 1996 before the 4–9 Rams were to face the Bears, I flew to yet another clandestine meeting with Shaw and Zygmunt. I didn't have to be worried about being discovered, because our rendezvous was purposely scheduled for the day before the team and the press descended on the city. Nevertheless, inside the thick three-ring notebook that contained my massive report I used numbers (1 through 7) instead of section titles so that if people caught a glimpse of it, they wouldn't be able to connect it back to the Rams or know what was contained within it.

Section 1 featured the background and a summary page for every successful coach currently working in the NFL: Bill Cowher, Mike Holmgren, Jimmy Johnson, Marv Levy, Bobby Ross, Marty Schottenheimer, and George Seifert. At the end of the section was an introduction to my tenets of coaching leadership.

Section 2 dealt with out-of-the-game coaches who might be available for hire. This featured a breakdown of their skill sets as well as a section called "If You Hire This Guy . . ." that described what things would be like working with that coach: how he operated, how he treated his staff and players, how driven he was. To go deeper into this topic, which I think is a key to hiring the right guy, I included a section with specific questions to ask during any potential interviews (see page 51). This chapter had Bill Parcells, Jim Mora Sr., Denny Green, Dan Reeves, and Mike Ditka, with the prospects ranked in order of who I would recommend, starting with Parcells.

Section 3 featured current coordinators who displayed the

leadership qualities I laid out in the first section. My guys (and in my ordered ranking): Chan Gailey, Pittsburgh Steelers' offensive coordinator; Emmitt Thomas, Philadelphia Eagles' defensive co-ordinator; Gary Kubiak, Denver Broncos' offensive coordinator; Pete Carroll, 49ers' defensive coordinator; Vic Fangio, New Orleans Saints' defensive coordinator; Sherman Lewis, Packers' offensive coordinator; Bill Belichick, Giants' assistant head coach; Jon Gruden, Eagles' offensive coordinator; and Cam Cameron, Washington's quarterback coach.

Section 4 covered college coaches and focused on Michigan State's Nick Saban, Northwestern's Gary Barnett, Florida's Steve Spurrier, Miami's Butch Davis, and Cal's Steve Mariucci. Most of my recommendations in this section included a caveat. Because I hadn't worked with most of those guys, I'd need to interview them before I could give them the full Lombardi stamp of approval.

Section 5 was devoted to organizational structures of success-ful NFL teams. It was a not-so-subtle message to the Rams' brain trust: This is how winning franchises operate.

Section 6 was my gratis breakdown of the Rams roster and how Shaw should tweak it if he wanted to win.

Section 7 was my official recommendations. I graded my top choices in all the leadership areas and offered examples to illus-trate my assessments. I explained that any candidate who wasn't strong in these pillars simply didn't make the final list. I included the career arc of each and insight from former coaches and play-ers. I also predicted the ability of each to handle the job.

I hoped I would have the chance to spell out for Shaw a couple of other broad takeaways as well. In particular, I wanted to talk about what happens when an owner hires a guy because he has at least shown proficiency managing one side of the ball with the hope that he will cover his blind spots with other talented coaches. The problem, though, is that such a setup makes creating a unified culture almost impossible. I call it the "Vienna problem." Austria's capital offers alluring highlights of many different countries: the coffee of Turkey, the intellectualism of Germany, the pastries of France, the brandy of Armenia, the art from all over the world. It is that cultural variety that makes Vienna an international tourist destination. But what works for cities doesn't cut it for teams.

Vienna would never win a Super Bowl. The little-of-this, little-of-that approach has a very slim chance of overall success. And that's what you get when you have lots of subcontractors and no visionary architect. Take Rex Ryan, former head coach of the New York Jets and Buffalo Bills. Ryan is great with a quote and quick with a prediction, and in his first two seasons with the Jets he appeared to have the qualities of a successful head coach. But in the end it was a mirage. Rex knows defense and loves coaching it. When he became a head coach, though, he still acted like a defensive coordinator. He left his offensive staff on an island. He subcontracted out half his team so that he could stay in his own familiar world. It got so bad that, in training camp, drills were set up for the defense to "win," and most of the important preparation for the season focused on that side of the ball. The offensive staff never felt like it was part of Ryan's inner circle.

I was ready to tell Shaw that this division never works. The coaching staff has to be united. Ryan's Vienna approach makes success impossible.

I also planned to warn against copycatting. Hire an assistant coach from a succcessful program, this thinking goes, and hope he'll duplicate that success. Kind of like how horse breeders count on former champions to produce future ones. It's a practice that makes for contented stallions and a whole bunch of colts who never get out of the gate. Check your racing form for one Marty Mornhinweg.

Many head coaching candidates come to their interviews with a huge notebook filled with a season's worth of practice sessions. I don't understand why this is perceived as a selling point, but I know how it became one. Blame it on Mike Holmgren's former teaching colleague Bob LaMonte, who quit his school job and began to represent Holmgren in 1992 after he became head coach of the Packers. Since then LaMonte has expanded his agent business, becoming a league power broker with a stable of young coaches and front-office candidates. He is known for spending lots of time preparing his candidates for their interviews, preaching attention to detail and thoughtful planning. He has even written a popular book on how to impress owners that pushes those skills.

LaMonte filled an important void in helping men prepare for the big job, holding summer seminars on team building. Andy Reid, now the head coach of the Chiefs, was an early LaMonte success story, hitting the ground running in his first head job with the Eagles even though he had never even been an NFL coordinator. But Reid has thrived at least as much because of his leadership qualities as because of LaMonte's curriculum. (He has never quite lived up to his early promise, though, for reasons I will discuss later.)

Mornhinweg, the former head coach of the Detroit Lions, is another of LaMonte's clients, well versed in the Holmgren school of detail and planning. (In fact, Mornhinweg's mannerisms and inflections remind you of Holmgren's.) Mornhinweg has always been a good offensive coordinator, but when it came time to don the headset, it didn't take long to see that he did not possess the leadership skills of a Holmgren or Reid, skills he couldn't learn at LaMonte Academy or read out of a notebook. When he won just five games in two years in Detroit, it reaffirmed for me that although organization is important, leadership is what really rules in the coaching ranks.

My first suggestion to Shaw would be to surreptitiously gauge Parcells's interest in running the entire organization. He checked off all the boxes, but there was no reason to court Parcells if, as I suspected, there was no chance he'd accept the position. It diminishes the team and whoever they eventually hire if it leaks out that the guy wasn't exactly their first choice. A little high schoolish? Yes, but optics matter.

After Parcells, my top picks were Saban, Belichick, Barnett, Carroll, Gailey, and Fangio.

I felt so strongly about Saban that I told Shaw not to let money or control get in the way. As for some of my other recommendations, Carroll certainly has proved my faith; Barnett has as well. Why Fangio never got a chance, I'll never know. And Gailey? If he never reached his potential as a head coach in Dallas, I'd suggest that not many do operating in Jerry Jones's world.

I didn't know then that history would vindicate my research, but in any case I was proud of the work I had put in and the product I'd produced. On the cab ride from O'Hare, I collected my thoughts and went over my presentation one more time. I was dressed in a coat and tie, hoping to project a sense of gravity, professionalism, and attention to detail. That made one of us.

I handed over the notebook and watched Shaw halfheartedly scan in seconds what took me months to compile. He seemed instantly disappointed. Shaw thought I had a blind spot for Belichick, and he was probably right. I favored a guy who would become the greatest coach of all time; go figure. Remember, though, this was a long time before all the Lombardi Trophies in New England, and at the time Belichick was a newly fired sub-.500 head coach who had a terrible reputation as a guy who couldn't get along with the media or persuade established players to buy into his concept. Belichick also had to answer for his handling of local hero Kosar's release, which infuriated the city of Cleveland. (Shaw and the other naysayers had no idea what a disruptive force Kosar had become in the locker room after losing his job to Vinny Testaverde.) Shaw dismissed my Belichick recommendation out of hand without reading one bit of the research.

As for Saban, he was even less enthused, if that was possible. Shaw's first experience with a college coach (Brooks) hadn't gone well, and he had no interest in hiring another. It didn't matter that Saban had coached more than five years in the NFL and had run a defense that allowed only 204 points in 1994. Saban arrived in Cleveland as Belichick's first hire. After one year as the head coach of the University of Toledo, he was chosen to be the Browns' defensive coordinator. From the first practice, any football observer could tell he had the makings of a fruitful head coach: He had a strong plan and an effective way of communicating that plan, and his ability to be self-critical earned the players' trust in a way that rivaled their feelings for Belichick. Saban was different from his old boss in many ways. For starters, he was more vocal and quicker to anger, and he was always well dressed and well groomed, never a hair out of place. Belichick was the opposite, hair usually messed up from sleeping on the couch, always in some form of team gear, with his trademark scissor-cut sleeves. But these two were similar in the ways that counted—intelligence, decision making, leadership—making them a true odd couple and an incredible team. Separately, they are simply two of the finest coaches I have ever seen.

But sitting in his hotel-suite chair, mindlessly leafing through my work, Shaw had the look of a guy who considered my information and conclusions to be worthless, which might explain why he never paid me a dime for any of it. And I had the distinct feeling he was going to throw away my notebook as soon as I left.

Eventually, Shaw convinced Dick Vermeil, the old Eagles coach, to come out of retirement to be the Rams head coach and director of football operations. (At least Shaw listened to me about the advantages of picking someone with head coaching experience.) Vermeil didn't do much initially to justify the hiring. In his first two seasons in St. Louis, he won a total of 9 games. In the third year, his leadership qualities began to shine through and he made the most of his own second chance, winning 13 games and the Super Bowl.

Things worked out well enough for Shaw and the Rams. As for

me, I left that hotel suite in Chicago and headed back to the airport without a job or a paycheck—at least, not until the next January, when the Eagles hired me as pro personnel director. What I did have, though, was something much more valuable: a notebook full of priceless research and insider knowledge regarding the evaluation and hiring of the most important position in sports—information that has benefited me every day since.

I'll never say that nothing good came out of that bizarre summer of 1996.

# WHAT TO ASK AN
# NFL HEAD COACH CANDIDATE

There's a popular social media meme that quotes Marcus Aurelius as having said, "The secret of all victory lies in the organization of the nonobvious." If Chapter 2 has shown anything, it's that sometimes the nonobvious looks pretty obvious from a different angle. But how can one possibly predict how a potential coach will handle the unpredictable? Our failures in the hiring process in Oakland led me to develop an addendum to my Rams notebook and my pillars of coaching leadership. To help with the interviewing of head coaching candidates, I created an extensive outline of inquiry that explores every nonobvious wrinkle of organization and team building that a head coach needs to control to conquer the modern-era NFL.

## PHILOSOPHY (GENERAL)

1. Offense
2. Defense
3. Kicking game
4. Player development
5. Player procurement

## OFF-SEASON

1. What kind of program?
   a. Define it: Goals and objectives?
   b. Fat guys: How are you handling them?
   c. What are your mandatory lifts?
   d. What schedule do you adhere to?
   e. Coaches' involvement?
   f. Individual player development: How and why we train?

2. OTA [organized team activity] days
   a. What is the objective of these?
   b. Team or individual?

3. Minicamps
   a. Objective: Team or individual?
   b. What is the emphasis?
   c. What players are to take part? Is it a veteran-based camp or a player-development camp?
   d. Meals: What do we want to pay for? Which meals?

4. Incentive clauses in contracts
   a. Mandatory?
   b. How much do we pay?
   c. What will the housing situation be like?

5. Rehab of injured reserve players
   a. Plan?
   b. Where and when does it start?
   c. Clearing of players: Who will make this choice?

## TRAINING CAMP

1. Philosophy
   a. Schedules
   b. Meetings
   c. Objectives
   d. Players who fail physical: How do we handle them?
      - Rules different for them?
      - Count on the 80-man roster?
   e. Breaking of team rules: Fines or waived?
   f. Veteran workdays: Different?
   g. Conditioning of team: Two-minute drill run or what?
      - If failed, what is the punishment?
      - Practice for players that are not in condition?
      - Treatment of players?
      - Deal with major injuries to starters?
   h. Do we stay at home or go away?

i. Meals: Who sets the menu? What extent do we spend?

j. Fan access?

k. Media access?

l. Family members' access?

- Coaches' kids ball boys?

m. College coaches?

- Give out any information to visitors?

n. Scrimmage philosophy:

- With another team?
- With our team?
- Contact? How much?
- Player development days?
- How much padded work?

2. **Player personnel movement in training camp**

a. Work roster? Improve the eightieth man? What do you want?

b. Move players' positions around during camp? Put players in right spot?

c. Depth chart evaluation: Who plays where? Do we reward practice or games?

d. Personnel meetings and evaluations?

e. Retired players at camp? How do we treat that with other players?

f. Preparation for opener in terms of personnel?

3. Preseason games

   a. Philosophy:

- Offense
- Defense
- Kicking game

   b. How do we travel?

- Who goes?
- Who stays behind?
- If not playing, then go?
- Kind of plane?

   c. Reps of veterans, reps of rookies?

   d. Schedule of game day, schedule of the day before the game?

   e. How do we handle injuries?

   f. Who cuts the players?

- Coaches talk to players cut?

## REGULAR SEASON

1. Philosophy of the week

2. What do you want from the pro personnel department?

   a. Scouting reports

- Meetings with director?

   b. Matchup notes

   c. Weekly workouts

   d. Emergency list

3. **Practice squad philosophy: For reps or player development?**
   a. After-practice schedule for practice squad?
   b. Young player workout? Who will work with them?

4. **Weekly schedule**
   a. Players
   b. Coaches
   c. Players who miss one day of practice, or two, or three, or on injured reserve
   d. Team meetings versus individual meetings
   e. Holiday schedules
   f. Bye week schedule

5. **Player discipline**
   a. Philosophy
   b. How do we handle:
      • Weight problems?
      • Sleeping in meetings?
      • Missing meetings?

6. **Travel**
   a. Dress code?
   b. Kind of plane?
   c. When do we leave?
   d. Who makes the trip?
      • Job at the game? Do they come?
      • No job at the game? Do they come?
      • Return policy:

- ◦ Can players stay in the town?
- ◦ Dress for return?
- ◦ Airport bars?

e. Curfew on trips?

f. Hotel rooms:

- Singles for players? Pay own or club?
- In city or out? Isolated part of town?
- Movies in the room?
- Who is allowed in meals?
- Family rates?
- Friend rates?
- Security on floor?
- Room check?
- Who gets suites?

g. Two-day philosophy and one-day philosophy?

h. Buses:

- Who rides them?
- How many do you want?
- Taxi for players? Mandatory for buses?

i. Monday Night game away?

j. Planes:

- Coaches in with players?
- Players' seats?
- What beverages are allowed on the plane?
- Boosters on plane?

## COACHES AND SUPPORT STAFF

1. **What is your role on game day: Calling plays, game management, or both?**

    a. Instant replay: Whose responsibility?

    b. Rules: Game day and during the week?

    c. Time-outs?

    d. Personnel?

    e. Special teams decisions: You or coaches?

    - Onside kicks: What is the primary option call?
    - End-of-the-game play: Do you have one?

    f. Fourth-down calls?

    - Who has final say, you or coordinator?

    g. Handling officials?

    - Report to the NFL office: Who?

    h. Conduct on the sideline?

    i. Who is allowed to be there?

    j. Where should coordinators sit?

    k. Pregame talk?

    l. Who decides on who gets introduced?
    Leave to PR?

    m. Halftime talk?

    n. Locker room access?

    o. Video of game?

    p. Handling of the computer printouts?

    q. Media after game:

    - How much time after game?
    - What staff members can talk to media?
    - Briefing before meeting the media: Who?
    - Radio show?
    - Any one-on-one media commitments?

2. Assistant coaches

   a. Do you have candidates for offensive, defensive, and special team coordinator?

- Who calls plays?
- Will you have overruling power?

   b. Who are your candidates for offensive and defensive line coaches?

- Your choice or coordinator's?
- Who will decide on the staff once the coordinators are picked?

   c. Salary of staff? Your call or GM's?

- Years of contracts?
- Rollovers?
- How many staff members?
  - Secretary or assistant?
- What kind of people are you looking for?
- What kinds of personalities are you looking for?
- Level of experience?
- Friends? Do you need to have known them?
- Film breakdown coaches?
- Who coaches the younger players?
- Evaluation of staff: Do you welcome any input?
- Off-season role for assistant coaches:
  - What do they work on?
  - Trends?
  - Visit other places?
- Evaluation of own team:
  - Draft role?
  - UFA [undrafted free agent] role?
- Media responsibility for assistant coaches:
  - Can they talk?
  - When and to whom?
  - Reporting process: How will it work?

3. **Player personnel staff**

   a. How do we work the roster?

   b. Players 46–58: Who controls them?

   c. What day is a workout day for emergency list?

4. **Training staff**

   a. Who will handle their schedule?

      • Vacation time?

      • Who handles the players before camp—July?

   b. What needs do you have?

   c. Treatment of players:

      • Schedule of times?

      • Home treatment?

   d. Players getting operated on: Who handles them?

      • What do we send to them in the hospital?

   e. Rehab in season: Who handles?

   f. Rehab out of season: Who handles?

   g. Medical meetings?

      • When?

      • Who is involved?

      • Who has final say on who is cleared to play?

      • Medical definitions of injuries?

   h. Out-of-town second opinions?

   i. View on second doctor doing the operations?

   j. Weight coach involved in rehab?

   k. How many trainers at camp?

   l. How many team medical people are involved?

m. View on massage and rub-down people?

  • Who pays: Players or team?

n. Dietary experts: Who handles?

5. **Equipment personnel**

a. Who will handle their schedule?

b. What needs do you have for them?

c. Who assigns jersey numbers?

d. Needs for players?

e. Shoes?

f. Equipment deals?

g. Game role in pregame, postgame?

h. Travel: Extra people?

i. Locker access: All allowed?

## ORGANIZATION

1. **Free agency**

a. Coaches involved?

b. Who will recruit them?

c. Pro board or coaches' board?

d. Salary cap knowledge:

  • Coaches know numbers?

  • Can agents call coaches? Can players?

2. **Projects**

a. Coaches' schedule in off-season?

b. What do they work on, not personnel-related?

c. Trends?

    d. Vacation time?

    e. Owners meetings?

3. **College draft**

    a. How much involved?

    b. Philosophy of draft: Aggressive, team needs?
       Best player?

    c. Coach reports: Grades?

    d. Coaches work out players?

    e. Coaches in draft room?

    f. Indy Combine?

    g. Interview of players?

    h. Who comes in to visit? Our 20-players list?

    i. College free agents:

- Who sets that list?
- Who recruits?

3

# TEAM BUILDING

## IN SEARCH OF PROGRAM GUYS

*We are not collecting talent; we are building a team.*

—BILL BELICHICK

El Camino Real, the King's Highway, is a well-known thorough-fare that stretches from San Diego to San Francisco. On a Tuesday in April 1986 the road that once linked California's Spanish missions carried me on an early-morning pilgrimage from my town house in Mountain View to the San Francisco 49ers' office in Redwood City. There is nothing easy or simple about the imperfect science of team building in the NFL except maybe the commute. In those days the NFL draft was still a midweek affair that began with a yawn and a whimper at 8 A.M. on a Tuesday in New York. The 5 A.M. start time for the 49ers staff put me, by then a West Coast college scout for the team, on El Camino Real at

2:30 A.M., when the normally jam-packed highway was empty, with nothing but green lights the entire way. Call it the calm before the most important draft in 49ers history.

Soon enough, NFL commissioner Pete Rozelle would walk to the podium at the Marriott Marquis in New York City's Times Square and announce Auburn running back Bo Jackson as the first pick of the Tampa Bay Buccaneers. But we were in a much trickier spot. For starters, the 49ers were picking eighteenth, a spot that didn't bode well for a burgeoning dynasty. If it was rather high for a team that had won a Super Bowl two years earlier, it was also a bit low for a team that had just finished second in the NFC West. (There were 28 teams in the NFL in 1986.) Under Bill Walsh's leadership, the 49ers franchise was no longer accustomed to second-place finishes or to being beaten decisively in the wild card playoffs by the New York Giants, with our high-octane offense held to three points in the process, as we were in 1985. It was clear as we headed into the off-season that the owner, Eddie DeBartolo Jr., would not tolerate another lackluster finish. Of course, the only person more eager than his boss to make the necessary draft-day tweaks to the team was Walsh himself.

The coach believed that securing a handful of new starters, including an elite pass rusher and upgrades in the backfield, was our ticket back to the Super Bowl. In 1986, the draft was really the only way to find those players and to build, or rebuild, a team. Despite all the changes to the economics of the game during the last 30 years, that's still very much the case. If anything, the finite resources teams now have under the salary cap (more on that in a bit) have only made the relatively inexpensive young talent in the draft even more valuable, and the grand art and science of talent evaluation and team building even more important. Back then, though, free agency didn't exist; when a player's contract expired, his team essentially retained control of him. There was the occasional difference-making trade, but for the most part, in 1986 draft picks were the gold. And Walsh needed to find his fortune.

It didn't matter that his scouts and personnel people were calling that year's draft the worst ever. That just made him crazy. I mean, he would go nuts, snapping back with "We only need to find 12 good players!" before stomping away in disgust. Walsh hated that kind of defeatist chatter, not least because if it was true, how could he ever improve his team? He didn't care what the rest of the league was doing or thinking or whining about; he simply wouldn't tolerate excuses. That extended even to speaking badly about a prospect. If someone needed to be critical of a player's talent, he was to keep it professional. Stay clean and to the point, and don't denigrate. Words such as *sucks* or *blows* had no part in a report. "It's our job to find talent, not dismiss it," he told me. His dignified single-mindedness led us to work harder than ever that spring.

Leading up to the 1986 draft, there was an unusual sense of urgency even for a workaholic like Walsh. That winter he seemed to always be calling me to fetch film of prospects or work the phones in search of more information. My job was to be on call at all times to help him with whatever he needed. That included invitation-only Saturday sessions in which Walsh and the 49ers staff discussed in great detail the players each of them had scouted over the previous week. Walsh controlled the meetings with his probing questions, reminding presenters always to highlight "what the player could do for the 49ers"—that is, how he specifically fit our schemes or needs. Through it all, he took notes on his ubiquitous 3-by-5 cards, leaning my way and whispering instructions whenever he needed supplemental information.

On draft day in 1986, driving through the inky, deserted darkness of El Camino Real, I thought a lot about those Saturday staff meetings and everything I had learned during the frantic three months of nonstop work that led up to the draft that would build a dynasty. I've never forgotten the main takeaway from that year. It remains just as relevant and vital more than three decades later. The game of football might be ruled by perfectionists, but at its core, success in the NFL comes down to managing the

maddening, inexact science of talent evaluation and team building. And when it comes to predicting human performance on a
football field, the only thing for certain is that nothing is ever for
certain. Despite the thousands of man-hours and millions of dol-
lars teams invest in the draft every year, a recent study showed,
teams still get it wrong on almost half of their top draft picks.

The imperfect nature of team building is why Walsh and all
the other great football minds I've been around have approached
the eternal puzzle of personnel the same way: Instead of trying to
"solve" or perfect the draft, they have figured out how to create an
edge by developing methods, strategies, and insights—things such
as deeper background checks, better character evaluations, and
more thorough off-season evaluations—that minimize risks and
improve the odds of building a better team. Few mastered these
techniques better than Walsh.

That's why, as I pulled into the San Francisco facility on the
morning of the 1986 draft, I was overcome by the strangest feeling
in our business: confidence.

One of Walsh's draft mentors was Al Davis himself, whom Walsh
had worked for earlier in his career. Having spent time with
both legends, I saw firsthand how Davis influenced Walsh's
ideas about team building, especially the importance put on a
prospect's pedigree. Both Davis and Walsh understood that digging deep into a draft pick's background could be indispensably
informative. For one thing, Davis believed that any player who
demonstrated rare talent in high school needed to be considered
carefully regardless of how he played in college. After all, his prep
potential could have been squandered by poor coaching or a mismatch in talent and scheme. Davis believed in this theory so deeply
that he carried around a file of old Sunday *Parade* magazines so
that in free moments he could pore over the tissue-thin pages that

listed past *Parade* high school All-America teams in hopes of un-
covering a forgotten diamond.

In 1985, Walsh had called me into his office to give me one
of his special assignments. He wanted me to give the top three
receivers in that draft—Al Toon, Eddie Brown, and Jerry Rice—
the Davis treatment. Calling high school coaches wouldn't do. I
was to go deep into their backgrounds and talk to teammates,
classmates, guidance counselors, girlfriends, ex-girlfriends, and
anyone else who could offer insight into those young men. After
finally getting to the NFL and what I thought was the big time, I
ended up spending almost a month collecting data on high school
wideouts. You'd be amazed at how much I was able to scare up.

I did my sleuthing on East Coast time, traveling the King's
Highway in the middle of the night, getting in before 5 A.M., and
working the phones from one of the back meeting rooms. Spiral
notebook open before me, I called possible sources, throwing the
49ers name around in hopes that it would loosen lips. More often
than not, it did. From guidance counselors and coaches alike, the
information flowed. I made and received calls all day long. Each
time I hung up, the phone would ring again. I always answered,
because I knew that if Walsh had the right information, he would
make the right decision. Somewhere in my stuffed notebook I was
going to have the right information. A little surprisingly, Brown
emerged as the clear local hero. He was revered at Miami High
School, eliciting raves from coaches who worked with him and
faced him. His athleticism and quickness were awe-inspiring. The
Bengals thought so, too. That is why, after the Jets took Toon with
the tenth overall pick, they grabbed Brown with the thirteenth,
leaving us with Rice. He worked out pretty well, I think we'd all
have to agree, but who knows what kind of a name Brown could
have made for himself in the NFL if he had dropped into our laps.

Another background area that Davis taught Walsh to care about
was track and field experience. Davis was forever on the lookout
for 100-meter champions from states he deemed "fast," such as

California, Florida, Lousiana, and Texas. (Impressive times from places such as Minnesota didn't carry the same weight because Davis assumed they were wind-aided.) Davis, by the way, also was obsessed with shot-putters, discus throwers, and state wrestling champs: athletes who displayed rare balance, great footwork, and explosive power. This scouting "cheat" had led the 49ers to Jeff Stover, the University of Oregon's Pac-10 shot-put champ, whom Walsh called the most consistent lineman on San Francisco's 1984 Super Bowl–winning team.

One of my all-time favorite Al Davis stories is also a cautionary tale about the imperfect science of player evaluation. In 1981 Davis selected Texas Tech cornerback Ted Watts with the twenty-first pick. When he finally got to meet Watts, Davis stuck out his hand and said, "Ah, the fastest man in Florida." To which Teddy replied, "Yeah, thank God that white boy slipped out of the blocks and pulled his hamstring." Davis was brought up so short that he almost pulled his own hamstring. He had made his pick on false pretenses. That white boy, it turns out, was Cris Collinsworth, who recently was named one of the top 50 Bengals of all time. Watts's NFL career never made it out of the starting blocks. He started just 22 games with the Raiders.

Walsh's first toe dip into the track and field pool didn't go much better. Renaldo Nehemiah, a favorite to win gold in the high hurdles at the 1980 Olympics until the American boycott took away his chance, didn't even play college football. But his breathtaking athleticism got him several NFL tryouts before the Niners signed him. Walsh tried desperately to mold Nehemiah into a receiver, but it was clear almost immediately that he just didn't have any instincts on a football field. After three years and only 43 catches, Nehemiah was out of San Francisco and back on the track.

Brown's stellar high school background and Nehemiah's mesmerizing physical presence on the track were proof that you can't judge a prospect on just one or two parameters no matter how incredible he may seem. A proper, successful evaluation has to include dozens of factors, countless hours of film study, and real-time confirmation from as many sets of eyes as possible.

If you ask me, Davis's most important lesson in scouting was this: Focus on the level of competition. It seems obvious now, but Davis was one of the first to understand the huge variation of talent in college—from program to program and conference to conference—and how not being able to compare apples to apples could severely affect draft evaluations. Davis was drawn to players who were at their best against the best. That was why he (and in turn Walsh and eventually almost the entire NFL) loved all-star games, especially the Senior Bowl. In fact, the Raiders would always begin their draft preparations the same way every year: with the complete scouting and coaching staffs in a room and Davis himself armed with the remote control and videotape of the Senior Bowl.

Senior Bowl week in Alabama offered insight that wasn't available during any other college visit. For starters, there's just no place to hide against competition that good. And if a player performed a skill once in such elevated company, coaches assumed that they could get him to replicate that in the pros. We looked at how quickly players learned new techniques and, most of all, how much they improved in the week leading up to the game. If a player could get better in four days, it was a safe bet he would take much bigger strides once he was being tutored full-time in the league.

Davis's idea about watching players compete against those at the highest level remains the key to effective personnel evaluation. Usually, the NFL teams with the lowest winning percentage in the previous season are given the opportunity to coach at the Senior Bowl (if they haven't been fired, that is). Just a couple of years ago that was the Dallas Cowboys. One of the players on their team was a young quarterback from Mississippi State. Dak Prescott had a distinguished college career, but questions lingered about his ability to adapt to the pro game, his football intelligence, and his overall skill level. After a week with Prescott at the Senior Bowl, though, the Cowboys had answers and insight on a quarterback prospect that no other NFL team could obtain. Armed with that information, they were able to secure a potential franchise quarterback with a fourth-round pick, the NFL equivalent of winning the Powerball.

I'm pretty sure I know exactly how Al, were he still alive, would feel about America's Team using his methods to find a marquee quarterback.

n 2003 Michael Lewis released *Moneyball,* the story of Oakland Athletics general manager Billy Beane's quest to gain an advantage for his revenue-poor baseball team with an outside-the-box analytical approach. In the book, Lewis explains the biases inherent in traditional baseball scouting. In his latest work, *The Undoing Project,* he delves deeper into the systematic biases of human decision making. In particular, he writes about confirmation bias, which holds that the human mind is just plain bad at seeing things it doesn't expect to see and a bit too eager to see what it wants to. Confirmation bias is absolutely insidious in my field even though it breaks the first rule of scouting: Never begin with the end in mind.

Most of the time we don't even realize it is occurring. Evaluators get caught up in groupthink, settle on an opinion about a prospect, and then arrange the evidence to support it, sometimes for years. Biases in scouting are the main reason many NFL teams fail to make substantial progress in the standings from one season to the next.

Certain coaches, for instance, have a particular weak spot for players with "football intelligence" and let that overshadow actual talent level. More than a few players have survived in the league by knowing a team's systems cold even when they lack the physical tools to actually make a play when it matters. I call those guys "bus drivers" because they can master the route to the stadium perfectly but can't do anything once they've arrived. When the game begins, they're stuck in park and have little effect on the outcome. Bus drivers make me crazy.

It's not just coaches who get fooled; personnel staffers can be mesmerized by biases as well. Blame the "card player." During game weeks, pro scouting executives watch practice squaders and other inactive players as they mimic the opposing offense or defense in drills. These scout team players are shown a card for their assignment and then execute it. They play fast because they don't have to think; they just do. Alas, this is not always an accurate indicator of their worth because it's assignment-free, pressure-free football, like the touch game you played in the backyard, with routes traced on the back of the quarterback's hand.

The greatest card player of all time—the man for whom the term was coined in 1991—was John Thornton, a defensive lineman from the University of Cincinnati (not to be confused with the John Thornton who played at West Virginia and later for the Cincinnati Bengals). John Earvin Thornton Jr., a college free agent nose tackle, had a typical-for-those-days nose tackle body—like a Coke machine. He was not an instinctive player, but at 6'3" and 300 pounds he could bull his way forward because he was stronger than almost everyone else. As a member of the Cleveland Browns practice squad, he was supposed to imitate the opposing defensive linemen. In practice he'd glance at the card for his alignment and path, then reenact whatever the card told him to do. Playing off the card, he was incredible and virtually impossible to block. So incredible, in fact, that we activated him off the practice squad. Big mistake. Once the game was live and the chess pieces started moving, Thornton had to think for himself. And when he was forced to rely on instincts and awareness of the scheme, he was far from the force we had hoped for. It was as if he were moving in slow motion, the easiest guy to block on the field. He lasted five games before we released him. But it was worth it, I suppose, because we learned something important about our own biases: Card players and football players are two very different things.

The second destructive form of bias we see all the time in NFL team building is "scouting blinders": whenever drafted players are kept around long after it has become obvious that the evaluation that got them where they are was dead wrong. Like many crimes, the cover-up is even worse than the initial mistake. When it came to players Al Davis discovered, there was no like, only love, and when he loved, he loved forever. Everyone in the Raiders front office called it "the scholarship." In 2001 we claimed Chad Slaughter, a 6'8" offensive tackle, from the Jets. (Normally, Davis hated to claim players from other teams because it gave the appearance, accurate or not, that other teams were better than his.) Slaughter was with us from 2001 until 2006, the longest stay he had with any team, but when it was time to redo his deal, I offered the minimum, because that was what he was worth. His agent, though, knew he was one of Al's favorite finds and held out for more. Smart. I eventually overpaid because, honestly, giving the money away beat having to deal with a belligerent Davis if we lost one of his scholarship players.

In 2014, the Jacksonville Jaguars drafted Central Florida quarterback Blake Bortles in the first round of the draft. He was the prize selection of Jags general manager David Caldwell, his first after being given complete authority to run the team. No matter how Bortles plays, though, Caldwell refuses to view him in a negative light. At this point that's actually quite an amazing feat. In spite of Bortles's losing career record, not to mention some of the worst fundamentals I've ever seen in a pro quarterback (and, yes, I saw what he did for Jacksonville in 2017; call me unconvinced), Caldwell has had difficulty removing his blinders because he doesn't want to believe he was wrong. In situations like this, GMs almost always blame coaches rather than players.

Love is blind in most NFL front offices, and the destruction caused by it gets compounded when the object of affection is the leader of the team. You can't bullshit an NFL locker room. Everybody on every team knows who the good players are, who the bad players are, and who the team's favorite (a.k.a. untouchable) players are. The best teams force players to prove their value. They don't give—or save—jobs on the basis of draft status. As a result, when a head coach stands in front of his team and supports a player— quarterback or otherwise—who doesn't deserve it, the rest of the players are almost assuredly mumbling their doubts under their breath to one another, and this lack of integrity and transparency erodes team chemistry faster than anything else in the game.

The truth is, you aren't officially an NFL general manager until you've made a huge blunder on draft day. It's just part of the gig. The best GMs just accept a mistake as a bad day at the office and move on. Bill Belichick will be the first to admit he blew it when he blows it, such as the year he selected Boston College defensive tackle Ron Brace in the second round, a pick Belichick calls his worst ever. Being able to talk about his mistakes—in Belichick speak: "I fucked that up"—makes it easier for him to hold honest discussions as a matter of course. And it is those discussions that minimize bad decision making.

Nate Silver's popular website FiveThirtyEight has calculated the success ratio of every position in every round. Drafting a quarterback in the first two rounds has less than a 50 percent chance of succeeding, and with each round those odds dwindle. Overall, the chances of finding a franchise quarterback in any round is closer to 40 percent. There are few parts of the game in which the public's perception of expertise and the actual data are further apart than in the NFL draft. Think about that FiveThirtyEight number for a second: With all the manpower and expertise that go into drafting the most critical position in professional sports, the experts still have a hard time beating a coin flip. You can blame a lot of things for why drafting is such an imperfect science, but in my mind, bias in the evaluation process is the biggest culprit. Making matters worse, bias-affected decisions inevitably snowball into a series of poor decisions that can bring down an entire team.

Have you seen *A Simple Plan*? It's a movie that is all about how bias can compound an original mistake. Three characters come upon a crashed plane in the woods. Inside, they find a dead pilot and over $4 million. Their "simple plan"—take the money before reporting the crash—begins to unravel almost immediately. And with each new move they make, it falls even further apart. In the end, two of the three are dead and the lone survivor realizes the haul is worthless. Everyone loses. And all because they doubled down instead of cutting their losses.

The same thing happens in football front offices.

A draft-day crash won't necessarily destroy a team. But sticking to a plan because of that disaster always will.

Character assessment is by far the hardest challenge for team builders. More than any other factor, inaccurate character assessment is why draft boards are to this day littered with so many mistakes. That's never going to change, either, because there are so many variables involved. For starters, let's be honest, there's a sliding scale of morality in the NFL (as in every industry), in which the more talented an employee is, the more he can get away with. Each team has its own method for determining the risk/reward ratio for signing or keeping players with questionable character. In New England, for example, Belichick has established such a strong locker room chemistry that he can take risks on players with questionable character because he knows they will be policed by their new teammates.

Just as each team situation is different, there are myriad ways to define character. A player might not be a Boy Scout off the field or have what fans in general deem to be great moral character, but if he has "football" character—he practices hard, knows his assignments, isn't a disruptive force in the locker room, and plays hurt—that's far more important even if no one in the NFL would be caught dead admitting it.

Because there are so many factors in assessing player character, it comes down to a case-by-case study. That's why proper scouting is so expensive and labor-intensive: Character can be assessed only face-to-face. A good example of this is when Belichick and I, representing the Browns, went into the 1996 Scouting Combine in Indianapolis hoping to learn more about two top prospects: Miami linebacker Ray Lewis and Nebraska running back Lawrence Phillips.

We had heard that, despite his lack of height and weight, Lewis was destined to be a star. No one had to train him to find the ball carrier; he knew where to go instinctively, usually a microsecond before anyone else. Lewis was also born to lead, to inspire others. A couple of months earlier, an assistant coach had attended *Playboy*'s Football All-America weekend at the Biltmore Hotel in Phoenix and come back with a glowing review: "He has an infectious personality that partied hard, played hard, and wants to win at everything he does, including Ping Pong," this coach wrote. Attending that weekend virtually incognito allowed our coach to examine the players in their most natural moments. Prospects are like the rest of us; when they know someone is judging them, they tend to behave better. Lewis's unguarded behavior passed every test. When I finally met Lewis at the Combine, he was precisely how the scout had described him in Phoenix: energetic and easy. Because we were the Browns, we had to beg and bribe (with free team swag) college players to come speak to us. But Lewis was happy to talk football and go over game tape, and he remembered the details of every game we watched together.

Phillips, in contrast, had all the physical gifts but a growing and well-documented reputation as a violent, unstable character risk. Still, just as we had confirmed our report on Lewis in person, we needed to see for ourselves and do our due diligence with Phillips. Well, however much enthusiasm Lewis showed in our meetings, Phillips was the exact inverse. He remembered nothing about games; not the name of the play, not the opponents, not even the thoughts behind the game plans. He seemed distracted, almost pissed, about being asked to sit with us and couldn't have cared less that we had the fourth overall pick.

By the time our face-to-face Combine interviews concluded, Lewis had leaped up our draft board and Phillips had fallen off completely.

Of course, there is no ignoring Lewis's subsequent connection to two stabbing deaths. In the end, he was convicted only of obstructing justice. I'm not giving him a pass, only the benefit of the doubt. What I know for sure is that, before and since, Lewis has carried himself with dignity, and on the field he was the consummate professional. But I also know enough to know there are no universal truths regarding character, no concrete lists of dos and don'ts, only a long string of independent anecdotes I've compiled over the years that confirm the importance of judging character on a player-by-player basis.

I'll start with one of my favorites: Randy Moss.

I traded for Moss when I was with the Raiders. No one disagreed about Moss the player. He was a consensus once-in-a-generation talent. But when it came to his character, there were many different takes. Some scouts around the league didn't think he could get along with his teammates; others thought he was a great clubhouse guy. Some thought him selfish; others thought he was team first all the way. Some didn't even think he was coachable.

In the end, Davis cared about one thing: talent. He believed, in that old-school way of his, that he could handle any player who got out of line. Whether he was right about that or delusional didn't matter; it allowed us to take chances. During Moss's first year with us he was one of our hardest and smartest workers and a great teammate. Unfortunately, he got injured before the season was half over. The next season under new head coach and former Raider great Art Shell, a different Moss showed up, one who wasn't buying what the inexperienced Shell was selling. If Moss respected you, he was all yours. If you lied to him, or tried to con him, or didn't respect his intelligence, well, you had a problem.

Thinking that Moss had lost a step, Davis was willing to trade him, and when Belichick called from New England in 2007, I told him that Moss was his kind of player and that all the other crap that was being spread about him was just that. Moss may not have been afraid to speak his mind, but I knew that he and Belichick would get along, in part because each would respect the other. In fact, Belichick later called Moss one of the smartest players he has ever coached.

Moss, of course, delivered big-time. In his first year in New England he had 98 catches and 23 touchdowns, averaging more than 15 yards per completion for one of the most prolific offenses in history. His physical gifts were off the charts, but even more remarkable was the way Moss and Belichick became kindred spirits, two football nerds underneath all those rough and torn edges. Anyone who bothers to see past the off-the-field issues knows that despite his rare physical gifts, Moss approached the mental part of the game like an underdog always looking for an edge. He often would come off the field yapping about how an opponent was trying to leverage him one way or another. He noted for quarterbacks and offensive coordinators in real time how defenses were reacting to his moves and dealing with his speed. It was Moss who helped teach Belichick how to see the downfield passing game from a player's standpoint, how the routes looked on the field in three dimensions, not just as a circle and lines on the blackboard. Moss loved to practice, he loved to engage his teammates, and he loved the game—and that love was infectious. He was quick to help younger players. He quickly won over Belichick and the entire

Patriots franchise. Even when his life was a mess, Moss was never sloppy as a player, a pro's pro.

Most of all, Moss displayed another Belichick staple: mental toughness, which the Patriots define as "doing what is best for the team when it might not be best for you." To the outside world Moss might have seemed like a basket case, but in Belichick's universe he had earned the highest compliment possible. In New England, Moss was a "program guy": someone who works hard, is a supportive teammate, and cares deeply about winning. In other words, someone with football character.

Moss is proof that character is such a key factor in the NFL that scouting now needs to be as much about a prospect's personality assessment as about his talent on the field. Maybe that means spending more time in the campus police office than the football office or more time at the local pub quizzing the bartenders who serve the players. Finding the real truth about a player's character can be done only with feet on the ground.

When cornerback Tyrann Mathieu tested positive for synthetic marijuana at LSU, he was removed from the Tigers' team and many NFL scouts moved him to the do-not-draft board. He went on to become a star for the Arizona Cardinals, a consummate pro who has never missed a game because of off-the-field issues. Many teams decided that his recreational drug use—in college!— defined his character. The Cardinals thought not, and they were proved right.

Another example: LSU's La'el Collins was a high-round offensive lineman on everybody's board in 2014. In the week before the draft, his romantic partner, Brittany Mills, was shot and killed in her apartment. When word leaked that Collins might be a suspect, teams were thrown into a panic. I had a great campus source, an auxiliary member of the program—a woman—who called right back to assure me the news was wrong. There was no way Collins could be involved, she said. She was around the players all the time, and she swore that Mills and Collins were no longer an item. This could not be the matter of jealous rage that it was being portrayed as.

With the draft just days away, every team had its security officers trying to learn more. Collins passed a lie detector test, but that wasn't likely to be enough to keep him in most teams' plans. On the day of the draft, Collins wasn't selected. No team decided the reward was worth the risk. A few days later, the Baton Rouge police quietly moved past Collins as a person of interest in the case. In New England we still didn't feel like we could sign him, but the Cowboys gave him a contract. Smart move. On the field, he's been nothing but stalwart.

With Mathieu and Collins the system to determine true character worked. With Aaron Hernandez it failed, miserably. When Hernandez was coming out of the University of Florida, there were rumors of some marijuana use and bar fights and documentation of a troubled childhood. But his head coach in Gainesville, Urban Meyer, and the members of Meyer's staff were staunchly supportive. Turned out Hernandez was good at keeping his secrets. No one on the Patriots staff had any idea how dark his past was before we drafted him or even when we rewarded him with a big contract. Sure, he was a loner who didn't hang out much with his teammates, but he was smart, knew his assignments, and loved to play. Hernandez was a great tight end, but he was also a murderer and a sociopath who somehow was able to sublimate his violent habits when he was at our football facility. In the Patriots' offense the tight end is such a key factor that it may have skewed our risk/reward scale, but I'm not looking for any kind of absolution here. (I also don't know to what extent brain injury contributed to Hernandez's undoing.) I'm just trying to show how easy it is even for teams that care about character to make big mistakes.

It's such a complicated task, in fact, that even an expert like Belichick relies on professional outside help. Bob Troutwine is a Ph.D. based in Kansas City, Missouri, and a cofounder of The Right Profile, creators and administrators of unique physiological profiles that "tap" the heart and mind of prospective players. We liked the TAP—Troutwine Athletic Profile—so much that we made everyone applying for a job in the organization take it.

Don't confuse the TAP with the Wonderlic, the better-known intelligence test that the NFL administers to potential draftees. The TAP offers more insight into personality, asking questions such as: If you could be an animal, which would you be: A. Cat; B. Dog; C. Lion. The questions are random and maybe a bit off the wall, but they lead to important conclusions about the prospect. And only Troutwine can decode the responses. In fact, one of his favorite tricks is being able to tell if a girlfriend, rather than the player himself, has filled out the test.

In Cleveland, Belichick gave the test to a young man who wanted a job in our personnel department. Troutwine called 10 minutes after we submitted the results for his review. In an excited voice, the normally calm doctor declared in no uncertain terms, "Don't let that kid out of the building; he will be the best employee you have." We didn't even give him a chance to get specific; we just dropped the phone and hired Jim Schwartz, who at the time was a former linebacker and economics major at Georgetown who finished third in his class. Despite a fistful of Wall Street job offers, Schwartz took a job as my college scouting assistant. Today he is one of the top defensive minds in the game.

Whether it's a coaching prodigy or a Pro Bowl player who ends up in prison, it all comes back to character. And because character issues can resonate so powerfully beyond the locker room, they often involve the entire team, from the public-relations department to the owner, and that complicates matters further. In Cincinnati, for example, owner Mike Brown believes in giving players second (and sometimes third and fourth) chances. As one of the league's more frugal owners he also likes the idea of getting highly talented players at reduced cost because of character issues. That's why Marvin Lewis is free to take risks on troubled players such as

Oklahoma running back Joe Mixon, who received a one-year suspension in college for punching a woman in the face.

It works both ways with owners, however. When Belichick was in Cleveland, he desperately wanted to draft Warren Sapp with the tenth pick overall in the 1995 draft. I can still hear Belichick raving about Sapp, a dominant college player at Miami. Before the draft, though, NFL assistant director of security Charlie Jackson whispered to Browns owner Art Modell that Sapp had off-the-field issues. Still hoping to secure public financing for a new stadium, the Browns couldn't afford the public-relations risk. Modell overruled a furious Belichick, who traded Cleveland's pick for a no-name linebacker. Sapp went on to become a locker room leader in Tampa and one of the greatest defensive players of all time. Eventually, he ended up in northeast Ohio, after all—at the Pro Football Hall of Fame in Canton.

While the rest of the sports world was still catching its breath the day after the Patriots' dramatic 28–24 win over the Seahawks in Super Bowl XLIX, Bill Belichick already had the next year on his mind. Knowing that special teams coach Scott O'Brien was planning to retire, he asked O'Brien on the plane ride home if he was okay with making the announcement the next day so that the team could begin to move forward. In Belichick's mind he wasn't being callous or unsympathetic; 2014 was ancient history, and he was already in planning mode for 2015. Like a Stoic, when Belichick proclaims, "We are on to Cincinnati" or "We are on to next year" or "Scott O'Brien has retired," he means it.

Whether the Patriots season ends with a Super Bowl parade or a first-round loss, Belichick's off-season approach to building his next team is always the same and always masterful. Every tactical assumption and roster decision made during the previous season is fair game. No one is grandfathered onto the next year's team—not for draft status, not for financial commitment. Year after year, roster spots are earned.

When the season ends, the Patriots coaching staff immediately holes up in the offensive team meeting room at Gillette Stadium to begin preparing for the next season. With Belichick and his trusty Mac laptop at the ready, the autopsy begins. Every facet of the organization is probed, examined, and challenged as he looks for ways to improve the team.

Belichick's off-season team-building meetings are probably better run than most Fortune 500 board meetings. They start with each positional assistant assessing each player in his unit: strong and weak points, relevant medical history, projected role for the upcoming season and beyond. The conversation eventually comes around to developing a plan specifically tailored to help each player get better. Off-season roster planning in New England always includes figuring out how to tweak the ways we teach our lessons. Like his mom and dad before him, at his core Belichick is a teacher and believes strongly in the idea of "taking the lessons from the meeting room to the classroom to the field."

Hulking defensive tackle Vince Wilfork, for example, never needed to get stronger but did need to lower his body fat, whereas linebacker Rob Ninkovich needed to be stronger and more flexible. When free agent corner Malcolm Butler arrived in New England, he learned the playbook better through one-on-one walk-throughs and independent study time. He needed one-on-one tutoring and special attention, so a plan was created for Butler to spend extra time with the assistant coaches. After two weeks we revisited the situation and realized that Butler learned best from seeing and doing rather than talking, so more time was devoted to on-field practice and less to classroom study. Each player retains information differently, and it's the coach's job to determine the best way to instruct him.

Belichick knows coaches tend to define their current problems as having binary solutions: A or B. It's the simplest way to break down the issues at hand. But though that might work at their level, general managers like Belichick can't fall into this "false duality" trap. They know there are often more than two solutions to any problem. At the GM's level the best way to solve a problem is often alternatives C, D, E, and F. Belichick's staff meetings allow him to push beyond the false duality to those more enlightening alternatives.

Belichick lets the coaches talk first, but invariably he has questions. He's in search of the right answers, not just any answers, and so he takes the time to listen to many different thoughts and ideas before coming to a conclusion. It's listening that leads to a clear choice when he is faced with a tough decision. In the end, Belichick is brutal in the decision making regarding his roster: When he knows a player's financial demands put him out of reach, for example, he instructs the coaches to move on. That player might be the most talented guy on our roster, one who played hurt and is beloved in the locker room, but by the time that meeting's done he might as well be dead to us. That's another one of Belichick's secrets: He can connect emotionally with players as a coach in a way that extracts their very best on the field, but then he can go upstairs, put his GM hat on, and make cold-blooded financial decisions regarding that same player without so much as a second thought. It's breathtakingly calculating and ruthless.

But it is also based on a wide range of intel. Belichick is not above asking a defensive coach, for instance, about an offensive player. He encourages everyone to have an opinion as long as there is data, insight, or experience to support it. No one dares to operate by the seat of his pants for fear of being called out by the boss. In essence, Belichick's open and transparent process at the beginning of each off-season helps remove personal biases so that the room can reach clean conclusions on how to spend the rest of the off-season.

The autopsy also covers the more ephemeral aspects of team building, such as attitude, relationships, and chemistry. Today we

operate in a world in which millennials dominate the NFL workforce. Brady, in contrast, is old enough to be the dad of some of the
young guys in the locker room. He's a Hall of Famer to you and
me but a geezer to some of his teammates. To get his job done,
though, he must relate to these kids just as any boss does. Therefore, after 2015, our off-season review included detailed discussions about how to work with millennials: how to reach them and
motivate them. I promise you, no other NFL team thinks this way.

Skill without the proper mental state gets you nowhere, and
Belichick knows it. Although his wardrobe never changes, Belichick often talks about how each year means a different team
makeup. For example, the 2016 team that defeated Atlanta in the
Super Bowl was in his words "tough and hardworking." He had little doubt that they would fight through bad performances, including the first three quarters of that Super Bowl. But his 2009 team,
the one that lost to the Ravens in the wild card game? That roster
was not nearly as tough. "I just can't seem to get them to focus,"
Belichick confessed to Brady in a walk-through before a game with
the Saints. When faced with the same problems in 2014, Belichick
solved his toughness problem the same way your high school coach
did: by making the team practice in inclement weather. He would
yell at his millionaire players, "Forget the elements; get your shit
on and get outside," and if it didn't necessarily produce the crisp-
est workouts, it did seem to hone their determination. There were
so many bad-weather practices with that team that by the end of
the season, as soon as it started raining or snowing, players beat
him to the punch, yelling to one another: "Get your shit on and
get out there."

Belichick takes all the information from the initial off-season
meetings and synthesizes it into three lists—for offense, defense,
and special teams—prioritizing the most deficient positions in
each unit. Then we spend the rest of the spring and summer fixing those problem spots. When I joined New England in 2014, at
the top of the need chart was a single word: *cornerback*. We had to

re-sign Aqib Talib or find his replacement. When we couldn't make a deal with Talib, Belichick simply moved on to former Jet Darrelle Revis—one more example of how Belichick the emotional coach never sways Belichick the pragmatic GM. All of my conversations with Belichick about Talib centered on the swagger he added to the locker room and how he brought out the best in the other defensive players. Those qualities were essential to our team makeup, and Belichick loved that Talib provided all of them. But love is never blind in the New England front office.

Belichick the general manager knew that the reason he was able to trade for Talib during the season was that the guy had a somewhat checkered past off the field. The risk/reward had been worth it. But not anymore. Not with the concern over his durability. (Talib had missed two of the most important games in his tenure, the 2012 and 2013 AFC championship games, suffering first-quarter injuries in both.) We pivoted to Revis. And that was that. Our contract offer to Talib reflected the new reality of the 2015 season. He signed with Denver, where he won another Super Bowl ring. Did we make the wrong decision? Belichick doesn't care. That's ancient history. He coaches with his heart, but he makes personnel decisions with his head and never looks back.

Granted, it wasn't yet a big-time need, because Brady was still playing at a peerless level, but Belichick believes that the best time to develop a young quarterback is when you already have one. So we were looking for more than talent. We needed someone who would not be intimidated by Brady. We needed mental toughness as well as physical skills. And we found it in a not-obvious person: Jimmy Garoppolo from Eastern Illinois.

How did we land on him? Well, I had just been fired unexpectedly from the Browns, a team in desperate need of a quarterback, and so I had done a tremendous amount of work on all the prospects. I knew this about Garoppolo: He was confident but not cocky; his teammates loved him; he had the work ethic and leadership qualities required for the position; his technique and fundamentals were excellent; and had a superior command of the offense. (Davis might not have liked him because he played at a lower level of comptetition, but that was the only thing not to like about Jimmy.)

After we brought Garoppolo to Foxborough, we knew he could handle it all. Again, it comes down to an individual assessment of each prospect's character. He wasn't going to be disrespectful toward one of the greatest players of all time, but he wasn't about to back down from the challenge of replacing him, either. We also brought in Johnny Manziel, the Heisman Trophy winner from Texas A&M. Both Manziel and Garoppolo did very well with the predraft routine the Patriots give all their prospects. But Garoppolo was clean off the field, a model player with the right demeanor, whereas Manziel had a few pretty blatant red flags. The choice was obvious.

Every team has a need list. What makes Belichick's different is that it is a living, changeable document. He revisits it constantly throughout the year, alone and with staff. There is a saying about college recruiting: "It's like shaving; if you don't do it every day, you look like a bum." Walsh believed that a team needed to make at least 10 postdraft moves. (No one knows how he came up with 10 as his magic number, but it would be easy to surmise that he wanted to add one upgrade to each position group except quarterback.) Belichick thinks of NFL team building the same way: as a never-ending process. Needs change as injuries arise and skill levels evolve. To ignore that is to fall behind.

Talk to any team's representatives over the summer and you'd think their moves had put the Super Bowl in reach. Talk to the Patriots and you might think they were an expansion team—not because they don't like their talent but because they are never satisfied.

Contentment is the enemy.

———

O kay, I think you're ready to appreciate the Niners epic 1986 draft.

When I arrived at our offices in those wee hours, 711 Nevada Street was a ghost town, empty besides the caterers. Coffee and my excitement were brewing in equal measure. As soon as Walsh entered the draft room, I handed him Will McDonough's mock draft from that morning's *Boston Globe*. In the days before the Internet, publicly posted mock drafts were a rarity and guys who had the inside scoops to inform them were rarer still. McDonough was one of those guys. Lucky for me, my college roommate, Massachusetts native Paul Brady, had turned me on to McDonough. Luckier still, Paul was an early riser and *Globe* subscriber who was eager to report how McDonough thought the first round would unfold. Walsh valued McDonough's opinion; he knew he was wired around the NFL. The tough South Boston scribe never backed down from a confrontation, just the kind of guy we figured no team would have the guts to flat-out lie to. (Keep their options open? Of course. But lie? No.) A year earlier, in fact, it was McDonough's intel that gave Walsh a sense of how high we had to move up to get Brown, Toon, or Rice. This is how crazy team building and the NFL draft can be: Even a genius like Walsh depended heavily on a crumpled roll of fax paper from Boston to help him make his selections. To this day I wonder if my buddy Paul realizes what a critical role he and his fax modem played in helping construct the 49ers dynasty.

Walsh had his eye on three players this time around. As the draft wound around to us, he directed me to the blackboard (yes, the blackboard; this was 1986: lots of fax machines, few greaseboards) to write the following names:

Gerald Robinson, DE Auburn

John L. Williams, RB Florida

Ronnie Harmon, RB Iowa

Sitting behind a large desk, Walsh appeared confident that at least one of them would be available when our turn arrived at 18. But drafts are like an open-sea cruise: It's smooth sailing until—whap!—a huge wave rocks the boat, and just like that you're navigating the squalls of a storm and taking on water. The first rogue wave landed when we heard the Vikings had selected Robinson with the fourteenth pick. We were prepared for that thanks to the *Boston Globe*. But it still stung: Our coveted pass rusher was off the board.

We rebounded quickly, knowing that with three picks to go we still had two of our guys available . . . until Seattle grabbed Williams at 15. Now the oxygen seemed to be sucked out of the room. Walsh pushed back from his desk and instructed our general manager, John McVay, to get on the phone to assess the market for trading down, just in case. McVay had barely begun to dial when—poof!—Buffalo snagged Harmon at 16.

Few moments epitomize the volatile art and science of team building quite like this: After three months of nonstop, backbreaking draft preparation, we were about to be on the clock and our blackboard was empty.

Now Walsh was up and pacing. It was like being in the middle of a busy ER. He barked to McVay that we needed to trade down, if only to buy some time—say, a half hour or at least two or three picks (each team has 15 minutes to make a choice)—to collect our thoughts and come up with a new plan. Right away, Dallas made us an offer to move to 20, but it only got us a fifth rounder. That went against McVay's own theories about value, but we were reeling a bit and it gave Walsh the cushion of time he needed, which was far more important than the compensation itself. Draft rule corollary: Know the objective of every trade. In this case, time trumped value.

McVay made the deal.

Unfortunately, time alone was not going to solve our problem; truth be told, we had no idea whom to pick. Our highest-rated player was Larry Roberts, a defensive end from Alabama, but McDonough had reported that he'd still be available in the second round. So Walsh asked McVay to move down again, this time as a value play. He told McVay he didn't even care if we slipped out of the first round altogether. A moment later our prayers were answered: The phone rang; we had an eager partner on the line. The Bills, picking twenty-ninth, were offering their second, third, and tenth rounders. Added bonus: The third-round pick was just in front of the Raiders, so Walsh could beat Davis in their annual draft-day oneupsmanship. We were desperate, but the Bills didn't know that. We tried to squeeze them for a ninth rounder instead of a tenth, but we were on the clock with zero leverage and were forced to agree to their offer. Everyone exhaled.

We had survived a nightmare scenario in the first round, and now we had extra picks and plenty of time to figure out what to do with them. One of the things that shows how Walsh and Belichick operate on a different level than the rest of the NFL is the way both coaches understand the value of trading down. If everyone in the NFL is missing on nearly half their draft picks, the only way to increase your odds is to make more picks, especially in the second to fourth rounds, where you generally find the best values (cost versus talent). It's simple math, but it's amazing how few NFL minds understand it.

After racing through most of the first round, now the clock seemed to stop in our draft room. The wait until our new spot at 29 seemed endless, but we were excited about the prospects we had to consider. Then the Lions called. They absolutely, positively had to have our pick and were willing to give us their own second rounder, number 39, and their third, 66, for it. McVay tried to maintain his game face but pounced on the deal and then, maintaining his momentum, traded our backup quarterback Matt Cavanaugh to the Eagles for another third and a second in the next year's draft. I don't know how he kept track of everything, but for good measure McVay then traded our own second rounder to

Washington for a first rounder in the next draft and an extra tenth before finally shipping the third-round pick we'd just aquired from the Lions for both of the Rams' fourth rounders and the rights to backup quarterback Jeff Kemp.

We had been at it for five full hours and had yet to make a single selection, but it was already one of the most successful drafts in 49ers history. Walsh and McVay had secured a new backup quarterback; a first-, second-, and third-round pick in the next year's draft; and a second, three thirds, three fourths, and a tenth in this year's draft.

Now all we had to do was make those picks count.

And did we ever.

In the second round, just as the intel from McDonough predicted, we were able to get Roberts, the highest-rated player left on our board. Next up: that third-round "beat Al Davis" choice. Walsh loved fullback Tom Rathman from Nebraska, thinking he would fit perfectly in the Niners' offense. From predraft conversations with Davis, Walsh knew he was looking at a fullback too, but the Raiders guru never mentioned his favorite by name. We snagged Rathman right before Davis inexplicably broke with his self-imposed level-of-competition standard to select Vance Mueller from tiny Division III Occidental College. A few months later we played the Raiders in the first preseason game, and Mueller ripped a nine-yard run right in front of our bench. Walsh vented wildly into his headset, letting us all know how much he hated the thought of Al getting the better player. But in the end it wasn't even close. Rathman had a much better career.

Still in the third round, we picked Tim McKyer, a fast and athletic corner from Texas at Arlington with iffy tackling skills. But that didn't bother Walsh at all. The speed was there, and his deep background check was positive. Plus, Walsh knew our Pro Bowl safety Ronnie Lott would demand physicality from the rookie. (He was right, as usual. McKyer's toughness earned him a spot on John Madden's All-Madden Team of gritty players a couple years later.)

With our last pick in the third we grabbed John Taylor, a wide receiver from Delaware State. In the fourth, we selected offensive lineman Steve Wallace, injured defensive tackle Kevin Fagan, and Charles Haley. Haley was another "beat Al Davis" pick. Davis loved pass rushers, and Walsh had been teasing him all spring about finding the next great QB killer. We were told Davis had everyone in his personnel department scrambling to uncover the mystery rusher, to no avail.

Each of the players we chose that day would be a longtime contributor to the dynasty Walsh was building. The 1986 Niners draft was a haul most football executives only dream about. We didn't know that at the time, of course, although we sensed we had done some excellent work. In fact, by the time we took Haley, everyone in the room was ecstatic. Everyone except our college scouting director and my immediate boss, Tony Razzano. Tony hated our draft to that point. For him, the only way to salvage the miserable day was for us to get Patrick Miller, a Florida linebacker, in the fifth round. Miller, though, had tested positive for marijuana at the Combine and had landed on Walsh's don't-draft list. Razzano was relentless in his support, however, and eventually Walsh acquiesced. This was the one time all day that we didn't use all of our tools to minimize risk and improve our odds. As soon as we turned in the card to make the pick official, Walsh pushed his chair back violently and headed for the board that held the names of the defensive back prospects. Fearing Walsh's rage, everyone scattered but me. (Not because I was brave but because it was my job to stick by his side at all times.)

As I stood there, Walsh stared at the list of free safeties. Head slightly tilted, he read the names in the "make-it-plus" category— that is, players we thought had more than an 80 percent chance to make the team. After a few moments of, I guess, channeling the football gods, Walsh's left index finger floated across the names like a giant Ouija board until—thwap!—it landed on the card of Don Griffin from Middle Tennessee State.

"What about this kid?" he asked.

I dutifully reported back that he was the Ohio Valley Conference player of the year and that both our scouts who visited the school liked him. But when Walsh actually suggested that we take him in the sixth, a pit formed in my stomach because, truth was, it had been eight months since anyone had seen or spoken to Griffin. (In our defense, this was pre–information age scouting.) I did the only thing I could think of: I raced to the side room, punched in the number we had on file for Griffin, and prayed. After three rings, someone picked up. I informed the person on the other end of the line who I was and what team I worked for as best I could over the party noises in the background. When Griffin came to the phone a moment later and assured me that he was healthy and ready to go, I let out the biggest sigh of relief in my life. Griffin, too, would become a Niner stalwart. Miller, not so much.

What a day. By the time our tenth-round pick came around, we had fully reloaded with more eventual starters than most teams get in two drafts, sometimes three. (And don't forget, we also had stockpiled three top picks for the following draft.) A relaxed and satisfied Walsh turned his attention to actor and draft obsessive Bradford Dillman, who was in the room with us. Dillman, a Yale grad who starred in the original *Escape from the Planet of the Apes*, *The Way We Were*, and a handful of Dirty Harry movies, had a deep love for the 49ers and over time had worked his way into the inner sanctum of the team. In each of the previous few drafts, Dillman had gone so far as to provide us with his own sleeper pick backed up by a funny but highly detailed analysis of why his player would make 49ers history.

His insight and presence were usually worth a good laugh or two. But at the start of the tenth round, he snapped open his briefcase and pulled out a typed dossier extolling the virtues of Harold Hallman, a defensive tackle from Auburn, who, the report stated, "could get more penetration than Warren Beatty at a sorority party." After a long, exhausting, and historic day, Walsh just kind of shrugged his shoulders. Hallman would be our final pick of the draft.

He never made the 49ers, but Hallman did go on to become rookie of the year and a four-time all star playing for Calgary and Toronto in the Canadian Football League. That made him just the right final selection in one of the greatest drafts in NFL history. Everything the 49ers touched that year, even our gag pick, turned to gold.

A day that began on a desolate stretch of El Camino Real ended with a clear path back to the Super Bowl.

# 4

# SPECIAL TEAMS

## THE MEANING OF ALL-IN

*It's not the strength of the individual players;*
*it's the strength of how they function together.*

—BILL BELICHICK

As the ball explodes off the right foot of Pittsburgh Steelers punter Mark Royals, the sold-out crowd inside Cleveland Municipal Stadium rises to its feet in a deafening roar, waiting to see what Eric Metcalf will do next.

With just over two minutes to play and the Browns trailing their rivals 23–21, darkness has begun to fall on the rickety old stadium and perhaps the team's 1993 season. Our defense has given up 26 first downs and more than 400 yards to the Steelers, and our offense has stalled after fading hometown hero Bernie Kosar replaced an injured Vinny Testaverde at quarterback. Most coaches would be out of options at this point. But not Bill Belichick. Everyone else in the NFL tends to dismiss special teams as an afterthought, but Belichick has an unparalleled respect for and commitment to special teams. To Belichick, special teams are the heart and soul of a team, the ideal way to establish culture, chemistry, and toughness and develop the talent of the entire roster. Oh, and just maybe to steal a game from a rival.

So as the punt soars past midfield and Metcalf, the Pro Bowl returner, rocks back and forth in anticipation on his own 25-yard line, I stand expectantly in the tiny coaches' booth near the roof of the stadium. Wiping the sooty condensation off the windows, I have a bird's-eye view of the play about to unfold and of Belichick's special teams' genius.

Before making his name as a defensive coordinator with the two-time Super Bowl champion New York Giants, Belichick spent several years in the league as a special teams coach. For Belichick, working on special teams was never a dues-paying grind. In fact, his affinity for that part of the game was instilled by the greatest influence of his life: his father, Steve, a renowned scout and coach and an associate professor at the Naval Academy. From the time he was nine, growing up in Annapolis, Bill would spend entire days watching his father conduct practice, scout opponents, and break down film. (Once in a while he even got to play catch with Navy quarterback Roger Staubach, his childhood hero.) Steve Belichick was never well-known to fans, but his football intellect, attention to detail, and ability to teach the game were highly respected by his peers. I really believe that Bill's deep respect for his father's career in the shadows and the tone set at the academy—a total, tireless, and selfless commitment to team and something greater than individual accolades and attention—are to this day what power his unique focus and appreciation of special teams.

Special teams led to Belichick's first job in the NFL. When he was 24 and still answering to "Billy," he was hired to be the assistant special teams coach of the Detroit Lions under Rick Forzano, a former Navy head coach. Among other things, Forzano and the Belichicks knew full well that the most important job that our military academies do is develop strong-minded soldiers. A study done by Angela Duckworth for her book *Grit* found that the factor most predictive of whether a pledge will endure at West Point is mental toughness. No surprise, then, that when Belichick finally became a head coach in Cleveland, he was on the lookout for players with that characteristic, particularly to man his special teams.

From the beginning Belichick has been a master at developing toughness. One of his first acts as head coach was to have a hill built beside the indoor facility in Ohio to hone the players' bodies and minds alike. Much like the hard-core training for Navy SEAL candidates, the hill was a test of determination. If players can fight past exhaustion, if they can focus when they're completely drained, well, that's mental toughness. It's easier to commit penalties when you're exhausted and easier to take a play off, too. There was no fooling the hill. (Today in New England, in fact, there are two hills.) The point was always to be able to disqualify players who could not handle the mental challenge before they saw real action and fell short when it mattered. If you can't make it through the training, you can't be a SEAL, and if Belichick's players couldn't handle the hill, they couldn't play on Sunday.

Backpedaling into place to receive the punt, it's clear that Metcalf is limping. A bad knee kept him out of practice until Friday, and truth be told, he probably shouldn't be playing. But all week long, Belichick has been buoyed by the feeling that the Steelers' special teams aren't as strong as ours. Seeing an advantage to exploit and a chance to build the culture of an eventual playoff-

caliber team, he's pushed our special teams units to make big
plays and set the physical tone against the Steelers—a challenge Metcalf has answered with an already gritty performance
on one healthy leg.

Belichick's other go-to toughness test was administered on the
field: the trial by fire of kick coverage and returns. No other play
in football demands that 10 big and fast men—apologies to all the
kickers out there—run full speed at and through 10 other big and
fast men to tackle a runner. Covering kicks is a show of bravery
that eliminates the weak. Watching a player perform that task can
answer a couple of questions at once: Does he play with abandon?
Does he love to get physical? If the answers were yes, Belichick
knew he had a guy with grit who would put his body on the line for
the greater good of the team. If you want to determine a player's
mental toughness, ask him to help out on kickoffs and punts. This
was one of the many grueling tests we gave newly arrived players
in Cleveland. Emphasizing special teams toughness helps instill
an "all-in" vibe up and down the roster. That was why Belichick
ruled that virtually every player must contribute to the various
special team units.

Metcalf was a former number one draft choice. So was Eric
Turner. Turner, Belichick's first pick as Browns head coach, would
become an All-Pro safety, but he was precisely the kind of strong,
athletic player Belichick loved to see on his special teams. In
Cleveland, we became so focused on developing our special teams
with that type of talent that our defensive coordinator, Nick
Saban, complained about how his side of the ball was always being
slighted, forced as it was to incorporate lesser players because they
also could help the kicking game.

Before he sent his punt return team onto the field, special
teams coach Scott O'Brien made sure his group understood
that he wanted them to set up a right sideline return. That

means the jammers (blockers) on both ends of the line have to do a great job of blocking the Steelers' gunners (the punt team's best cover men and generally the first defenders downfield). Earlier in the game, Metcalf took one back 91 yards for a touchdown with a left sideline return, and O'Brien knows that if Royals makes a tactical mistake and punts down the middle of the field, a right return, the play he called, will be the shortest path to the end zone.

But on the right return the responsibility of jamming the gunners falls to a couple of exhausted defenders, Turner and fellow safety Stevon Moore. Turner and Moore have played their hearts out all day. These stars of the defense are also special teams stalwarts. Being exhausted is no excuse; their teammates need them. In reality, they secretly love the violent chaos of punt return duty. If all goes as planned, Turner will go to the left side of the Steelers line, jam his man, peel off, and race across the field to help set up a "fence" of blockers that will lead Metcalf up the right sideline in front of the Cleveland bench. Moore will align to the right side and jam his man inside toward the middle of the field and then race backward to help seal the sideline for Metcalf.

Belichick has called off any rush of the punter to better set up the return, hoping the extra time causes Royals to relax a bit and overswing on the kick rather than direct it to a sideline. And the tactic works. Royals's kick is headed exactly where we'd hoped it would go: straight down the middle of the field toward the most explosive talent in the NFL.

Many NFL teams give certain players dispensation to avoid particular team drills, but I've never seen that do anything except divide the group into haves and have-nots. That was certainly the case in Oakland. During the 2005 season, I was driving home from

Friday practice to have dinner with my family when I got a call from Al Davis. "How could you let them work him so hard?" Davis yelled into the phone. To which I naturally asked, "Who is him?" In his angrier-by-the-second Brooklyn accent, Davis answered simply: "Alvis." Ah, Alvis Whitted, our fourth wide receiver. My still-flummoxed response: "Do what?" only got him more riled. "Let him run down kickoffs!" he clarified. "We have to save his legs!"

When I pointed out that we needed guys to cover kicks, too, Al followed with his signature "Ah, fuck" and hung up.

Whitted did have incredible speed, but he was the fourth or fifth option at his position—exactly the kind of guy who fills coverage units. We couldn't exempt him. Here's what separates the most subtle football thinkers from the rest: They know that special teams account for nearly 20 percent of all plays during a game, and they're not willing to forgo the chance to gain an advantage over an opponent in one-fifth of the available opportunities. But most coaches (and owners) are happy just to get off the field with clean exchanges—that is, no turnovers. They're not even overly concerned with field position, because you can turn field position with one deep pass. Davis was one of those guys. He wasn't interested in risking the health of his starters—and primary backups such as Whitted—on a unit that to him didn't matter strategically. He certainly wasn't thinking about building a foundation of teamwork atop the unit. Guys like Belichick, though, believe firmly that an "all-in" culture is an essential piece of the championship equation and that special teams are the fastest path to it.

Davis, in all fairness, loved specialists. He drafted a punter, Ray Guy, and a kicker, Sebastian Janikowski, in the first round, and so it would be hard to knock him for not loving the special teams. He just didn't love using his "fast" players from the offense to cover kicks. He found his edge in other places. For one thing, he saw the advantages of forcing opponents to field a ball kicked by a left-footed punter, particularly when they'd had no experience at it. Davis understood that the ball comes off a left foot with a different rotation, making it a challenge to catch. Plus, left footers are rare, which means returners don't have a lot of practice dealing with that rotation. Davis would hire left footers when he could, and he always made sure to bring one in to practice the week before we were set to face one. And now Belichick does that, too.

Another reason for Belichick's obsession with specials teams is that they allow coaches to interact with more of the team at once. Offensive and defensive coordinators just manage guys in their unit, but the kicking games use players from both sides of the ball. Aside from a full team meeting, the special teams meeting is the largest regular gathering. Sure, most of the players at that meeting are from the back end of the roster, but a second tier that is strong and nourished pushes frontline players as well as any cash bonus or contract incentive.

Belichick isn't the first coach I saw use special teams to change the broader culture. When Kansas State hired Bill Snyder to be its head coach in 1989, the program was among the worst in college football. Snyder took over a program that had gone 27 games without a win. In the 53 years before his arrival, the Wildcats won 137 games, total. A couple of years earlier I had sat in the stands in Manhattan, Kansas, watching practice as a Niners scout and wondering if anyone could ever have success there. And then Snyder put up 136 W's in 17 seasons. He won many of those games with a wide-open offense and by taking advantage of the instant upgrades that junior college transfers offered.

But it was from the kicking game that he concocted that all-important, all-in atmosphere. Just recently, Snyder shared with me that he knew going into the project that turning around Kansas State would mean building tough-minded players. He also knew that excelling in the kicking game was something all coaches said they wanted but rarely spent the effort to achieve. That is why Snyder walked the walk from the beginning, devoting as much practice time to that unit as he did to the others. Snyder still boasts about how much time he has spent on the kicking game.

There is no magic to any of it; it's simply a function of the head coach's level of attention. Snyder once said, "You think about the number of repetitions in the course of a ball game that you get in some aspect of special teams, and it is pretty substantial, so it deserves the time you invest in it." When Snyder landed in Kansas, he was determined to make starters play on special teams because that was how he was going to create what I call the tornado effect.

All-in teams are in fact a bit like tornadoes: disparate energies that band together into a single destructive force that cuts down everything in its path. The greatest example of this concept is the 1980 U.S. Olympic hockey team. Coach Herb Brooks didn't collect the best hockey players in America for his squad. Rather, he found the *right* players. To help put together the roster, Brooks, a psychology major, gave each prospect a lengthy test in which he was looking for high scores in three areas: open-mindedness, willingness to learn, and coachability. He felt those interrelated qualities would allow him to build a team that could overcome the large talent gap it would confront as college kids playing against the best teams from around the globe.

The Soviets had won every hockey gold since 1964, outscoring opponents 175–44 in international play and crushing the NHL All Stars 6–0 in 1979—with a backup goalie, no less. That Soviet team was the best hockey team in history, but Brooks beat it with a bench full of misfits and maybe the greatest all-in culture ever created. No wonder, then, that Belichick admired the 1980 U.S. Olympic hockey team. He admired it so much that he gave its players access to the most protected inner sanctum in sports: his locker room.

In New England, Belichick invited goalie Jim Craig to tell the Patriots about how he flat-out refused to take Brooks's famous test. The coach relented, but just before the Winter Games were to begin, he told Craig that he was thinking of starting someone else in net. Craig went nuts, yelling, "Is it because I didn't take your stupid test?" Brooks answered, "No, it's because I want the guy back who *refused* to take the test!" Craig was losing his fire, and Brooks wanted to ignite it like Lake Placid's Olympic torch. Craig was a tremendous storyteller, but he spent very little time talking about his legendary 36-save performance against the Russians, one of the greatest Olympic performances of all time. Two minutes into his speech, though, every Browns player saw what Belichick had seen in Craig: a kindred spirit. Just like most of the players in Cleveland, Craig was a special teamer at heart. Instead of talking about himself, he focused on the power of the 1980 team's all-in nature and the unique collection of teammates that built it. Belichick was trying to build something equally cyclonic in Cleveland, and he wanted his special teams to spur the teamwide storm.

I have been part of four Super Bowl teams, and all were all-in types. There simply has to be a thread of unity running through any successful team, from the best players to the practice squad. I'm not saying they all have to like one another, but there has to at least be some level of mutual respect. So when a head coach like Belichick makes special teams a priority, treating these mostly unknown and underpaid players with the same respect as the All-Pros on offense and defense (and sometimes with more), it's a powerful message about trust and accountability that resonates with all 53 men in the locker room.

Turner, the big, fast, hard-hitting safety from UCLA, was football and book smart, fully prepared to lead the defense even though he was younger than everyone else on the unit. But he was exceptional in another way, too. From the beginning, he wanted to play on special teams. And he was very good at it. We counted on him to contribute to both of our coverage units, and he elevated them both. If he needed a break, we'd give him one, but at critical points of every game he wanted to be out there, and we were happy to oblige.

All of the best, most competitive players I've been around are exactly the same, willing to do whatever it takes. I was at the University of Miami in 1988, working out some Hurricanes on the

"Box," which is basically an electronic timer that clocks a series of drills. This was data solely about athletic skill, not football instinct. The key to Box drills was that they were run on a wood surface for consistency's sake, and that meant I often found myself conducting workouts on campus basketball courts (a massive highlight for this serious college hoops fan). Even today when I watch games on TV, I think fondly of my Boxing days and all the janitors I pissed off by ripping the gloss off their shiny floors when I pulled up the tape I'd laid down as players' marks.

Anyway, Michael Irvin, Miami's star receiver, wasn't likely to agree to participate, so I had to improvise. When I made my call to set up a workout, I was not 100 percent truthful. You see, I gave Irvin the impression that I was actually Marty Schottenheimer, the head coach of the Browns. Irvin had no reason to doubt me and, without caller ID, no way to check even if he did. But when Irvin arrived at the gym to find a fat low-level Italian, he was like "Uh-uh—no way am I working out for you" before walking over to join a hoops game with some of his football teammates. I still had to work out other players, and as I put them through their paces, I kept noticing Irvin sneaking glances at the Box. He was curious, but more than that he was competitive; he wanted to prove he could test better than anyone else. Before I left that day, Irvin had completed the test. (And yes, his scores were outstanding.)

Irvin accepted the challenge to prove his talent, and that's not unusual for the great ones. It's the main reason that creating an all-in team with a buy-in from the stars—even when that means getting them to participate on special teams—isn't as hard as you might expect. Great competitors want to conquer every challenge, and that is a win-win for the special teams coach, because getting the most talented guys to line up with the kicking units can make them dominant.

If relying on their competitive streak fails, sometimes a piece of clothing may be enough to get the message across. You'd think the modern football professional would be too rich and too adult to fall for typical high school motivational methods. Never. NFL players are still helpless before the power of the T-shirt. To help create the culture he wanted in Cleveland, Belichick gave the special teams a nickname, the Strike Force, and each week rewarded top achievers with a brown shirt that proclaimed "Strike Force Champion" across the chest. The top performer got a leather jacket. From high school to college to the pros, locker rooms don't change. Sure, NFLers own expensive cars and thick financial portfolios. It doesn't matter; competitive sorts aren't about to let the opportunity to snag a free shirt pass. In fact, stars might covet those shirts most of all. Belichick required players to participate on at least one kicking team unit, but by season's end, even the best players were pushing to be on more, hoping to raise their chances of earning a T-shirt or that prized jacket.

Like a smooth major league center fielder, Metcalf has taken two steps backward, calculating precisely where the ball will drop into his soft hands. His eyes never leave the ball. Instead, he lets his internal clock tell him exactly how close the defenders are getting. To do this he must trust completely that his teammates will protect him. The other key, he knows, is the first five yards of the return. If he can get a clean takeoff, Metcalf has an excellent chance to gobble up some major yardage. Turner and Stevon Moore, along with fellow defensive backs Stacey Hairston and Terry Taylor, have done the dirty work, battling the Steelers' gunners tooth and nail on the line, preventing them from getting a clean, quick path down the field.

Metcalf catches the ball on the Browns' 25-yard line and takes two quick decoy steps straight up the center of the field. It's a gutsy game of chicken meant to draw tacklers away from the "right return" coming together on the edge. Metcalf hopes that the rest of the unit can stand tall and hold back the onslaught of tacklers.

The Strike Force comes through.

All around Metcalf is a barrage of human projectiles colliding in a kaleidoscope of brown and yellow jerseys. Bodies fly by in all directions at maximum velocity. The violence of a punt return is breathtaking, really. Everywhere you look players are putting their bodies—and their livelihood—on the line to protect or destroy the returner. You can't force players to do this; they have to want to do it for one another. Moore even doubles back to race 50 yards downfield just in time to make a perfect diving—and legal—block that springs Metcalf toward the safety of the sidelines and the protection of his blockers, including 295-pound defensive tackle James Jones.

That Moore and Jones were perfectly positioned to help spring Metcalf's return was no coincidence. Rather, it was a by-product of years of careful game planning and roster building by our staff.

My first job in football was as a volunteer coach at the University of Nevada–Las Vegas, in charge of making coffee for head coach Harvey Hyde. (I was also car washer, fill-up-the-gas-tank guy, and errand boy.) The job was neither glamorous nor high-paying, but it was a start. After my two successful seasons as barista in chief, a young coach from the University of Wisconsin–Superior drove his shiny new Corvette into town, looking for something to do while his wife attended graduate school. That coach was Scott O'Brien.

O'Brien and I quickly formed a football friendship that became a lifelong relationship. (It didn't hurt that he soon replaced me as official coffee maker, although I always thought he skimped a bit on the grounds.) He had been on the Packers' practice squad, on the defensive line, but he loved special teams. I mean, he really loved them. Some aspiring coaches are forever drawing plays on scraps of paper. Hell, if someone had snatched any of my notebooks in college, they would have had no luck finding the daily lessons amid the pages and pages of play diagrams. (Did I mention that I was an awful student?) Similarly, O'Brien's journals featured alley returns for kickoffs and attacking schemes for punt blocks and ways to check into the best return on kickoffs no matter where the opponent kicked the ball. He had an excellent understanding of schemes and what players needed to do to make those schemes work. He was special teams 24/7 and couldn't wait to teach what he knew, which was quite a bit.

After I left UNLV for the 49ers, O'Brien and I kept in close touch. His career took him to Rice, then to the University of Pittsburgh, where the head coach was another good friend, Mike Gottfried. (Naturally, when he was looking for a special teams coach, I told him to interview O'Brien.) By the time O'Brien was in Pittsburgh, I was close by in Cleveland, so we saw each other more frequently, and when the Browns hired longtime NFL defensive coordinator Bud Carson as head coach in 1989, I saw my chance to get O'Brien to Cleveland. I had no prior relationship with Carson, so I knew it would be a hard sell. Deciding I'd take the same tack that worked with Gottfried—just meet the guy—I marched into Carson's office. I wasn't four sentences in when Carson said, "What the fuck would I want with some college guy coaching my special teams?" Two years later I got a second chance when Belichick replaced Carson. Belichick and I had no prior relationship, either, but this time when I talked up my friend, I had an interested audience.

A few days later O'Brien arrived at the Berea, Ohio, training facility. Belichick, dressed in a coat and tie, immediately escorted him into his office. Every so often I peeked down the hall to see if the door had opened, but . . . nothing. Two hours went by, then three, then four. Finally, after six hours of nonstop nerding out about special teams, Belichick walked down to my office to thank me for the recommendation. O'Brien got the job.

On top of being a great special teams coach, O'Brien was a great talent evaluator. A few years into the job, he made a particularly astute recommendation. When our punter's leg began to age out, we went shopping for a replacement. O'Brien wanted us to sign Tom Tupa, a local kid from Brecksville, Ohio. Tupa had been a great punter at Ohio State, but he also had been a decent quarterback and the Phoenix Cardinals chose him in the third round in 1988 to fill that higher-profile position. In his first six years in the NFL, Tupa punted just six times, and when he was released (by the Colts), we brought him to camp as our backup quarterback. He didn't make the team and ended up sitting out the 1993 season. But while he was around for those few weeks of camp, O'Brien urged him to get back to punting. The next season, his booming leg and the bonus of a viable passing dimension as a holder of kicks made him a vital piece of the team. It was the first year of the two-point conversion, and naturally, Tupa was the first to score one. Soon, he was "Tommy Two Point" around the office.

The kicking game allows teams to improve their overall talent level without having to navigate the usual intraleague competition for available players. The NFL procurement system is designed to favor the losers, as poor records earn higher draft positions. But in the draft, those teams are looking for immediate help, players who can make an offense or defense better *now*. What they are not looking for are players whose skill sets can be honed over time on special teams. This lack of interest in that kind of player creates a variance in the market for those looking for, well, let's just call it "special" talent.

O'Brien's ability to find these hidden gems was so uncanny that we built a whole strategy around it. We believed that if a player was a standout in the kicking game, he had a good chance of developing into an effective four-down player (assuming he was smart enough to learn the relevant playbook). And the more four-down players we accumulated, the better we would be. Take Stevon Moore, for example. His trajectory illustrates a best-case scenario in Belichick's universe. Moore had been a free agent, most recently with Miami. As he did with every potential pickup, O'Brien graded him according to how many kicking teams he thought he could contribute to. Meanwhile, the position coach graded him on strictly defensive criteria. Then Belichick and I assigned a grade that was based on projected overall contribution for the upcoming season and the one after. We also built a specific plan for growing Moore into a four-down guy, which included one of O'Brien's assistants, Kevin Spencer, teaching him—along with a promising group of 10 or 12 others—the rest of the playbook. Moore eventually was a starting strong safety for us, but he never stopped being an excellent special teams player.

We had to coach up Moore to make him the player he would become, but we never had any doubt that he was a Belichick player. Most of them scream out to you the moment you lay eyes on them. In the spring before our first draft together in 1991, Belichick and I did a one-day, three-city tour of Iowa, kind of like we were on the campaign trail for the state's caucus. We were coming mainly for Iowa's star running back Nick Bell. Bell was a big man—not just for a running back but for any position. The problem was, he never played as big or as tough as his size. We had an internal disagreement in the scouting department over his value and role, and this trip was meant to decide whether he would make our final draft board. When we touched down in Iowa City, we learned that Bell was not too interested in working out for us; he especially didn't want to be timed in the 40-yard dash.

Throughout my career, I've found that most prospects are willing to do skill work and strength work but hate the 40, not least because they know that a bad time can offset every good time in their file. We didn't need to time Bell—his athleticism was not an issue for us—but his lack of desire to run was telling. Unfortunately for him, it also gave us more time to interview him and assess his competitiveness.

Leaving Iowa City, we headed north, and as I drove along Highway 380, we talked about what we had just learned: (1) Bell was neither particularly physically or mentally tough, so (2) he wasn't a good fit for our special teams. Before our car pulled into a parking spot near the University of Northern Iowa's indoor stadium, it was decided: We would not be drafting Nick Bell.

We had only one player to work out in Cedar Rapids. That was James Jones, who—his agent Jack Worth kept telling me—was going to be the steal of the draft. Worth was selling his client, sure, but he was a good judge of talent. He scouted players himself, attending games and handpicking his client base. We were already a little intrigued; Jones was excellent on tape, dominating the competition and playing with intensity. But we needed to project his skill set to the next level. Could he play that way against pros? The workout would give us clues. As we entered the football office to meet Jones, he was waiting for us in the small reception area. A good sign. We followed Jones down to the field, where I set up our usual preworkout drill: four large circular bags laid on the ground for players to maneuver over and between. It loosens them up for the rest of the workout while allowing us to judge their quickness, balance, and athleticism. A Belichick workout never began without the bags.

Jones killed in all the drills, from the bags to position-specific tests. During those workouts, Belichick is particularly interested in a prospect's power. We set up two cones five yards apart. Then, from a two-point stance, the player follows Belichick as he walks from one cone to the other. At some point Belichick turns parallel to the player, at which point the player is supposed to punch the coach's chest and keep moving. This tight jab gives Belichick an idea of the prospect's quick-strike force—and often sore ribs. On this day, Jones was Mike Tyson, delivering a blow that I thought was going to earn an eight count. When the workout was over, the guy was on our draft board and Belichick was walking a little hunched over. We drafted Jones in the third round in 1991, and he immediately became a four-down player and a hero, I suppose, to everyone in football who has ever fantasized about hitting Belichick really, really hard.

Jones clears the way for Metcalf to get to the sidelines before lugging his nearly 300-pound frame upfield to find someone else to pancake. As the return is developing, Steelers linebacker Reggie Barnes has the best shot at Metcalf. But the returner's elite speed catapults him out of reach. The interaction lasts for only a fraction of a second, but it is a definitive justification of Belichick's singular approach to special teams: Metcalf is a former first-round pick surrounded by blockers who double as starters, but the one guy the Steelers have asked to prevent the game-winning touchdown is Barnes, an undrafted rookie free agent thrown onto special teams as an afterthought, who takes a sloppy tackling angle and comes up with nothing but air.

At midfield, Metcalf cuts inside, allowing the Browns to plow a few Steelers halfway onto the Cleveland bench. Out of no-where and maybe trying to make up for his poorly aimed punt, Royals appears in front of Metcalf. That's when he is atomized by Jones. Somehow, Jones stays on his feet and manages to stiff-arm Steelers tight end Tim Jorden (yet another undrafted rookie free agent) before he can get a clean shot at Metcalf. At the 15, one last Steeler backup dives for Metcalf's legs, but he is chopped down by Taylor, who has covered nearly 115 yards and blocked four different tacklers in less than 10 seconds.

Metcalf high-steps his way through the end zone, stopped by the only thing that has been able to accomplish that in the game: the bursting barricades of the infamous Cleveland Dawg Pound, its boisterous celebration seemingly slingshotting Met-calf back into the end zone, where he's mobbed by teammates. To make this moment even more perfect—for me at least—the stadium speakers blast Springsteen's "Born to Run."

# 5

# OFFENSE

## FINDING THE SEAMS

*If we are all thinking alike, no one is thinking.*

—BILL WALSH

ill wants a meeting.

Combine those two words—*Bill* and *wants*—and stuff happened; everyone who worked for the 49ers perked up, paying close attention to whatever came next. "Bill wants" could move mountains. "Bill wants" could make or break careers.

Just days before the critical 1987 draft, what Bill wanted was everyone on the 49ers staff crammed inside a second-floor office facility for an emergency meeting. The tiny impromptu conference room was no match for a "Bill wants" all-points bulletin. At my utterance of those two words every assistant in the building came running, which meant there weren't nearly enough seats for everyone.

Luckily, Walsh was quick and to the point.

Bill wanted Steve Young.

We were all highly skeptical but also intrigued. A big part of Walsh's genius was his uncanny ability to spot a quarterback in a crowd. Even from a distance and after only a few throws, he could sense immediately if a quarterback could run his offense. Guys like Walsh and Belichick are unusual this way: They can visualize how skill sets fit in their schemes in a way that both maximizes those abilities and fuels the system. Walsh was secretive about that particular gift of his; he never shared what he saw. So he seemed like a railbird at the track who could discern the best horses just by studying their gait around the paddock. It might have been footwork, a kinetically clean throwing motion, the way a quarterback carried himself in the pocket, or, more likely, some mystical balance of several QB qualities floating around in his head—but whatever it was, Walsh knew it when he saw it.

In Walsh's first season as the head coach and GM of the 49ers, in 1979, he took a trip to UCLA to work out Olympic hurdler turned wide receiver James Owens. Owens was incredibly fast, but Walsh wanted to see if he had the other skills necessary to be an NFL receiver. He forgot one small thing, though: He needed an arm to throw to the guy. As luck would have it Notre Dame's quarterback, Joe Montana, was working out nearby, preparing for the draft, too. Walsh asked him to stop by. I'm not exactly sure what Walsh zeroed in on that day with Montana, but after a few throws he was so focused on the quarterback that he practically forgot Owens was there. (As a talent evaluator you never want to rely on this kind of divine, or dumb, luck—accidentally borrowing a future Hall of Fame quarterback as a workout passer or, say, drafting Tom Brady in the sixth round—but you don't want to be closed off to it, either. Heck, as great as he was and as seriously as he took his profession, Walsh wasn't above a little scouting serendipity.)

Before the workout at UCLA began, Walsh was leaning toward drafting Stanford quarterback Steve Dils, who had played for Walsh and knew his offense inside and out. But after one or two routes at UCLA that day, Walsh knew he had found what he was looking for: his franchise quarterback.

Nearly a decade later, he needed to find another.

Prior to the 1987 draft, I traveled to Indianapolis with Walsh for the NFL Combine. Part of my duties at my first NFL stop was to caddy around Walsh's notebooks. This was the mid-1980s, and backpacks were an accessory for Marty McFly in *Back to the Future*, no one else. Coach Walsh was not a backpack kind of guy, anyway. But that was okay. It meant I had a good job—lugging around a huge briefcase stuffed with his things and mine—and lots of one-on-one time with "the man." As we entered the old Hoosier Dome that day, Walsh was in a hurry, striding with purpose toward our coaches in the stands who were there to evaluate the rookie class of quarterbacks. The whole idea of having to look for a quarterback put Walsh in a sour mood. The 1986 Niners had been injury plagued, especially at quarterback, and Walsh wasn't sure how Montana would recover from back surgery. Walsh would never actually say it, but he sensed Montana was nearing the end.

As we hurried to our seats in the stands, Walsh stopped short and turned to stare at the field. Across the stadium a few of the rookie quarterbacks, including an unknown passer from Delaware, were already on the field working out. Walsh stood like a statue, as if he had gone into a trance. I had no idea who or what was holding his attention until he turned to me and barked, "Make sure Holmgren goes to see that quarterback throwing right now." In one glimpse across a field, Walsh had seen a level of athleticism and timing from Rich Gannon that it would take the rest of the NFL a decade to figure out.

When I relayed the news to our quarterbacks coach, Mike Holmgren, about Bill wanting (once again, "Bill wants") him to travel to Newark, Delaware, he was none too happy, blaming me for his itinerary, as he thought I had promoted the local boy. The charge was utterly false. Sure, as a South Jersey kid I had a fondness for all things from the Philadelphia area, but I wasn't nearly bold enough to sell a Blue Hen quarterback to Walsh even if I wanted to. Walsh was the expert.

Holmgren did eventually go to Delaware, and he liked Gannon. But he didn't love him (Gannon had prototype size and arm strength, but Delaware's wing-T offense and the old Yankee Conference weren't exactly ideal preparation for the NFL), and so Gannon was selected by the Patriots—to play defensive back. Gannon had no interest in that, and after bouncing around the league from New England to Minnesota to Washington to Kansas City, he ended up paying off with the Raiders, under Jon Gruden, who finally inserted Gannon into the scheme that perfectly fit his skills: Walsh's West Coast offense. In 2002, Gannon was named the NFL's MVP after leading the Raiders out of nearly a decade of mediocrity and back to the Super Bowl. I was with the Raiders staff at the time, and remembering how Walsh had spotted Gannon's talent in an instant that day in Indiana, I couldn't help but wonder just how many potentially great quarterbacks have wasted away in the wrong system. Would Gannon's late-career success have happened much earlier if we had drafted him in San Francisco?

At the time, of course, Walsh really only had eyes for Steve Young.

That was the message he wanted to relay to our entire staff inside that crowded second-floor conference room. As Walsh made his announcement, the faces of the assembled football minds were those of schoolboys who had sipped sour milk. Steve Young? The running QB? Steve Young who was a disaster as the quarterback of the Tampa Bay Buccaneers? That Steve Young?

A little background: Young's college career was sensational. After leading the Brigham Young Cougars as a senior to an 11–1 record that included an impressive win over Missouri in the

Holiday Bowl, he was the consensus top quarterback in the draft. But before that could happen J. William Oldenburg bought the Los Angeles team in the upstart United States Football League and gave Young one of the biggest sports contracts ever to lead it. (The four-year deal negotiated by Young's agent, Leigh Steinberg, appeared to be worth $40 million.) But then the league folded and Young signed with the Bucs, who selected him with the first pick in the 1984 supplemental draft of USFL talent. In two years in Tampa, though, Young displayed better running skills than passing skills, and the Bucs had seen enough to decide it was time to try someone new.

That meant Young would be a relatively cheap pickup (essentially costing a second rounder and a fourth rounder plus some of owner Edward DeBartolo Jr.'s hard-earned cash). Yes, the former most-sought-after player in football was on the bargain rack, mainly because every other "expert" in the league felt he would never fit the traditional role. That included 99 percent of our staff. Now that Young is in Canton, there's a lot of revisionist history about how he came to be a 49er. For starters, Walsh has said that once he informed DeBartolo about Young, the deal was done in "minutes." The truth is that he labored over the decision. In fact, he eventually held that emergency meeting to get his staff's opinion on the trade. And though lots of people will claim they knew all along that Young was destined for greatness in the NFL, I'm here to tell you that when Walsh asked for a show of hands of those who supported making the deal, none went up.

Not one.

Walsh actually stormed out of the room—and made the deal anyway.

What Walsh knew better than anyone in the game was that the key to success in the passing era of the NFL was to marry the right quarterback to the right scheme. (It's much harder than it sounds, trust me.) Most of the time, when the quarterback and the system clash, it's the quarterback who goes. Walsh approached challenges like this one from an entirely different perspective. That's why he had such a huge impact on the game.

Early on in his coaching career, when faced with a quarter-back in Cincinnati who didn't match his offense, Walsh flipped the script: He kept the quarterback and changed the offense instead, transforming the NFL along the way.

In 1968 Walsh was an assistant coach for the expansion Bengals. Besides his talent as an evaluator, Walsh was a deep thinker, a student of the game, and a problem solver. His specialty was counterintuition, and it helped him solve what appeared to be an insurmountable problem in Cincinnati: a roster of castoffs that featured much less talent than every other team in the league.

At that time, the NFL was still a run-dominated league; passing was a tactic of last resort. As former Ohio State coach Woody Hayes said, "Three things can happen when you attempt a pass, and two of them are bad." Reliance on the forward pass was actually considered a bit cowardly. But the expansion Bengals had an undersized line and not much hope of generating a productive ground game. Walsh took a look at the dire situation and saw one thing: opportunity. Whereas most coaches would have thought that moving the ball in Cincinnati would depend on either compiling a stronger roster or throwing the ball more often, Walsh sought a less obvious solution—and, most important, one that was likely to work. He had a player pool of parts—some good, some bad—and no chance in the short term to add anyone else to the mix. But if he couldn't change his players, maybe he could change the offense.

In a story Walsh repeated many times, including in his post-humous book *The Score Takes Care of Itself,* the inspiration for his West Coast offense was the Bengals quarterback Virgil Carter. Carter was one of the first in the long line of great quarterbacks who played at Brigham Young. At just over six feet, he was not an impressive physical specimen, yet he still set a host of school, conference, and NCAA records and led the Cougars to their first-ever conference title in 1965. Drafted by the Bears in 1967, he played 10 games in Chicago over two seasons, throwing 193 passes with 6 touchdowns and 10 interceptions, before being traded to the Bengals after the 1969 season.

Carter did not have a particularly strong arm, and that was a deal breaker for most teams. Much of the league gravitated toward cannon-armed throwers because passing attacks back then almost always came down to "everybody go long." To this day, a quarterback who can't throw with velocity usually doesn't last. But Carter had a different kind of skill set and a demeanor that intrigued Walsh. He was deadly accurate on short passes, physically and mentally nimble, and impervious to pressure. Walsh thought he could develop an offense around such a combination, one that would control the ball despite a useless running game. And controlling the ball enough—say, gaining 25 first downs a game—and playing well on special teams would put them in position to find a way to win at the end. The Bengals couldn't attack the defense vertically with strength the way everyone else did, so they would attack it horizontally with speed, using an intricately timed short passing game that essentially turned short passes into long handoffs. And just like that, as Steve Jobs and Steve Wozniak changed the world from inside that small garage in northern California, Walsh ushered in the future of football from a cramped office in Cincinnati.

A future that would come to be known as the West Coast offense: the last and perhaps greatest innovation in pro football, conceived in Middle America.

Weirdly, Walsh's offensive success—and his unique perspective on the passing attack—stemmed in part from his experience as a defensive coach. (He was a defensive coordinator for Marv Levy at California and the defensive backfield coach at Stanford under John Ralston.) Belichick also used his defensive knowledge to design one of the most prolific offenses in modern football. Both men understood the checks and adjustments that occurred within defensive schemes. They built a counterattack by knowing their enemy. Most coaches today have been trained on only one side of the ball. Because they don't know both, they can't always effectively game-plan against what the opposition is attempting.

Through his defensive lens, Walsh built a system that took into account the things Carter could offer: his football intelligence first and foremost. Football intelligence is way different from book smarts, but in this case Carter, an academic All American, had both. He quickly grasped the ins and outs of complex schemes, knowing what every defender was likely to do. He could do that because he was able to transfer what he learned in the classroom to the field. That is what's known as football smarts. Anyone can memorize a playbook. That's checkers. The West Coast offense is chess, and it requires a quarterback who can instantly react, without thinking, to any of the dozen or so twists and disguises a defense throws at him before and after the snap. With his football smarts, after internalizing opponents' tendencies in tape sessions, Carter could make those game-speed decisions and adjustments that are in and of themselves the nervous system of Walsh's offense.

If Walsh's quarterbacks needed to be quick-witted, they also needed to be quick-footed. The ability to throw in rhythm was the essential ingredient in his system. You see it when a quarterback releases the ball on the proper step of his drop, quickly, accurately, and in synchrony with the receiver's route. In the West Coast offense, the passer's and receiver's footwork is synced up like that of dance partners. As soon as Carter's back foot planted at the end of his drop, his intended target would be coming out of his break. Think of the way an orchestra depends on each section of instruments working off the others. The attack that Walsh invented needed to be as finely tuned. He was forever reminding the quarterbacks to focus on their footwork, with each pass play requiring its own precise mechanics.

Walsh let the rest of the football world focus on a quarterback's arm. He was focused on the feet. It was a paradigm shift born from his lifelong love of boxing. Walsh often shadowboxed his way down the halls of Niners headquarters, and whenever he found a fitting boxing metaphor to motivate his team, he was happy. He broke down boxers as he watched fights: their footwork, their quickness, how they moved, timing, balance. Like a boxer who can throw a flurry of punches as he deftly shuffles his feet, Walsh's quarterbacks needed their body parts to work in a similarly surgical unison. Quick feet, quick arm. Balanced feet, balanced arm. Coordinated feet, coordinated attack.

Every play in Walsh's offense was designed around precise timing. All routes were synchronized such that as the quarterback hit his third (or fifth) step, the ball would be out of his hand and on to a ball catcher. That quick-hit rhythm solved one of the Bengals' main weaknesses—blocking—by relieving the offensive line of having to hold blocks too long. It also allowed the receiver to become a runner beyond the line of scrimmage, in stride and in the open field. As a result, Walsh's offensive schemes elevated the relevance of yards after catch as they slowly transformed a run-first league into a pass-happy one.

Once again, though, Walsh and his new offense were the beneficiary of great luck: Just as the West Coast was developing, the NFL made several rule changes to encourage more passing and scoring. Offensive linemen were now allowed to extend their arms and use their hands in pass blocking (essentially legalized holding) to protect the passer, and defenders no longer could redirect receivers once they got beyond five yards of the line of scrimmage. With more time to throw and with pass catchers free to run across the shallow part of the field—the bread and butter of Walsh's scheme—the West Coast offense began to thrive and expand.

Walsh drew up one play after another, and before long he had a binder full of short passes that quickly got the ball out of Carter's hand and to his receivers just as they reached an open seam in the defense. He sent all his skill position players out on routes, lining them up in unusual and changeable spots to stretch the field horizontally rather than vertically, the league norm. The alignments gave Carter a better presnap view of the defense. Walsh had created the ideal situation for a guy with a diagnostic mind and a quick, accurate arm.

I have come to believe that all great coaches think alike regardless of what sport they're in. Basketball Hall of Fame coach Phil Jackson made his fame with the triangle offense. Created by Sam Barry at the University of Southern California and enhanced by Tex Winter, an assistant on Jackson's staff in Chicago and Los Angeles, the triangle was basketball's way of creating clear passing lanes. Simply described, when the ball is thrown into the post, that player and two others on the same side of the ball form the points of a well-spaced triangle. Walsh's passing game was essentially the triangle on turf.

When you break down any of the fundamental plays of the West Coast offense, the same geometric shape forms inside the defense: a triangle. For example, say you have two backs in split formation in the backfield and the tight end on the line to the right. Now, the Z receiver (the one on the tight end's side) runs a 12-yard curl while the tight end runs to a spot that is exactly in front of the location of the snap when the play started, at a depth of five yards, where he can't be legally bumped off his route. Meanwhile, one back swings out toward the sideline of the Z receiver's curl. Hit pause and draw a line from that back to the Z receiver to the tight end and what do you get? An isosceles triangle.

The formation means the West Coast quarterback is never looking at a particular receiver. Rather, he looks toward the apex of the triangle and then decides where the ball should go, depending on the coverage or the spacing. Walsh hated to see quarterbacks locking in on a receiver early in his route because defenses can see that, too. But when quarterbacks instead key on an area of the field—the triangle—defenders don't quite know what or who they are guarding, especially if a receiver makes a late break, coming free just as the quarterback hits the launch step in his drop.

## PASS PLAY CALLING SYSTEM

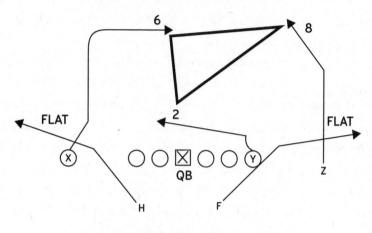

SPLIT RIGHT 628 BACKS FLAT

Spacing, timing, and rhythm. Seems simple enough, but it actually put stagnant, slow defenses, unaccustomed to adaptation, at a huge disadvantage. So much so, in fact, that in the first year of the new offense—just the third year of the team's existence—Carter, Walsh, and the Bengals won the AFC Central. In so doing, Walsh had proved something revolutionary in the typically risk- and innovation-averse NFL: that quarterbacks with a different skill set could lead successful attacks so long as the passer matched the scheme. When it comes to evaluating quarterbacks, pedigree and prototypical size, speed, and arm strength will always matter, but thanks to Walsh, things such as intelligence, poise, and precision also became important.

More than anything, Walsh coveted accuracy from his passers; it's what allowed receivers the opportunity to run with the ball after the catch. If a tight end with his back turned to the defense was open in an empty zone, Walsh expected the quarterback to throw away from an oncoming defender to let the pass catcher know where that defender was and which way he should run to avoid him.

Fans of a certain age have the play known simply as "the Catch" indelibly etched in the part of their brain reserved for important historical moments. In the 1981 NFC championship game against the Cowboys, 49ers quarterback Joe Montana threw the ball so high and toward the back of the end zone that it almost appeared to be a throwaway. But that throwaway was in fact precisely where Walsh wanted it, because the only person who could catch it was receiver Dwight Clark. For Walsh, throwing to the back end line always meant throwing high, whereas throwing near the goal line meant throwing low because, in both cases, the ball could be caught by a 49er or it would be incomplete. High throws near the goal line could be tipped and intercepted. For similar reasons, he was never a big believer in small receivers, because wing span and catch radius could only help the quarterback. He left no detail to chance, and all those details were harmoniously linked.

To push the game forward Walsh was constantly looking back through history for guidance and inspiration. Walsh pored over the old tapes of teams coached by Clark Shaughnessy, a longtime college mainstay and a big believer in the T formation—quarterback behind center, two running backs spread perpendicularly behind him—finding them intriguing even though there were few forward passes in any of them. Rather, he watched for the blocking schemes, which set off offensive linemen at angles to defenders instead of having them face the rush head-on. Those side blocks made it easier for less talented players to seal off defenders while providing a more unobstructed path for the back to follow. Many disparaged the West Coast offense as more finesse than power, partially because angle blocks outnumbered drive blocks. But helping players get an edge is not finesse; it's just smart. Similarly, with the old T formation, the ball handling confused the linebackers, as they watched the ball instead of the blocking scheme, causing them to be slightly out of position. And in the run game, being even a little bit in the wrong spot can create a lane big enough for a back to scoot through.

In the end, though, the most significant influence for Walsh was his time spent with the Raiders. Oakland's passing game—which, to be fair, was preceded by Sid Gillman's air attack—was a precursor to the West Coast offense in the way it freed the linemen from having to protect the quarterback for too long through the use of short passes and quick releases. Yes, Davis much preferred throwing the ball down the field, but he, too, believed strongly in the timing between quarterback and receiver. Everybody had to be in sync. That included tight ends and running backs, which in those days was a rarity. With those players involved, there were often five route runners who had to be covered, thus overwhelming defenses.

Of course, that was when things worked just right—which they rarely do. But even in the typical chaos that takes place on a football field, Walsh still managed to find something useful. In another story that Walsh loved to tell and write about, Cincinnati's tight end Bob Trumpy, facing the Raiders, once broke the huddle and lined up on the right side instead of on the left, where the play called for him to be. The quarterback shifted him to the other side in time to run the play correctly, and when Trumpy came to the sideline when the series was over, he was apologetic. The Bengals coaches, though, particularly the offensive line coach, Bill Johnson, barely heard him because they were still marveling at the fact that when Trumpy moved, four defenders followed him (and actually ran into one another in the confusion), which meant that when he ran back to where he was supposed to be, the Raiders were not where *they* were supposed to be.

Defenses always set their fronts and coverage packages against the strength of the offense—that is, the side on which the tight end lines up. When Trumpy moved, the strength of the defense moved, too, and when he moved back, it had to realign. The shift added another complicated layer to the defense's communication while forcing the defense to tip its hand just before the snap. Once Johnson and Walsh saw this, they knew they could mess with the defense—get it out of position and confuse its communication.

Thus, out of a broken play the shift was reborn as a major weapon in the West Coast offense.

Believe it or not, the run was also a weapon in Walsh's new scheme. Walsh was weaned in a time when establishing the run was agreed to be the most critical component of winning football. But he was the first to realize that everyone was chasing a lie. He correctly understood that teams interested only in establishing the run were creating nothing more than a chance to kick a field goal. Think about it: The odds of covering 80 yards, more or less, on the ground are not good; one negative play pretty much stalls a drive. One pass play of, say, 20 yards, though, dramatically changes field position and a team's chances of driving to a touchdown. Walsh's West Coast offense wasn't anti-run. He just wanted to run the ball with a creativity that would give the players the best chance to succeed. Running every play between the tackles was not for him. In fact, he saw the traditional run game as the lazy coach's way, putting the onus on players to execute or rely on brute force for yardage. That was something Walsh always wanted to avoid.

That's why Walsh's teams—not to mention the best teams in football today—came out throwing. If you were to plot the rushing attempts of recent playoff teams by quarter, it would look like this: first quarter, a rush-to-pass percentage in the bottom third of the league; second quarter, same; third quarter, middle of the pack; fourth quarter, top third, more or less. Examine the regular-season breakdowns of the teams that made it to the Super Bowl after the 2016 season. In the first half, the Patriots threw the ball 57 percent of the time and ran it 43 percent. The Falcons threw 61 percent of the time and rushed just 39 percent. But in the second half, the Pats were more 50/50, and the Falcons 54/46. Walsh was the first NFL coach to foresee the paradigm shift on offense and how the run one day would become more about preserving the lead than establishing it. (Maybe if the Falcons had stuck to the plan and run the ball more in the fourth quarter of Super Bowl LI they would have won the game.)

Old schoolers think establishing the run is a quarterback's best friend. But what kind of a friend is third and long when everyone in the stadium knows you have to pass the ball? In truth, conservative play calling is a quarterback's worst enemy. The best thing an offense can do for its quarterback is throw on traditional run downs so that the QB doesn't have to deal with obvious passing situations. Throwing the ball makes running the ball easier, and that's how Walsh succeeded with the Bengals.

In the first few years of what was derisively called the dink-and-dunk offense, Walsh found success not so much in scoring points but in getting first downs and keeping the ball away from the opponent. Defenses were slow to adjust, continuing to play as if they were expecting the Bengals to throw down the field. Pretty soon the defenses found themselves in even worse trouble as the Bengals added more talented pieces to the offense, receivers such as Isaac Curtis, Charlie Joiner, and Chip Myers, whose speed allowed Walsh to add a downfield element to his short game. The first-down machine had been transformed into a scoring machine.

Thanks to what Walsh did in Cincinnati, NFL teams started to think of their offenses the way baseball executives think of their stadiums. Baseball teams collect talent that makes the most sense for the quirks of their home parks. The Red Sox stockpile right-handed hitters because the Green Monster in left is so close. More cavernous stadiums become homes to speedier players. Stadiums dictate style. Same thing for football offenses. Quarterbacks have to be slipped into systems that best feature their skills. Very, very few players can make a bad fit work. Too often, though, teams think that the player makes the system rather than the other way around. It sends them hunting for a guy with obvious tools—a gun for an arm, mobility—around whom they figure they will build an offense.

Walsh and his West Coast offense have proved that's just not how it works.

W alsh always cautioned me: "Very few people can coach the quarterback, and even fewer can evaluate them." After more than 30 years in football I can verify that that statement is 100 percent accurate. When it comes to the most important position in sports, biases, rationalizations, and willful ignorance all get in the way of dispassionate and accurate analysis. Even a genius like Walsh knew that it was an imperfect science with exceptions to every rule. Drew Brees, it turns out, was not too short. Philip Rivers's slightly sidearm delivery works just fine. Kurt Warner's Arena League pedigree was good enough to get him to the Hall of Fame. But along the way, while studying Belichick as he searched for Brady's replacement, and by watching Walsh, Montana, and Young operating inside the West Coast offense, I've managed to compile a list of "7 QB Qualities" that, though not foolproof, have helped me formalize my beliefs on the quarterback evaluation process.

## 1. A WINNING WAY

"Winning is a habit," Vince Lombardi said. "Unfortunately, so is losing." Bill Parcells's golden rule was to draft prospects with at least 23 wins in college. It told him that a player knew what it took to be successful and was committed to doing the little things that got the job done. Now, 23 wins isn't a magic number, but it's a pretty good indicator. You can't bluff your way to 23 wins, not even in Pop Warner. Jameis Winston was 26–1 as a college starter, Marcus Mariota was 36–5, and Kirk Cousins was 27–12. That's a trio that is holding fairly steady in the pros after succeeding against the top tier of college competition.

The flip side may be the Chicago Bears' 2017 first rounder Mitch Trubisky. Trubisky started only one year at North Carolina, and his numbers caved against top-25 competition. Let's look at his yards per attempt in particular. This statistic is telling because it is a representation of what a quarterback is seeing and where he is looking. It's an eye-level test. Higher yards per attempt—say, 7.5 or better—indicate a quarterback who is looking long, looking for big plays. Lower numbers indicate a quarterback who may be too concerned about being hit or is playing it safe and thus takes the quickest completion.

In Cleveland, we learned the power of this statistic the hard way. When once-great quarterback Bernie Kosar was nearing the end of his career, he was more concerned about his completion percentage than yards per attempt. During a game against Miami, Kosar was struggling, and Belichick pulled him from the game.

Kosar argued, "How can you pull me? I'm 15 of 19."

To which Belichick immediately snapped back out of the side of his mouth, "Yeah, for 82 yards."

Kosar was spending too much time not getting sacked to realize that he was no longer doing the job we were paying him to do.

Trubisky's yards-per-attempt average dropped from 8.3 to 6.2 against top-25 teams. Similarly, when he played from ahead, he averaged 9.1 yards per attempt versus 7.2 when he was behind. That's a fairly significant spread. Fans of Trubisky will blame the talent level that supported him for the discrepancy, but that's not how it works. The same teammates helped him to the good numbers, too. Meanwhile, Houston Texan Deshaun Watson, drafted the same year as Trubisky, averaged 7.7 yards per attempt when his team was ahead and 9.4 when it was down. In other words, he turned up the heat when his team needed it the most, when it was time to catch up.

By the way, Watson won 32 games in college. Trubisky? Eight.

If you believe in the rule of 23, you don't need to watch the next five seasons to know how these stories end.

## 2. A THICK SKIN

"The measure of who we are is how we react to something that does not go our way," says San Antonio Spurs head coach Gregg Popovich. It's definitely a good measure of a quarterback as well. I always tried to find a prospect who had already overcome adversity, and not only on the field. If past performance is the best indicator of future achievement, those who have fought through bad times are likely to be able to do so again. The one thing every young NFL quarterback can be certain of is that he will struggle mightily at some point. Even Peyton Manning went 3–13 as a rookie. Poor Troy Aikman finished 0–11 his first year. So I wanted to know how a prospect handled criticism and whether he let bad plays get to him.

Winston won those 26 games in college despite throwing 28 interceptions. Yes, that's way too many, and yes, such misfires, which have continued in the pros, will keep him from the pinnacle of his profession if he doesn't clean them up. But say this about him: Those mistakes don't bother him. He comes off the field acting as if they are just part of the game—which they are. His mental toughness allows him to keep taking chances, to keep moving forward.

Nobody questions Tom Brady's mental toughness, but after one of his rare interceptions he tends to be a bit more careful with the ball for a couple of series, avoiding throws into especially tight spots. I hate turnovers, but when I evaluate quarterbacks, I hate thin skin even more.

## 3. WORK ETHIC

"Your best player has to set a tone for intolerance for anything that gets in the way of winning," says NBA coach and TV analyst Jeff Van Gundy. Okay, so this is not an earth-shattering revelation, but you'd be surprised how many scouts ignore it. Do you think JaMarcus Russell was the hardest worker at LSU? Or Johnny Manziel at Texas A&M? Here's a hint: Taking care of your body is a pretty accurate indicator of commitment to the job. Being lazy gets in the way of winning. Think of the recent quarterback busts. How many were truly hard workers? Ryan Leaf was 20 pounds overweight *at his initial weigh-in.* What kind of group rationalization did the Chargers' brain trust have to engage in to convince itself that he was a worthy second overall pick? Your star quarterback needs to be a gym rat, pure and simple—first at practice, last to leave. (It's not the only quality he needs, of course. Case in point: Tim Tebow.) Too often, football suits believe they can change a player's work habits. Al Davis thought he could make Russell love the game enough to work as hard as he needed to. He found out soon enough that he couldn't.

Why do teams like the Raiders and Chargers convince themselves that they can change a player's character? Hubris, for one thing. But it's mainly because every once in a while a team gets lucky and pulls it off. There are, of course, exceptions to every one of these 7 QB Qualities. None is bigger than Brett Favre's "discovered" work ethic.

The Falcons drafted Favre near the top of the second round in 1991, but all he was in his rookie season was a disaster off the field. As Favre himself described it a few years later to a reporter, "I missed the team picture. I missed a couple of other things. I was late for meetings. I was surprised it took them that long to trade me." Of course, after getting traded to Green Bay, Favre became an all-time great. Guess the Packers ironed out his character flaws, right? Not so fast. Favre's issues were with alcohol, and he had to solve them for himself before he could become the player he did. Falcons coach Jerry Glanville tried everything in Atlanta, going so far as to drive around town asking bartenders not to serve his quarterback, but in the end he didn't have that kind of power. No one does. Assuming you can change a guy is magical thinking.

## 4. FOOTBALL SMARTS

Here's the thing: Everyone watches game tape, but precious few benefit from it. Watching and studying are two different things. A quarterback who really studies tape will learn what the defense is trying to do. If he knows what he's looking for, he also can note individual strengths and weaknesses as well as the particulars of the attack. New Orleans quarterback Drew Brees is a tape nerd. He knows the personnel of every team's schemes and can ID all the adjustments made in each of them. Brees gets so obsessed as to be annoying, the kid in the front of the class with all the answers, asking for more homework. Brady, too. (The 7 QB Qualities often overlap like this: You need a great work ethic to study film long enough to build your football smarts.) But on Sunday that translates into wins. There is nothing the defense can do that will catch you by surprise.

(Well, almost nothing. Here's another classic exception to my 7 QB Qualities: In Super Bowl LI, on third and six with just over two minutes left in the first half, Brady was expecting the same coverage from the Falcons—straight man to man—that they played 99 percent of the time in those situations. But as Brady let the ball go toward Danny Amendola, he didn't realize that the Falcons had made a slight modification to the safety's responsibilities. The next thing anyone knew, that safety, Robert Alford, was running the ball back 82 yards for a pick-six. Let it be a lesson to everyone: If you want to beat Brady and the Pats, you have to try something a little different. Staying conventional is suicide.)

Brady, like Brees, Aaron Rodgers, and a few others, knows that success on Sunday comes from time spent Monday through Saturday preparing yourself to think and play faster. A quick mind comes with preparation. You prepare so well that you don't have to think; you just react.

This is hard for young players, though, because they often enter the NFL with little or no understanding of what it means to study tape even though they obviously watch plenty of it in college. Don't blame their coaches. Blame the time restrictions of the NCAA, not to mention classroom responsibilities. Today's college offenses are controlled from the sidelines—every play, every audible. Quarterbacks never have to call anything. But in the pros, radio communication between the coach and quarterback is shut off with 15 seconds on the play clock, and so quarterbacks are on their own. NFL games aren't just more complicated, they're also faster, so how quickly a quarterback can process information and make decisions often makes the difference between winning and losing. And that processing can happen only if a quarterback is football smart.

It's not until they get to the NFL that quarterbacks begin to understand the game's tiny crucial details, such as the leverage points of defensive backs or the side of the receiver defenders want to take away, the same way a basketball defender tries to take away an opponent's "stronger" hand. It takes time for a young passer to understand that when a blitz comes from the defensive backfield, the defender responsible for the blitzer's vacated area will cheat to that side, creating a hole in coverage and thus tipping off the blitz.

Subtleties gleaned from studying tape the correct way often make the difference between a Pro Bowl QB and a draft bust. The truly scary thing from a personnel standpoint is that no matter how much you vet a college quarterback, it will always be a 50/50 gamble. Why? Because you simply can't measure his ultimate football smarts and how he'll react to the speed and complications of the pro game until he gets under the center on a Sunday.

## 5. INNATE ABILITY

"Some quarterbacks are just born with such instincts and intuition," Walsh wrote in his book *Finding the Winning Edge.* "As a rule, there is not much coaches can do to develop this area." I'm no geneticist, but I can tell you that when Tom Brady's mom first took him in her arms, he already had somewhere in his DNA the fundamental quarterback requirements—tangible and intangible. Obviously, he would need to develop some tools—the arm, the foot movement, the rush-avoiding quickness, the sense of timing—but the core of what makes him who he is on the field today was pretty much there already. I understand how subjective this "born with it" quality is, but I don't care. Walsh couldn't define it, either, but he knew it when he saw it. And I believe in it, too.

Speaking of "it," from all indications, Deshaun Watson has it. I mean, the guy started in high school and college as a freshman. On the other hand, Miami Dolphins fans will tell you that Ryan Tannehill was no quarterback in the crib. Athlete, yes, but a natural for the position? Don't think so. In fact, in high school, Tannehill didn't become the starter until his junior year, and he was only a three-star recruit—listed as an athlete, not a quarterback. At Texas A&M, he was even moved to wide receiver for two years before starting six games at quarterback as a junior. Sure, he impressed a lot of people as the starter on a solid team as a senior, but you couldn't exactly argue that Tannehill was a natural. Whatever that certain something is, he lacks it, and that is what's holding him back in the pros. Because he is not an instinctive player, he doesn't play as fast as he needs to. Don't get me wrong; he is capable of good things. It's just that he doesn't seem capable of fast things. The best indication of this is his play on third down, when blitzes and passing situations speed up considerably. Tannehill's career third-down numbers: 26 interceptions, one-half yard less per attempt than his overall average, and a 58 percent completion rate (versus 63 percent overall). When the game pushes him, Tannehill is less productive. If Walsh were still around, he would be telling the Dolphins they need to start looking for a new quarterback, one with more innate ability.

## 6. CARRIAGE

The University of Connecticut's women's basketball coach, Geno Auriemma, benches players—even stars—if he doesn't like the way they are carrying themselves, correcting the problem before it subverts the team. How long, do you imagine, would quarterback Jay Cutler be stuck on Geno's bench? You don't think body language is important? Ask Bears fans. I think Cutler would still be playing in Soldier Field if his sideline posture indicated he was even a little interested. At times he has looked as if he'd sooner sit in a dentist's chair than get back in the game. Cutler has problems on the field, too, sure, but they are compounded by the way he responds to them. He acts like he just doesn't give a damn. I don't get it. His coaches in Chicago and Miami must have known that his lousy body language would kill credibility among teammates almost faster than his poor play would. Quarterbacks have to inspire. And if they can't always do it with pinpoint throws and blitz-facing courage—everyone has a bad day—they can always look as if they have it all under control and that somehow they will figure out how to lead the team to victory. No one wants to follow a sulker. (Exception: Cam Newton is a Heisman Trophy winner, a number one overall NFL draft pick, and an MVP even though he hunkers down under a towel, argues with coaches, and storms out of press conferences. Go figure. However, he hasn't yet led his team to a Super Bowl, so . . .)

## 7. LEADERSHIP

Quarterbacks who fail to gain the respect of teammates leave a team rudderless. When teams I worked for were in the market for a quarterback, we made sure we knew what the teammates of any prospective hires were saying about the guy (off the record, of course). Is his competitiveness contagious or overbearing? Are players willing to go to war with him? Does he command the huddle? Finding the truth isn't easy. College coaches used to be a good source for this kind of stuff, but lately they have become adept at talking up their prospects because they want their guys to make it to the league—and not just for the players' sake. Pros promote programs. Therefore, scouts have to dig deeper to get what they need even if it's not what we want to hear.

A recent very high pick was dinged by his college teammates. Check that. They flat-out hated him. They refused to attend his private workouts, for heaven's sake. But the team that drafted him chose to ignore all that, and today most of the teammates he's had feel exactly the same way his college teammates did. Trust me, injuries are not the only reason Robert Griffin III has had such a hard time finding a job.

Gil Brandt, the Cowboys' legendary personnel guy, once told me: "The best time to draft a quarterback is when you don't need one." It's actually one piece of advice I got to pass along to Belichick. In New England before the 2014 draft, we had a meeting to make sure we were focused on finding a player to replace Tom Brady (on the assumption that someday, eventually, perhaps, he was actually going to have to retire). The current backup, Ryan Mallett, was entering his final season under contract, and we knew he was not the answer. When we drafted Mallett, he looked to have all the skills. Unfortunately, he lacked the maturity and work ethic to play at the next level. Guys like that are exceedingly frustrating to coach because they never see that they are wasting their talents. We gave Mallett time to shape up, but he didn't and it became time to move on. Brady was coming off a subpar season for him, with his lowest quarterback rating since 2003. But nobody thought he was anywhere close to finished, so the timing was perfect. Whoever we selected would have at least a couple of years to get ready away from the spotlight.

The draft had many prospects: Blake Bortles of Central Florida, Johnny Manziel of Texas A&M, Teddy Bridgewater of Louisville, Derek Carr of Fresno State, and Jimmy Garoppolo of Eastern Illinois. Choosing near the bottom of the first round was going to prevent us from having our pick of the group. Still, the offensive staff, mostly Josh McDaniels, the quarterback coach and offensive coordinator, spent time watching tape on them all and then narrowing the field. Fresh off my time in Cleveland, I was up to speed on our options because I had spent considerable time assessing each quarterback for the Browns. By the time McDaniels and Belichick had completed their tape study, we were down to two: Manziel and Garoppolo.

I admit that I was fascinated by Manziel despite his lack of height and loved how Garoppolo dominated his level of competition. (That might not have swayed Al Davis, but it was enough for me.) Manziel had a boatload of off-the-field issues that we had to research to separate fact from fiction. Garoppolo stood out in almost every area, but spending time with him would help us determine whether he could duplicate his skill set at this level and grow in our offense. One directive Belichick kept pounding into us was that we were not looking to duplicate Brady; whoever we drafted, the offense would have to do some adapting to his strengths. (Spoken like a true Walsh devotee.) That is not to suggest that we would overhaul the offense, but once we understood the new guy's strengths, we would feature plays and wrinkles to highlight them. When Brady took over for Drew Bledsoe, the Patriots tweaked the offense by making it slightly less vertical, increasing the focus on timing routes and the tight end as a weapon. When big play wide receiver Randy Moss arrived, the Patriots tweaked their attack once more to take advantage of his incredible speed and downfield threat. Belichick might not be much for change, but he's a big believer in adaptation.

When potential draft picks come to New England for a visit, it is not a recruiting trip. Belichick has zero interest in being a salesman for the program. His just wants to find the truth about each player. Players meet with all divisions of the football operation, then sit alone with McDaniels as they watch tape. At some point they have to explain the plays they are watching and then learn some basics of our playbook. After lunch the players are put through a walk-through of the plays they learned. Once this is over, they meet with Belichick, who, like any great trial lawyer, has all the answers to the questions before he asks them.

After Manziel and Garoppolo headed to their next NFL destinations, Belichick held a meeting to review the day. All the coaches in the session felt that both men passed muster as far as being able to learn the offense and not being overwhelmed by their potential proximity to a legend.

But Manziel had those issues that would not be cleared in a one-day visit.

Garoppolo, in contrast, just had it. I swear he seemed like the living embodiment of my 7 QB Qualities. And after we selected him in the second round, it became clear that everything we thought about him was dead-on. There was a quiet confidence in whatever he did. He was a great worker, his football smarts were off the charts, and he carried himself like a leader at all times. (Was he throwing spirals from the crib? Probably.) He quickly bonded with the offensive linemen and was respectful toward Brady even as he competed to win a spot as his backup. For someone who has studied quarterback prospects for 30 years—how to find them, evaluate them, and develop them—it was a very exciting and interesting time.

Everything just felt right. Everything except the timing, it turns out.

More on that in Chapter 9, but I will say this: Watching Garoppolo's style and mannerisms, Walsh would have wanted this kid, and remember—spoiler alert—whatever Bill wants, Bill gets.

# 6

# DEFENSE

## WHERE SIMPLICITY IS COMPLEX

*Times were simpler, defenses didn't move as fast,*
*and the quarterback was often the best athlete.*
*Now he's being chased by the best athletes.*

—BILL WALSH

You know that game people play where they name their dream dinner companions? In the spring of 2016, I actually got to live one of mine. Before the draft that year, Bill Belichick and I traveled to the University of Alabama to evaluate the school's talent at its annual Pro Day. There we also caught up with Nick Saban, a friend of mine, who was the defensive coordinator on the Cleveland Browns staff and a friend of Bill's even before that. When the Crimson Tide's Pro Day was over, the three of us headed to Saban's house near campus for dinner and conversation about—what else?—football. Whenever I finish a lengthy phone call with Belichick, my wife, Millie, always asks me, "Do you two talk about anything other than football?" The answer, of course, is no. Hey, you talk about what you love, and we love football. The only other person I know who loves to chat about the gridiron as much as we do is Saban. As we left campus, he informed us that his wife, Ms. Terry, was not going to be home. That meant the three of us football nerds didn't even have to pretend to be interested in anything but ball.

We practically raced to Saban's house. It was going to be a real man-cave dinner with a single course: defense.

Imagine my luck that evening: being a fly on the wall at a long and uninterrupted dinner with perhaps the two greatest football coaches in history, men who have enjoyed a long, symbiotic, and successful history of pushing and challenging each other to perfect their sometimes disparate defensive styles and philosophies.

Even before they were together in Cleveland, Belichick and Saban would meet at West Point or at points along the road to discuss different ways to create the all-important pass rush. Saban and Belichick agreed that pressuring the quarterback was the best way to slow down any aerial attack in the pass-happy era. They just didn't quite agree on how to accomplish it. On this matter, Belichick offered a staunch conservative counterpoint to Saban's screamingly liberal all-out-pressure-on-every-down-and-from-everywhere approach. But each saw the merits of the other's position, and ultimately neither was above borrowing a little from the other and blending it into his own philosophy.

When they reconnected for dinner in Alabama, the timing couldn't have been better. Saban had just defeated the high-powered Clemson offense for the national championship, although the Tigers, led by Deshaun Watson, put 40 points on the famed Crimson Tide defense. It sounds incredible, but despite the win Saban was still fuming over that defensive performance. As I said, sometimes these guys seem like twins. For both of them, their moods are never a reflection of the score—it's about the execution. And Saban is far too savvy to pretend that his team wasn't lucky to prevail.

Clemson ran over and through Saban's defense by using the spread attack that has been popular in the college game for some time. What made the dinner conversation so intriguing to Belichick was that the up-tempo spread was becoming increasingly commonplace in the NFL as well, ever since Chip Kelly, late of the Oregon Ducks, had brought his version to the Philadelphia Eagles a few years earlier. Belichick could not have cared less about the menu that night or Saban's spectacular home. He wanted to pick Nick's brain about stopping the game's newest offensive wrinkle.

The NFL has a version of the run-pass option: Two plays are called in the huddle—one run, one pass—and the quarterback determines which to go with once he gets to the line and peruses the defensive formation. In college, though, the run-pass option adds a wrinkle, the spread formations from which teams either hand off the ball or fake the handoff and throw a pass. They can do this because unlike in the NFL, college offensive linemen can be as much as three yards downfield, which means they can always block as if for a run play—regardless of whether the offense ends up throwing a pass. In professional football, it's illegal for linemen to be so far downfield, and anyway, most, if not all, teams would be reluctant to run the option this way for fear of getting their quarterback clobbered.

Nevertheless, Belichick was eager to understand how Saban planned his counterattack. Between bites, Saban went into all of it in depth. Trying not to sound like too much of a fanboy, I have to say that his discourse was amazing: not just the scheme but the way he could make even the most complicated pieces of this puzzle seem simple and easy to digest. Belichick wasn't particularly interested in the micro, the countless adjustments to each of the calls. What he wanted to hear more about was Saban's broad philosophy. Belichick would figure out the particulars himself.

That was how they always did things when they worked together.

In 1991, when Belichick became the head coach in Cleveland, he inherited a team that allowed 462 points (28.8 points per game). In just one year, he and Saban dropped that number to 298. And in 1994, the last time Cleveland won a playoff game, the Belichick/Saban defense gave up just 204 points (12.7 per game). They did it with a defense they invented called Red 2.

Red 2, which is often credited to Saban but was truthfully a joint creation, was a "match coverage." Depending on the pass routes, receivers would be defended man to man or passed off as they crossed into and through different areas of the field. Essentially, it was football's version of a matchup zone in basketball, and it was used mainly when football offenses were in the red zone. It had different rules and guiding principles than a typical Cover 2 because it defended a more contracted space, and it was hard for the players to understand at first. In fact, my colleagues got sick of me walking around the office saying that learning Red 2 could double as the entrance exam for Harvard. But before long it became clear that Red 2 was a keeper.

In the Red 2, a corner was responsible for carrying a receiver for a distance before passing him to a safety and waiting for another receiver to enter his area and become his responsibility. What made the Red 2 so hard to learn—but nearly impossible to game-plan against—was that each week it could be tailored specifically to the opponent's passing designs. One week the corner might carry a receiver for 10 yards through his "zone," and the next week he might cover him for just 8. Depending on any number of factors—matchups, scores, personnel, speed, injuries—the parameters could and often would change. It was taxing on the brain but very effective on the field.

That night he boiled it down for us to a single tenet: More than anything, the goal was to make sure that the "run force" player (the defender who "forced" a rushing play in a certain direction) was never compromised. Setting an edge to contain an outside run and redirecting it inside toward the teeth of the defense had to be that defender's primary focus, so much so that he needed to be free of the responsibility of handling pass plays, too. Whatever adjustments or sacrifices needed to occur in coverage schemes to make that happen, well, they just had to get done.

Between courses, Belichick peppered Saban with so many questions—"If they double your defensive end, then what?" and "What do you do if the quarterback steps up in the pocket?" and "Could a screen work if you threw it over the end?"—that we were dishing out dessert before I knew it.

Looking back, my dream dinner had little to do with the food and everything to do with the high-level theoretical conversation. The meal was tasty, yes, but the seminar offered by two of the greatest football minds ever was much more filling and fulfilling.

And it inspired me to create my own philosophy about the 11 essential rules of good defense.

Bon appetit.

## 1. THE DISGUISE IS AS IMPORTANT AS THE DEFENSE

In the movie *The Usual Suspects,* the small-time con artist with cerebral palsy, Roger "Verbal" Kint, regales U.S. customs agent Dave Kujan with tales of an elaborate heist scheme and a mysterious man named Keyser Söze. Verbal's grand story about the villainous, enigmatic Söze includes one of the most classic movie quotes of all time: "The greatest trick the Devil ever pulled was convincing the world he didn't exist" (which—fun fact—is actually a rephrasing of a line from the nineteenth-century French poet Charles Baudelaire).

When it comes to disguising defenses, Belichick is the NFL's version of Keyser Söze, without the murderous impulses, of course. At his peak as a defensive coordinator in the mid-1980s, with everyone watching and trying to reverse engineer his schemes, the tight-lipped Belichick convinced everyone that the New York Giants' defense was nothing more than a 3-4 Cover 2, with no complexity to it. He convinced the football world that the important wrinkles in his attack didn't exist by aligning in the same front and showing the same coverage look on every play. Most teams vary their fronts and coverage shells on first and second down to confuse the opposing quarterback. Not Belichick. He brings a level of confusion and disguise *after* every snap that keeps most quarterbacks up at night.

Belichick kept up the Keyser Söze act even with his friends and colleagues. When I asked about disguising his defense in 1991, he told me that, in fact, the 3-4 Cover 2 was his only call. He wasn't lying, but in what some might consider classic Belichick fashion, he wasn't being entirely truthful, either. Yes, the call was 3-4 Cover 2, but what the defense did out of it depended on the strengths and weaknesses of the particular opponent, not just from week to week but from play to play. For example, just before the snap on an obvious passing down in Belichick's base 3-4, it might look like the outside linebacker was lined up to rush the edge, but a split second after the snap Belichick would drop the outside backer into coverage and blitz the inside backer through the interior line— all because the last-second switch created a better matchup with a lesser blocker. On the next play, he might slant his entire defensive front to the strong side to combat a strong side run team. The layers of complexities were subtle and the modifications slight, but they allowed Belichick to use what seemed like 35 custom defenses in a single game, which shifted the tactical advantage to his team's side. Anyone who wanted to believe the tweaks didn't exist was making a huge mistake, just like the saps in *The Usual Suspects*.

Belichick's simplicity-first ruse on defense was inspired by Washington Redskins Hall of Fame head coach Joe Gibbs. Gibbs was a masterful offensive tactician, with a scheme that featured a power running game that won three Super Bowls under three different quarterbacks, none of whom are household names. (Think about that next time you're engaged in one of those best-football-coaches-of-all-time debates.) His offense appeared complex on first glance, but when Belichick broke it down, he found that it all could be reduced to 13 base plays (3 runs, 10 passes). Gibbs believed, as Belichick does, that repetition breeds execution. All those basic Redskins plays, however, were executed out of (and disguised by) myriad formations, looks, shifts, and personnel groupings that turned 13 vanilla plays into 130 complicated and mysterious plays. For the quarterback, though, no matter what went on before the snap, by the time he dropped back to pass, all the routes in front of him looked just like they always did. Similarly, by the time the ball was in the running back's hands, the blocking scheme and running lanes before him looked exactly the same. Gibb's playbook had 13 pages. Everything else was window dressing used to keep defenses in the dark and on their heels, constantly worried that the devil they didn't think existed was actually playing tricks on them.

Before he became a head coach, remember, Belichick competed against Gibbs twice a year as the Giants' defensive coordinator, and what he saw in that camouflaged offense had a major impact on him. On his first day as a head coach, in fact, Belichick walked into the Browns' headquarters and declared that we would adopt the Skins model: core plays disguised with various looks and personnel groups to create confusion.

New plays don't win consistently, he preached; using old plays in new ways does.

## 2. STUDYING AN OFFENSE IS THE FIRST STEP
##    TOWARD STOPPING IT

Battles on the gridiron are much like battles on a chessboard. In each case, grandmasters know their opponent's tendencies and spend time studying games played in styles reminiscent of their own. When Belichick sits down to study an offense, he doesn't read the press clippings or fixate on the win-loss record. Instead, he watches tape of teams that play a scheme similar to his own base scheme to learn how his upcoming opponent attacked it. Knowing the opponent's offensive or defensive coordinator is critical, too, so he maintains a thick file on all the men holding those jobs. The more he knows about them, the better he can anticipate what they'll do in key game situations. When Belichick arrived in Cleveland and I was the pro personnel advance man, we would meet each week to discuss the next opponent, and those meetings began with a debrief about the coordinators. From background to football influences and finally to recent games, he wanted to know as much about the coaches as he did the players because, like chess champion Bobby Fischer, he wanted to know how he was going to be attacked.

The movie *A Beautiful Mind* was based on the life of another troubled genius, John Nash, the renowned mathematician who made fundamental contributions to game theory and the study of partial differential equations. (Yeah, me neither.) In the film, Nash's office shows a desk covered with papers and drawings and a blackboard filled with all sorts of equations and no more room to write. Maybe all geniuses think and work alike, but I swear, Belichick's office looks just like Nash's. The coach's conference table was always covered in stacks of paper—or as we all called them, "the pads." The pads are Belichick's version of Warren Buffett's massive in-depth preinvestment research, the due diligence required to make a correct evaluation of a company, though in this case the company is an opposing team. To "own" an offense, first you have to know how it works. But incredibly, most teams misidentify what opponents do best because they don't spend enough time studying them.

Every week defensive coaches around the NFL talk about "stopping the run." But which run? From what formation and toward what direction? And even if you do go deep enough with your analysis, that's only half the work. Now you have figure out the right way to counter. Say they love to run left. Do you match your primary run defender against their best blocker—like against like—or do you try to free him? Nor is the answer to simply show an eight-man front. If that idea worked all the time, no team would ever gain a yard on the ground. In fact, general solutions often create more problems. No, it's never as simple as "stop the run."

The pads all over Belichick's cluttered office were his defense against this kind of fatal flaw. Essentially, they were plays from game tape printed out on an 8½-by-11 sheet of paper with the precise movements of each member of the offense and defense delineated. And when I say precise, I mean precise. "Padding" the games was a job for young wannabe coaches. It took at least four or five hours to do a game, to make sure Belichick would have the exact details he needed in front of him. The notes on each play went far beyond just basic X's and O's. For starters, Belichick wants to know how, when, where, and why every player on the field moved during every play. He wants to know, for example, if there is a variation of even a couple of inches in the offensive line's splits or if the quarterback likes to throw to his right or is especially deadly on out patterns.

Josh McDaniels, the Patriots offensive coordinator, began his coaching career padding games. After handing over the first few, he got them returned with color-coded Post-its highlighting his various mistakes and omissions. Belichick takes great pride and pleasure in helping and developing young assistants, and with McDaniels he had basically graded his work, adding colored lines to indicate more accurately the movement of the play on both sides of the ball and entering a host of extra data. McDaniels is a proud and competitive man. It didn't take long until he was padding a game in under four hours, fully confident that there would be no boomerang Post-it notes.

Belichick believes that coaches who learn their craft by padding games are much better coaches on Sunday, even though the task is so labor-intensive that it basically requires them to go without sleep. It's exhausting work, and Belichick knows it because he often padded games himself. But to him, learning every detail of how an offense plans to attack is far more valuable than rest.

## 3. DON'T COACH DEFENSE, TEACH IT

"In a very real way," Bill Walsh once wrote, "everything I did was teaching in some manner or other." The truth is that at their core all good coaches are great teachers and communicators. The trait ran deep in Belichick's family. His mom, Jeannette, was a teacher who spoke seven languages and had a lifetime subscription to *The New Yorker*. Lou Holtz, the former Notre Dame head coach, often asked his assistants, "Are you a schemer or a teacher?" He wanted to know if they were more interested in doodling plays or teaching teams how to win. Blackboard coaching is a killer. Schemes drawn up in classrooms are undefeated; whoever has the chalk last wins. On blackboards across the league there are elaborate defenses being created that, in two dimensions at least, seem certain to shut down any offense. In real life? Doodles usually don't translate. But teaching always does.

Sometimes that's because although they might look incredible, what the play diagrams represent on the field isn't so smart at all. Or, worse, players can't properly execute what the doodle demands. But more often than not, the problem is that players don't understand what they're being asked to do. And that's the fault of the coach, not the doodles. When the TV cameras cut to a coach on a sideline after his defense has just allowed a big play, even amateur lip-readers can see the frustrated man saying some version of "What are we doing?" We can't hear the response, obviously, but honestly, it doesn't matter. If the coach is asking that question, it's probably because in some ways the players were, too. If someone has been left wide open, it's because the players didn't know what they were doing, and that happened because the coaches didn't help them understand their responsibilities when they had the chance.

George Seifert, Walsh's defensive coordinator with the Niners before becoming his successor, was a brilliant assistant: innovative, creative, and not intimidated by a West Coast offense his unit had to face every day in practice. What really set him apart as a coordinator, though, was his teaching skills. Seifert knew how to transfer what was in those elaborate schemes he drew up—the concepts, the assignments, the visual keys, and even the physical requirements—into execution on the field by his players, much to the chagrin of the crusty scouts on the payroll. Those old-timers often complained to me that Seifert's playbook was too big and too hard to learn and that defense was a reactionary game, not a thinking game. Seifert proved them wrong year in and year out. He didn't just draw a doodle of a race car; he knew how to build it and how to teach people to drive it. He knew how to implement his schemes.

In Cleveland, our defensive backfield coach—and later defensive coordinator—was a great teacher named Rick Venturi. Over the years Venturi had mastered the extremely complicated Red 2 scheme from top to bottom and even added his own variations and twists to it. But Venturi's real genius lay in knowing the defense so well that he understood its one shortcoming: It was really difficult to teach. He often warned young members of his staff that "learning Red 2 is not natural for the players; it's hard to understand and harder to perform." Not everyone was ready to learn or even play match coverage, and even fewer of us were ready to teach it. How well we taught our players was going to make the difference between success and failure. Venturi knew that just because something like "handing off receivers" looked great on the blackboard, that didn't mean it would necessarily look great on the field. What Venturi taught us all in Cleveland is that the greatest scheme in the world is only as good as the coaches teaching it.

## 4. MAKE THE OFFENSE PLAY LEFT-HANDED

This is a classic Belichick tactic: taking offenses out of their comfort zones by preventing them from doing what they do best. Former longtime NFL offensive coordinator Jim Shofner, who was the interim head coach of the Browns before Belichick, described what his successor did as "making you play left-handed." Of course, everyone in the game is trying to do this. But what makes Belichick different, what makes him worthy of Shofner's catchphrase, is the way he commits to his plan.

Take the way the Patriots played the Colts with Peyton Manning under center, running back Edgerrin James, and receivers Reggie Wayne and Marvin Harrison. That's some offensive firepower, but after padding a few of the Colts games, Belichick learned that he could neutralize that explosiveness by setting a hard edge to keep James from getting around the corner and up the field. Belichick game-planned to set that edge no matter what; even if he had to commit two extra players and run the rest of his scheme with nine defenders, he would do it. And if Manning hit a few long passes or if the Colts gashed the middle of the defense for back-to-back first downs, so be it. Most coaches, of course, would instantly abandon their edge-first scheme at the first sign of weakness, but not Belichick.

If the Colts had ever discovered the discipline to ditch the outside running game and just blast away on the inside instead, the Patriots would have been in big trouble all those years. Because he knew Manning and the Colts almost better than they knew themselves, though, Belichick counted on them growing bored with an inside run game. So the Patriots would double Harrison, use their best corner to contain Wayne, and wait for Manning to force the ball into double coverage. All that study and Belichick's brilliant mind led to a game plan with one goal: take away what the Colts do best, and force other players to step up. That's making them play left-handed. (Belichick's overall record against the Manning-led Colts? 12–8.)

Belichick takes away what the opposing team does best, but he also takes away what specific players do best. It's a subtle but crucial difference. He personally breaks down every offensive player to understand his strengths within his team's scheme. Then he moves around his defense's talents to best serve the system he has created for the week. Most teams put their best corner on the best receiver. Naturally, Belichick does the opposite. As he did with the Colts, he doubles the best receiver with his second and third corners so that he can line up his best corner against the second-best receiver and create two matchup advantages. Similarly, Belichick doesn't see All-Pro Atlanta receiver Julio Jones as a classic Z receiver; he sees him as the one man the defense needs to stop. When the Falcons have to make a play, wise men expect the ball to go to Jones. Belichick is a wise man. Hence the double coverage on Jones. Take away the player who can hurt you, force Matt Ryan to find someone else, and the Falcons are playing left-handed.

Say the opponent is an excellent running team, which the folks watching at home know because the announcers have thrown the "relevant" stats at them: *Team X is third in the NFL in rushing.* But that fact means nothing to Belichick. He wants to know where they gain those yards. Off right tackle? Over the left guard? Once he has isolated the player who triggers an offense's tendencies, he can put his best run-down player, for many years nose tackle Vince Wilfork, at the exact spot that will cause the most debilitating roadblock.

## 5. TIMING IS EVERYTHING, SO DISRUPT YOUR OPPONENT'S

When Manning came to Foxborough for the 2004 AFC divisional playoff game, the Colts' offense had been virtually impossible to slow down during the season or in their wild card victory against the Broncos, when they scored seven touchdowns in 10 possessions. That offense was nowhere to be found on January 16 against the Patriots; the Colts had the ball for barely 22 minutes and scored three points. One week the Colts were unstoppable; the next they were on their way home.

Did Belichick install an elaborate scheme that befuddled Manning? No. In fact, he simplified his plan by going old school and roughing up receivers—legally—as they ran their routes. Again, here's Belichick the pragmatist: If the Colts' record-setting offense is based on timing between the quarterback and the receivers, the easiest way to defend it is to throw a wrench into that intricate mechanism. Belichick did it through the art of rerouting: hitting a receiver on his route to alter his prescribed direction. Rerouting is not holding or interference; it's a stab or a push intended to momentarily disrupt—and effectively blow up—the precise timing of a pass play.

It's a technique he mastered under Bill Parcells in New York: A little messed-up timing plus an onrushing linebacker meant big trouble for the offense, plain and simple. It got its best workout in the Giants' many high-stakes battles against Bill Walsh's West Coast offense. Belichick realized that the only way to slow down such a well-choreographed attack was to bully its receivers. Need more proof? Just ask Isaac Bruce, Torry Holt, and the rest of those Greatest Show on Turf Rams, the ones who lost to the Patriots in Super Bowl XXXVI.

I got a full-blown education on the art of rerouting during my second season with Belichick in Cleveland. After each game, I joined the defensive staffers, ostensibly to help them review our performance but mostly to listen and learn from their analyses.

With Saban controlling the video, I sat, mostly quietly, as line-backer coach Al Groh and line coach Jim Bates went over every detail of their units' work. Rerouting had already become such a huge element of our schemes that opponents would specifically at-tack the area of the field where the reroute occurred. For instance, offenses would run a seam route down the middle of the field just to occupy the linebacker. Meanwhile, they'd send a receiver across the field to the exact spot the linebacker had vacated. I love this kind of check/checkmate aspect of football strategy. The play—which we called a seam crosser—was a surefire way to exploit Belichick's emphasis on rerouting, but only if they could get the rerouter to commit on the seam route. So, checkmate: Saban and Groh instructed their linebackers to punch, disrupt, and then turn back to cover the next crosser.

This heavy-handed physical tactic enraged many pass-happy teams but none more than the Peyton Manning–era Colts and their general manager Bill Polian. Polian grew tired of seeing Belichick's Patriots bang around his receivers. After the 2004 AFC playoff game, he only said: "I give the Patriots credit for what they did; I won't go beyond that." Unfortunately for New England, Po-lian also happened to be a member of the NFL's competition com-mittee, and by the next season, wouldn't you know it, the NFL was instructing officials to enforce its illegal contact rule more strictly.

In the current era of intricately timed passing offenses, disrup-tion remains the key. But Polian made sure that playing defense beyond the five-yard grace area, especially against rhythm pass-ing games, would be much more difficult from then on. It didn't matter that Polian was thinking only about his Colts when he led the charge to enforce illegal contact and help hurry-up offenses and intricately timed passing schemes. Suddenly, the scales were tipped toward the passing game, and further rule book tweaks just put a thumb on that scale.

Belichick being Belichick, though, he didn't complain or whine or lobby the competition committee. He rebuilt his own offense using the rule change he inspired and won three more Super Bowls with it.

## 6. DEFUSE EXPLOSIVE PLAYS

In 1994, when the Browns headed to Dallas for a late Saturday afternoon game, making the Cowboys play left-handed wasn't going to be easy. That offense featured Michael Irvin at wideout; Jay Novacek at tight end; the man who would become the NFL's all-time leading rusher, Emmitt Smith; and (maybe most of all) future Hall of Famer Troy Aikman. The Boys were so loaded that they didn't have a left hand. The closest thing they had to a left hand was wide receiver Alvin Harper, who would have been a primary option on most other teams.

If we couldn't make them play left-handed, we could do the next best thing: take away their big play potential with sure tackling and an awareness of where their chunk plays came from. Most NFL teams convert about 35 percent of their third downs, and that's not going to get you down the field. A drive is far more likely to end up putting points on the board if it includes at least one run or pass of more than 20 yards. When coaches talk about a game or an entire season coming down to just a handful of key plays, this is what they're talking about. Belichick's plan for Dallas was simple: We'd let them have their catches and yards as long as they didn't get too many yards all at once. And it worked. Smith got his 100-plus yards, but it took him 26 carries to get them. Irvin had seven catches, but the longest went for 18 yards. The longest play of the day was a 26-yard run by Smith. We held the Boys to 14 points and won.

I always laugh when a defensive coach says, "Besides that one 55-yard play, we played great run defense." A great run defense doesn't give up 55-yard runs. You know what else great run defenses don't do? They don't erase outlying plays from their record of the game; they focus on them and try to understand how they were allowed to happen so that they don't happen again. On the jubilant plane ride back from Dallas, Belichick did not say, "If you ignore that one long run from Smith, we held him to 86 yards on 25 carries." He said, "We did a good job of fixing the edge after Smith gained those 26 yards on the second drive of the game, which is why we held him to 86 yards on 25 carries the rest of the way."

## 7. REMEMBER NEWTON'S SECOND LAW

When Saban ran our defense in Cleveland, he wanted to be in the perfect defense for each play. The thought of giving up 5 yards drove him as crazy as giving up 50. His impossible dream manifested in countless checks and adjustments before the snap of the ball. Decades later, you can still watch an Alabama game and see all the defenders looking toward the sideline for his last-second adjustments. Belichick is the exact opposite. In fact, before we hired him as our head coach in Cleveland, I told Belichick that I had watched him on the sidelines at a Giants game and noticed his hands in the pockets of his red Starter jacket and asked where he kept his call sheet. And in classic Belichick fashion, he said, "I call the same thing every play; why do I need a call sheet?" Belichick prefers to work with few checks and adjustments because above all he wants his defense playing fast. He wants them doing, not wondering what to do. He wants them reacting, not thinking. He hates mistakes, but if they happen, he wants them to happen while his defense is going 110 miles per hour.

Defensive team speed starts with the middle linebacker, the Mike. He is the quarterback of the defense and needs to be both mentally and physically fast. He is the one responsible for calling the defenses and getting everyone positioned correctly before the snap. But he is also the one who dictates the tempo. A Mike who can get from sideline to sideline in the run game and fulfill coverage or attacking assignments in the pass game keeps a team moving apace.

The best indicator of a fast defense: forced fumbles. I'm sure you're familiar with Newton's second law of motion, but in case it has slipped your mind, here's a refresher: Acceleration is directly proportional to net force because net force equals mass times acceleration. Newton probably wasn't thinking about football, but he could have been. When a defender hits a ball carrier, the best thing that can happen is that the ball comes loose. And when a faster, bigger defender hits a ball carrier, Newton says the ball is that much more likely to come loose. Show me a defense with a low number of forced fumbles and I will show you a defense with a slower-than-average Mike. Show me a fast-thinking, fast-moving defense and I will show you harder hits, more balls on the ground, and—all other things being equal—more wins.

## 8. THINK PRESSURE FIRST, SACKS SECOND

It seems like every great coach in history has an opinion on the art and science of blitzing. Vince Lombardi once said, "Blitzing is a form of weakness." When he coached, that might have been true. Back then, a blitz meant sending six or seven men toward the quarterback while the secondary covered the receivers man to man. If the defensive front couldn't get to the quarterback, the whole unit was in trouble. Of course, in those days, with the limitations placed on offensive linemen in regard to using their hands, not being able to get to the quarterback was never much of a problem for the defensive front. That is no longer the case. Changes to the rules have opened up the passing game, and defenses need to be creative in the ways they pressure the passer to make him throw before he wants to. That means being smarter about the kinds of blitzes sent at opponents.

When offensive coordinators call a play that results in a touchdown or a long gain, we compliment the "great call." When a defensive coordinator calls a blitz that sacks the quarterback, we often just move on to the next down. But the particular details and timing of the call deserve our praise, too. Specific blitzes attack weaknesses in protection, and that means that defenses have to understand what those protections are trying to do and when the best time to attack them would be.

The thing is, most of the time coaches don't have a good enough grasp of those particulars, and so they can't be strategic about their blitz calls. They just blindly send as many guys at the quarterback as they can and hope for the best. In that sense, Lombardi was right: Random blitzes are a sign of weakness. But well-designed strategic blitzes most definitely are not.

Al Davis was also not a big believer in total pressure. He saw blitzing the way Lombardi did, as an admission of some inadequacy. In fact, he had a steadfast edict for all his defensive coordinators: Never leave the middle of the field open. And that contained an implicit corollary: no all-out pressures. It was Raider Law. That's not to say that Davis forbade his defense to blitz; they just had to be sure to leave the free safety in the middle of the field when they did. Davis had reasons for his mandate, particularly his second rule of defense: no big plays. He felt a man in the middle of the field was an important last line of defense against big plays. Not surprisingly, though, his no-all-out-blitz decree handcuffed his defensive coaches and drove them all crazy. To them it felt like an impossible-to-overcome handicap. Every Raiders opponent knew of Davis's no-all-out-blitz rule, and that meant that they didn't need to prepare for that type of pressure.

In 1955, the legendary Paul Brown predicted that as quarterbacks became more mobile and accurate, sending extra men to pressure the passer would become a necessary evil. Writing for

*Collier's* magazine, Brown stated: "The great quarterbacks in future years will have to run as well as pass to survive pro lines, which seem to get rougher and faster every season. The defense places a greater emphasis on rushing the passer. . . . The new development in pro football, therefore, will have to be the running quarterback." The guy knew what he was talking about. But his crystal-ball certainty depended on a game in which the value of defensive linemen never wavered.

To this day there is nothing more powerful than a defense that can bring adequate pressure with a four-man front. When you can create pressure with just four players, that means you can flood passing zones with the remaining seven defenders, which makes a quarterback feel like he's facing a 13-man defense. It's such a powerful advantage that it tends to create nickname-worthy defenses such as the Fearsome Foursome of the Los Angeles Rams, the Steel Curtain in Pittsburgh, and Dallas's Doomsday Defense. Today, though, the economics of the game (salary cap and free agency) make it hard to afford four top-flight rushers on one roster, and that's why blitzing has become a difference maker. Only now the goal of blitz pressure isn't to sack the quarterback; it's to make him throw the ball prematurely and under duress. Forcing a quarterback to throw the ball "hot" is a huge win for the defense, especially on third down, because it will force a receiver to catch the ball short of the sticks and get the defense off the field.

In today's pass-first football, pressure matters more than sacks do, as long as it's strategic. What does it mean to be strategic with pressure? Simply put, it means to run the blitz that will attack the pass protection most effectively and give you the greatest chance to get a defender to the passer unblocked. Of course, that's not simple at all. And it begins with understanding how the offense intends to protect the passer. What good is a pass-rush stunt blitz, after all, if the defensive end who is looping runs into an offensive tackle–tight end double-team block that is just waiting for him?

On TV you can hear the sideline microphones pick up a quarterback in passing situations screaming at his line, making sure they know where the Mike backer is. That's because most pass protections designate a specific player—the running back or one of the linemen—to block the blitzer. The "point out" isolates the focal point of the defense, and all blocking schemes and responsibilities stem from that identification. Who picks up the blitz changes with the protection scheme, keeping the defense from knowing who it needs to worry about—for example, whether or not the tight end is participating in protection, too. All this means that the defense has a lot to decipher before it can choose a blitz with confidence. And choosing the correct blitz is only half of it. The defense needs to call it at a time that maximizes its chance of success. Play callers never get enough credit for making the correct call on the correct down on either side of the ball. Knowing "when" is a product of lots of film study.

One way to be strategic with pressure is to save something for the second half of the game. In Cleveland, we once faced a team whose offensive line coach wasn't all that adept at in-game adjustments. The line coach was a former player, a good old boy, and the players fought hard for him, but he was not the quickest thinker. During the week, when he had time to review blitzes on film and work the problem in his own time, he figured out how to have his team ready for Sunday. But during a game he was at a disadvantage, so Belichick saved some calls for critical moments later in the game when the guy had no time to whip up a counter.

Bill Walsh loved putting all-out pressure on the quarterback, but mostly because it was a sign his game plan had gone well. He counted on his team getting a lead that would force opponents into playing catch-up through the air, leaving them vulnerable to defensive pressure. During my first year in the league, Fred Dean, our best pass rusher, held out for more money. Ray Rhodes, the secondary coach and one of my early defensive teachers, kept saying that we needed Dean back in the lineup to get interceptions.

No, the 230-pound future Hall of Famer wasn't being switched to safety. (Although I would have liked to see that.) Ray Bob—that was Rhodes's nickname—explained that although Dean's sacks were important, they weren't nearly as disruptive as the constant pressure he brought even when he didn't get to the quarterback. Time your blitzes for maximum impact while keeping a quarterback under constant pressure, and sooner or later he'll crack.

## 9. ELIMINATE FOUR-POINT PLAYS

All third downs are not alike. A third down when you're backed up in your own territory is more important than a third down at midfield, because if you fail to convert, your opponent will have excellent field position. The leg strength of most of today's placekickers means there is a possibility of putting up points without the offense having to move the ball much. In fact, analytics will tell you that the outcome of a third down in the red zone can swing the score by four points, and you don't have to be a math whiz to see how. If a team holds an opponent on third down in the red zone, it takes the prospect of a touchdown largely off the table, leaving the offense to settle for three—a difference of four points. That's huge. Most NFL games are decided by a lot less than four points, yet most teams defend all third downs the same way.

The "high" red zone begins at the 30-yard line, the border at which a field goal seems likely for today's kickers. From there, offenses are attacking on what is essentially a 40-yard field (30 yards plus 10 yards of the end zone). This smaller field tends to limit the number of offensive plays a team can call, because you cannot stretch the defense or clear out zones, and that in turn shrinks the windows a quarterback can throw into and forces him to elevate his accuracy. A smaller field favors the defense—less ground to defend—especially if it tackles well and doesn't allow yards after the catch or contact.

Playing defense in the middle of a regular field means having to defend length and width, whereas a defense in the red zone gets to focus more on width than on length. A throw to the back of the end zone has to be perfect; a receiver doesn't have room to run under the catch. The back line is a defensive coach's accomplice. Therefore, the trend today in the NFL is for teams to play more zone in the red zone, drop eight men into coverage, and let the offense wear itself out looking for a knockout punch. It's like the Muhammad Ali tactic—you know, the rope-a-dope he used against George Foreman in Zaire. "Force them to take small, harmless gains in the red zone," Belichick often told his defense, "and they will get impatient and make a mistake." Then we counterpunch.

In 1991 Belichick transformed the Browns' defense from one of the worst in the league to one in its top half with a slight talent improvement but a much greater emphasis on red zone third-down execution. By 1994, Belichick realized that four-point plays—stopping opponents on third down in the red zone and preventing field goals from turning into touchdowns—often came down to keeping a quarterback in the pocket.

Quarterback movement is a killer for a third-down defense because once the guy gets out of the pocket, all hell breaks loose. Think back to when you played touch football in the backyard. If you are covering a receiver, once the pass rusher yells his fifth Mississippi, the play becomes something else entirely. The quarterback scrambles, the receivers break their routes to get open, and chaos reigns. In the NFL, because teams often use eight men in coverage, that chaos can be epic. Zones break down into man to man, defenders have to chase down a scrambling quarterback, and holes open everywhere.

In a four-point-play situation, the goal is to not let the quarterback break the pocket. And that demands that defensive linemen attack as they would, say, a field goal—down the middle and always in front of the passer, keeping his sight lines narrow and his escape routes few. If the defense can build an umbrella around the quarterback, he cannot escape. Keeping a quarterback from running is not luck—it's planned. Too many linemen run up the field, using swim moves to get by offensive linemen, creating space between themselves and other defensive attackers. But that space is an escape route for the quarterback. When the quarterback, afforded space, throws a touchdown from outside the pocket, the lineman walks off the field telling everyone, "I almost had him." "Almost"s don't make it onto the stat sheet for a reason.

This is why in Belichick's scheme, defensive ends don't have nearly as much freedom as they would like in any part of the field but especially in the red zone. In fact, ends who arrive in New England after playing for other teams have been known to complain about not being allowed to attack. But they learn soon enough that this kind of rush creates more problems than solutions.

Compounding the drama, the battleground is at its most intense on third down because the offense knows it needs to succeed to keep the ball and thus will do whatever it takes to extend the play. Most quarterbacks run only when it matters, and red zone third downs matter most, particularly in a situation when the difference can be four points and probably the game. Letting a quarterback convert a third down in the red zone with his feet absolutely breaks a defense's back.

In Super Bowl XLIX, Russell Wilson presented a unique problem that required a foolproof rush plan for the Patriots. Stopping Seattle on offense was mainly about stopping Wilson from moving around in the pocket. We were more worried about his feet than about his arm, and more worried about him in the red zone than in the middle of the field. Only two Seahawks had more than one rushing touchdown that season: Marshawn Lynch, the star running back, who had 13, and Wilson, who had 6. Stopping Lynch from running the ball in the red zone would be difficult, but at least we knew what he would do: run. Wilson, in contrast, could feign like he was going to run and then throw a pass. Wilson isn't tall (forget what the program says; he's slightly under six feet), so he has a hard time seeing over the linemen. That means he needs to move left or right to find windows in the rush that afford him a view down the field. He does this with great success; his hit chart—a plotting of where he throws from—indicates that he is actually better when defensive pressure forces him from the pocket. If you want to handle Wilson, you better know what you want to accomplish with your pass rush.

To use a basketball metaphor, in Super Bowl XLIX the Patriots' rush plan was to stop Wilson by getting their defensive linemen "in the paint," or within one yard of and directly in front of the quarterback. That prevented him from stepping forward and seeing downfield. All quarterbacks hate dealing with someone in their face. They can deal with pass rushers running at them from the sides because they have room to step up and away. At the same time, from the defense's standpoint, the worst place for any defender to be is two yards past the quarterback. You just rushed yourself right out of the play. Now it's 10 on 11. Against Wilson, Belichick had his defensive ends play down the middle, inside the offensive tackles, forcing the quarterback to step into the paint, where our defensive tackles were waiting. Wilson finished the Super Bowl with just 12 completions, a manageable 39 yards rushing, and zero four-point plays.

## 10. GAMES ARE WON OR LOST IN THE FINAL FOUR MINUTES— OF THE FIRST HALF

To this day, when the Patriots win a coin toss, they often defer possession to the second half. The choice goes against conventional wisdom and usually is dismissed as nothing more than a Belichick quirk, but in fact, it's a pretty ingenious tactical maneuver. All those years of facing Peyton Manning taught Belichick a great deal, but most specifically they taught him that the best plan on defense is to keep the offense on the bench. Forget blitzes, timing, and defensive disguises; the simple truth is that Manning was never less dangerous than when he was standing next to his coach, Tony Dungy.

Over time, Belichick actually built an entire game management theory around this simple realization. If the Patriots could manage a drive at the end of the first half and another at the beginning of the second, that would keep the opposing offense off the field for almost an hour of real time. For a guy like Manning, that's an eternity. No offense, no points. No plays, no rhythm. When Manning does finally get back in the game, he and his offense have lost their edge.

Beyond that, Belichick's tactic usually tips the number of total possessions in the Patriots' favor. In chess, the player with the white pieces goes first, and that extra move often gives him or her a slightly better chance to win the game. Belichick's coin-toss trick does the same thing in football, in which both teams usually end up with the same number (12) of possessions.

On the road, there's a third benefit to deferring after winning the toss: It outlasts the crowd. (This is Belichick's genius in a nutshell. He's taken something as simple as the coin toss, something 99 percent of coaches don't even think about, and found a way to extract considerable extra value from it.) At the start of the game, home fans are riled and loud. An away team that elects to receive has to deal with the crowd at its most rested and clear-throated. It's a recipe for going three and out without even being able to hear the play calls. In other words, a precious series of downs has been squandered. At the start of the second half, though, the stadium has a different feel. Fans are still in the bathroom or on the concession lines, and the stands are half empty; it's certainly not as intimidating as it is at the beginning. Visitors who have deferred receiving the kickoff don't have to contend with a wall of noise and thus are better able to get into a rhythm before the fans are back in their seats.

But the thing is that Belichick's tactic pays off only if the receiving team in the second half ends the first half with the ball. Too few teams play defense in the final minutes of the half with that in mind. How often have you cursed your favorite team when it goes into its prevent defense, willing to sacrifice yards for points, as the half winds down? Better question: How often have those curses turned into murderous rage when those "meaningless" yards turn into very real points? Far too often, right? Well, that's because the best four-minute defense is not a prevent defense. It is a defense that fights to get the ball back for the offense.

To do that, defenses need to use a weapon most people see only as an offensive advantage: time-outs. (When Belichick deploys the tactic, it doubles as a disruptive influence as well.) Teams that play the Patriots know that if they don't run the clock out and New England gets the ball back with more than a few seconds on the clock, the Patriots are capable of cashing in because no one runs the hurry-up better *and* their kicker can hit from the parking lot.

In basketball, coaches talk all the time about closing out quarters, but in football, the concept doesn't garner much attention. Except from Belichick, who sees it is an opportunity to take over the game. For starters, by the time there's four minutes left in the half, he expects his defense to know the offense's game plan inside and out. If they don't, he is there to remind them. Over the headsets, Belichick will say things like "This is a Landry game" when the Patriots are playing the Dolphins and he suspects that wide receiver Jarvis Landry will be the focal point. The ends of the halves are when those talented players rear their heads. For another thing, he knows that most offenses wait to take advantage of the way teams simplify their defensive calls in two-minute drills. He, of course, does the opposite. Meanwhile, at the end of the half, offenses looking to move downfield quickly think pass first and foremost. And when an offense becomes one-dimensional, it's advantage defense.

When Belichick tells his team that games are won and lost in the final four minutes—and trust me, he does that a lot—he often means the *first* half more than the second.

## 11. IF YOU'RE NOT TALKING, YOU'RE NOT WINNING

Once in New England, Belichick ripped all the numbers off the preseason practice jerseys. Everyone thought it was intended to confuse the media and other onlookers, but really it was to force the Patriots defenders to learn one another's names and get used to talking during the play. Belichick always said that if you want to know how well a defense is working, just listen. Defenses succeed only if the players know the scheme. But they really thrive when the players are talking to one another on the field. When it comes to adjustments, reads, and coverages, everybody needs to be on the same page in the lead-up and in the moment.

Belichick's jersey trick didn't always work, though. You'd be surprised how many players, even great ones, would rather just do their thing and not worry about anything or anyone else. Darrelle Revis was one of the best corners I've ever seen close up. He had fantastic awareness and instincts, and he could jam at the line to disrupt the timing of a pass as well as anyone. Quick feet, balance, the ability to play the ball—he had it all. Each week Revis would study his assignment and then go out and shut down the best receiver on the other side. For most of his career, his focus was on one man and one man only. He didn't worry about what the rest of his teammates on defense were trying to do.

When he came to New England in 2014, though, he had to learn to communicate with our other new corner, Brandon Browner. Big and physical, Browner wasn't as gifted as Revis, but he was a force on and off the field. One day in practice before a game against Peyton Manning and the Broncos, Revis went radio silent again in the defensive backfield, and the scout team hit them for a big play.

That's not supposed to happen, and you could sense the tension from across the field. Revis was worried only about his own assignments, not about helping the rest of the unit, and as practice wore on, the tension between Revis and Browner escalated.

When it finally boiled over, Browner flattened Revis with a massive roundhouse right to the temple. Revis got up, and the two continued to fight. I mean, really fight. This wasn't like linemen pawing at each other in training camp; this was a bar brawl, one of the most brutal I've ever seen on a practice field. It went on until the coaches and players separated them.

Both guys were sent off the field; Belichick does not tolerate fighting. But sometimes he appreciates it. Revis might have been the better player, but Browner was the team leader and the leader had spoken, albeit with his fists.

And the message was heard. For the rest of the season, Revis was one of the chattiest defenders in the entire NFL.

Some lessons about playing defense are more painful than others.

# 7

# GAME PLANNING

## PREPARING TO IMPROVISE

*Everybody has a plan until they get punched in the mouth.*

—MIKE TYSON

hey will be confident, riding high after a win." That's what Belichick told the Patriots players and staff who gathered in the team meeting room in Foxborough two days before the new year. In 2014 we earned the top seed in the AFC and a bye in the wild card playoffs, which left us in the strange position of preparing for a game without knowing who our opponent would be. But that didn't stop Belichick, the most experienced and successful playoff coach in NFL history (26–10 lifetime), from putting his game plan into action. First things first: He wanted us to make sure we understood exactly what lay ahead, whoever our opponent would be. "They'll have the momentum, so we have to be ready to play," he continued. "We need to bring a great attitude and great energy. We need to be communicating and functioning as a complete team."

There is a delicate balance to a bye week. You need to give the players a chance to rest and recharge while making sure they are properly focused for the next game. No one is better at this part of the game than Belichick. It's just a fact: When he gets in the postseason, he wins. Only twice during his long career has he failed to win at least one game in the playoffs. That was in the back-to-back seasons of 2009 and 2010, a rare downturn that Belichick responded to by leading the Patriots to the Super Bowl (where they lost to the Giants, but still) the next year.

Believe me, the ghosts of squandered postseasons will forever haunt this coach's dreams, spurring his unparalleled postseason preparation until the day he retires. Losses take a toll on any coach. But for Belichick, who is constantly asking what more he could have done, the toll is extreme. He never blames the players, instead pointing a finger at himself for not preparing them to win. There are members of that 2011 team, in fact, who still become emotional when recalling a broken and teary-eyed Belichick apologizing to everyone in the locker room after losing to the Giants.

Those rare playoff losses haunt Belichick and push him to another level of intensity when the postseason begins. You can sense the change in his demeanor and delivery when the calendar flips to January. So despite the impending time off, he had a captive audience in that meeting room. Everyone listened intently, afraid of being caught flat-footed by one of the signature gotcha questions with which Belichick peppers his meetings. When he calls on you and you don't know the answer, he doesn't get loud or berate you; he does something way more humiliating: He simply ghosts you and moves on to someone else. Most of the time, anyway. When veteran linebacker Rob Ninkovich was quoted in the paper saying that the defense needed to handle screen plays better, Belichick asked him in one of the next meetings how we should go about doing that. Rob had no answer and sank into his seat. After that, every time the subject came up, Belichick would turn to the linebacker and quip, "So, Rob, you have strong opinions on screens; what do you think?" The team would laugh—to themselves, of course. Point made. And made. And made again.

As he addressed the team during the 2014 bye week, Belichick warned about becoming complacent. He didn't want his team falling for the common postseason wisdom that playing at home is as good as a victory. "Playing well with precise execution and avoiding mistakes will determine the winner," he reminded the players, "not where the game is played." He then made it clear that the holidays could not be a priority. He wanted his team focused on nothing but being the best they could be when next they hit the turf. "We can celebrate the new year some other time," he said while staring right at Rob Gronkowski, a tight end known for his enthusiasm for partying. "Put everything in a back drawer for now. Focus on preparation. Nothing. Else. Matters."

Playoff football is a completely different animal from regular-season football. In the single-elimination playoffs, games are lost far more often than they are won. Mental mistakes, turnovers, an abandonment of fundamentals—these problems are hard to overcome in the regular season and nearly impossible to survive in the no-wiggle-room scenario of the playoffs. There's a huge responsibility on players to have their best week of preparation and even more pressure on coaching staffs to create and implement the perfect game plan.

Even though he's got more playoff experience than anyone in NFL history, Belichick will be the first to tell you that experience is not preparation. Having previously participated in a playoff game means nothing. Conversely, he told the team, having no prior postseason reps does not necessarily preclude immediate success. Belichick then recounted the story of Hall of Fame linebacker Lawrence Taylor's first playoff game in 1981. Taylor dominated the Philadelphia Eagles for 60 minutes, playing like he'd been there before because Belichick noted he had spent the week practicing as if he wanted to be there. That's what he expected us to do.

We were the number one seed, and so we would play the lowest remaining seed. Of the three possibilities—the Baltimore Ravens, the Cincinnati Bengals, and the Indianapolis Colts—we were most concerned about the Ravens. Going by wins and losses, they were the weakest team in the playoffs, but they always gave us a hard time. In fact, in one of the years New England failed to advance beyond the first weekend of the playoffs, it was the Ravens who sent them home with a 33–14 thumping. Until we knew for sure, we would train our attention on the Ravens.

In the meeting, Belichick gave the players their practice schedule for the week. Later in the day he gave his staff their marching orders. But long before that, he had given me my postseason assignment: a complete analysis of the Patriots' previous playoff performances, due the day after Christmas.

During the NFL season, there are no breaks. Luckily, my wife, Millie, always understood the time requirements of my job. As long as we had the opportunity to spend a little time with Santa as a family, she never objected when I inevitably had to head back to work. With home field advantage locked up, I had started my research a few weeks earlier, and despite the time away from home, I was having a lot of fun with this project.

The first thing I learned was that Belichick's playoff game planning is informed by three things: (1) what his team does well (these things will require time to hone but not in-depth work), (2) what it doesn't do well (these things will be the focus of practice), and (3) what he thinks it will take to win the playoffs in a particular year. The thick document I presented to him addressed each of these categories as they related to the 2014 team. The dossier was many pages long, so I won't burden you with all of it. But here are the word-for-word summary and recommendations—

unedited to this day, I hasten to add—that I delivered into Belichick's hands at the start of our Super Bowl run.

## SUMMARY

In New England's playoff teams, the winners and losers, there are commonalities among each team that wins and others among each one that falls short. All were good teams, but the winning teams were "complete teams" that could win a game with the offense or defense and made an impact on special teams. The 2003-2004-2006 teams had the best defenses overall and the 03 and 04 teams won Super Bowls. The 06 team lost the conference championship game in Indy after a few defensive players were injured. Offense might have carried us into the playoffs, but winning the Conference Championship or the Super Bowl has been a result of great defense—simply put, keeping people from scoring: covering, rushing and tackling.

We have scored over 500 points during the season 4 times since 1999, 07-10-11-12, and two of those teams lost the Super Bowl. Obviously we need to score points, but we struggled to finish in the playoffs when we could not get control of the game with our offense and our defense was not strong enough to play well for 60 minutes. We have only held the ball over 30 minutes 1 time in the last four playoff games, which has caused the weaker part of the team—the defense—to play more and have more chances to make a mistake. In the 2011 postseason, we scrapped for 60 minutes against Baltimore and won, but when we played them again the next year, we controlled the game until the midway point of the third, then could not score again and lost. That time, we played great in the red zone to keep us in the game but fell way short on offense.

That game was a classic example of our offense not converting opportunities, not finishing drives, not executing at key parts of the game and allowing the Ravens to play within their comfort zone. We had chances to put the game away early, but we failed to execute big plays and failed to convert pressure third downs, which would have allowed us to end up in scoring position.

## RECOMMENDATIONS

- Our defense needs to make **3rd and 4 or less** as competitive as we can.
- MAKE PRACTICE AS COMPETITIVE AS WE CAN THIS WEEK. **Playoffs are a different level of competition; our practices have to simulate the change.**
- We know we won't make many throws over 10 yards
- We need to use tennis rackets at practice to simulate linemen's arms so we can prevent tipped passes in the game.
- We must stay fresh, healthy and vibrant. We need our key players to play well—Gronk, Revis, [Jamie] Collins, Edelman and Brady. Second half of the games we have been poor on both sides of the ball. We NEED to be better in the second half.
- WE NEED TO KEEP FINDING WAYS TO CREATE NEGATIVE PLAYS.
- WHEN WE MAKE TEAMS PLAY LEFT HANDED, WE CAN WIN. In all three of our losses this year we never made the opponent play outside their comfort zone. When we do, we are hard to play. In Miami we never stopped the run. In KC we never forced Alex Smith to make a play. In GB we allowed them to have balance early in the game.

- TACKLING DRILLS EVERY DAY. We will need to be the best tackling team in the playoffs and that means pad level work. Seattle is the best tackling team in the NFL; we are 14th.

## EMPHASIS FOR PLAYOFF BYE

1. RED ZONE WINS—Teams that play well in the RZ during the playoffs win. We allowed Baltimore to be 4 for 4 the last time we played them in a Championship game.

2. CONVERT 3RD AND 2 OR LESS—We have to be able to convert third and short. Overall we might appear to be doing well, but in the first quarter of the last two Conference Championship Games, we were 3 for 10 on 3rd and short, which does not allow us to gain control of the game or confidence.

3. SIMPLE GAME PLANS WIN—Players knowing what to do and doing it at a high tempo win. We must simplify and play without hesitation.

4. PRACTICE CRISP, FAST AND SHORTER—Need to be fresh in the game. In 2013, we allowed 56 points in the entire playoffs, and 29 came in the 4th quarter. And we have not started fast either, because of poor third down execution. In four games we have scored 24 points in the first, and allowed 13. In games we lose, we don't start fast, nor do we finish strong.

5. SPECIAL TEAMS MUST WORK ON KICK-OFF RETURN— Had 10 KO returns in 4 games and didn't average over 20 yards. Meanwhile we allowed a 94-yard return to Danieal Manning. WE HAVE NOT DOMINATED IN THE KICKING GAME COME PLAYOFF TIME. We have had no depth and it shows. WE MUST MAKE A PLAY HERE.

One of the many things I loved about working for Belichick is that I never had to hold back. All he wanted was the truth—whatever it was. With Belichick, every interaction is about trying to win and get better. Bring him a way to do either, and you get his full attention. In fact, until I handed him my self-scouting memo, he had no preconceived ideas about how to approach this particular postseason. After reading it, he began to set a course over the next two weeks. The data I had uncovered meant that regardless of the opponent, the Patriots would need to focus their effort on three areas: red zone, third and short, and the kicking game.

Before we sent the players away for a few precious days off prior to our first playoff game, we conducted one practice at our stadium on Thursday. It was a scrimmage to go over all the areas in my memo. Belichick usually reserves competitive intrasquad scrimmages for the summer as a way to get a feel for the lesser-known players trying to make the team. But in this case Belichick thought a postseason blue-white affair would be a good way to refocus everyone on the things that now mattered most, in particular those third-and-short situations. Third and short is a unique problem for the defense, in part because both the run and the pass are viable options. Belichick's theme all week was that at this time of year an entire season can be lost on one play, and so players have to be prepared at every moment for every possibility. On days like this, the field is an extension of Belichick's classroom, with each scenario analyzed and made actionable. Our goal was clear: Don't squander any opportunity.

We also worked on ways to create such opportunities by inserting a few trick plays into the game plan. The first was a wide receiver pass from Julian Edelman, a college quarterback, to Danny Amendola. In week 4 we had actually called it against Kansas City, but the Chiefs seemed to sense what was coming, so Brady threw the ball to Brandon LaFell on a slant instead. That was great because it meant there was no film of that flea-flicker anywhere. If we ran it in the playoffs, it would be a total surprise.

The other trick play Belichick wanted to install came to him one Saturday as he was getting his fix of the college game. On that night he got home just in time to see the Crimson Tide head into overtime. During their first possession in the extra session, Nick Saban, Belichick's friend and fellow football savant, called for a pass to what appeared to be the left tackle, who was actually a legally eligible tight end in an unbalanced formation. Alabama flexed its right tackle to the left of the defense, lining him up inside two receivers, while putting the tight end where the left tackle normally stands. On the snap, the tackle (lined up way outside like a receiver) just stepped back away from the line and the tight end (lined up inside like a blocker) ran down the seam and caught the ball for a huge gain. It was devilishly clever and all perfectly legit because, if you looked closely, Alabama had the requisite seven men on the line—just not in their normal spots. The next day Belichick breathlessly recounted the play to his offensive coaches and told them he wanted to start working on it right away.

After the quick-paced scrimmage, Belichick and the team headed over to the movie complex by the stadium to watch the soon-to-be-released *American Sniper*. The movie is loosely based on the life of Chris Kyle, a Navy SEAL who was awarded a Silver Star and four Bronze Stars, among other medals. The movie was a classic Belichick choice because it highlights teamwork, sacrifice, and overcoming obstacles. Kyle is the star of his unit, an expert marksman who can hit a target almost a mile away. But he doesn't act like a hotshot. He's just one member of a team in which everyone has to do his job for the whole unit to succeed. The movie affected us all. It would have been easy to focus on Kyle's impressive record as a sniper or the horrific and sad fact that after returning to Texas he was murdered by a former Marine he was trying to help. But as we strolled back to the facility afterward in the dark, all I heard was players talking about how Kyle's unit kept working together even through chaos and life-threatening danger.

The movie stayed in the back of my mind for the whole weekend, even as I watched the Ravens pull away from the Steelers in the wild card game. By the end of the third quarter, I announced to Millie and our sons that we were going to be game planning for Baltimore. I knew what kind of a challenge we faced over the next week, and I must have been eager to get started, because that night my internal alarm clock went off at the ungodly hour of 3:45 A.M.

There was no time to waste. Kickoff was less than a week away.

Here's a behind-the-scenes look at everything that happened next as we prepared to play the Ravens.

## SUNDAY: SIX DAYS BEFORE KICKOFF

Most of the players don't report until tomorrow, but the staff spends all of today preparing game plans and scouting reports. It's a short week, as our game is on Saturday, but that doesn't change our to-do list. The Ravens-Steelers wild card game is already loaded into the video system, and the staff gets to work, preparing for Belichick to call a meeting to map out the rest of the week. Right now, though, he's busy familiarizing himself with every detail of the Ravens' different units, planning out our preparation, and forming a vision of the game in his head. When the staff comes together later in the afternoon, he will offer a few of his initial thoughts and then see how they jibe with the approach his coordinators have mapped out.

But first Belichick will conduct a meeting that has become the signature of his game-planning regimen: a private skull session with Brady. The backup QBs are also in the room, but it's really just two of the all-time greats riffing and brainstorming about the challenges and opportunities in the upcoming game. Belichick begins by sharing his own handcrafted report on the Ravens' defensive back seven. In exquisite detail he goes over the players, showing tape to accentuate his points as he discusses how to attack each of them and the unit as a whole. This is not a game plan meeting; it's a scouting meeting—maybe the most exclusive in sports. Not even Josh McDaniels, the coordinator, is invited. Most coordinators are protective of their players and want to control who talks to them or whispers in their ear, but in New England that's not an issue. Everyone knows Belichick's vision and preparation have quite a track record and that whatever he has to say will only benefit the players, the team, and the coordinator, for that matter. When the players leave the session, they probably know more about the Baltimore secondary than most of the people on the Ravens' staff. This private session includes Belichick's unique approach to game planning: He starts at the end. Six days before facing Baltimore, he and his field general have already synchronized their brains and their focus. And this week that means moving right past first down—where most game plans begin—and to an increased emphasis on third downs.

After his one-on-one with Brady, Belichick studies tape while running on the treadmill. At five o'clock Belichick, still a little damp from his workout, is already seated at the head of the table as his coaches wander in for the full staff meeting. As soon as everyone fills his usual seat, he begins.

The first topic is inactives for the game. Belichick says that five players will not dress for sure and that the status of a few others will need to be determined during the week. It's mundane but relevant because, with limited time to prepare, coaches don't want to waste practice reps on guys who won't see the field. Peeking at his typed notes, Belichick appears to be in a relatively good mood as he goes over what he wants to spend time on. Dressed in his signature look—frumpy workout gear—and sipping a protein shake, the first thing he tells McDaniels is not to take starting tight end Rob Gronkowski off the field. Never. Not once. "Make them defend him on every play," he says.

The plan for Gronk is clear. The question Belichick has is which tight end he wants lining up alongside him. Based on the talk around the table, the coaches prefer reliable Michael

Hoomanawanui—Hoo-Man to his buddies. He isn't the fastest or most athletic guy in the league, but he understands the system, which gives the coaches comfort, and his hands are outstanding. Most important, Brady trusts him. That's no small thing. If Tom doesn't trust you, he won't throw to you. For any veteran quarterback, trust is everything. For Brady, it is the only thing, and you don't earn it easily. Just being on the team won't cut it. Heck, just making the Pro Bowl won't cut it, either. You must prove that you have made the offense a part of you, made it second nature, knowing where to be at all times. Brian Tyms was a receiver who made our team one year after an excellent preseason. He was raw—a track star in college—but he was hardworking and athletic. It wasn't enough. He never quite got it, not to Brady's satisfaction anyway, so he never saw the field, let alone the ball. This week our other choice at backup tight end is Tim Wright, a converted wide receiver who isn't much of a blocker. We have plenty of talented receivers. What we need is help with the Ravens' ferocious pass rush. Belichick, in full command, listens intently to the talk in the room, then makes the call. Even on major decisions he's quick and decisive and leaves no room for lingering debate or doubt. When there's an issue with the game plan, the staff talks it over, Belichick listens, then he rules, and that's that. Against the Ravens' edge rushers, an extra blocker makes the most sense. Hoo-Man, it is.

Finished with the tight ends, Belichick changes subjects abruptly. Turning to Scott O'Brien, he says he wants special teams to go right at Baltimore's long snapper, Patrick Scales. That's right, in the first meeting of the biggest week of the year, the long snapper is a topic of conversation. Don't get me wrong. For me, a former college long snapper, I think it is a perfectly reasonable subject. And it's pretty standard fare for a special teams savant such as Belichick. But everyone else thinks it's a little random until Belichick starts talking about how pressuring the poor guy just might pay dividends. Belichick, a failed college lineman turned long snapper, is speaking from experience, but believe

it or not, he actually knows something about Scales because he and O'Brien keep an updated database of every long snapper in the league just in case we need a new one. In fact, Belichick's pro scouting department often brings in snappers for evaluation because, not surprisingly, the Patriots treat the long snapper with the same level of importance as a punter or kicker. Belichick and O'Brien must have uncovered something about Scales that tells them he can be rattled; not surprisingly, Belichick isn't sharing that something with anyone.

Defensively, Belichick is concerned about the Ravens' cut blocks, primarily how his hulking defensive tackle Vince Wilfork will handle the borderline dirty technique. He wonders out loud how we can simulate this in practice, duplicating the Ravens' offensive tempo and tactics without injuring any of our players. For starters, we'll need to spend extra time with our practice players to make sure they imitate the Ravens' technique precisely—"cutting" a defender off near the knees, knocking him to the ground and thus out of the play—and that means a special meeting after the full team meeting. Nothing is left to chance; we need these practice players to give us an accurate but safe look. Belichick talks to the defensive coaches and Dave DeGuglielmo, our offensive line coach, to make sure everyone is on the same page. This is a mainstay of the Belichick process: Practice execution becomes game-day reality. Unless we can make our practice cut blocks convincing, we won't be prepared to defend the Ravens' go-to running play.

Once he checks off all the items on his list, we plan a week's worth of practice, as Belichick's son Steve, an assistant, transcribes it all on a grease board. As everyone expected, especially those who read my memo, third and short and third down in the red zone garner their own five-minute periods. Now, five minutes might not sound like much time to spend on something deemed so important. Let me assure you that in the football world, it's a lifetime. Team preparation is a never-ending math problem, with practice time limited by restrictions imposed by the players' union and the needs of a recovering human body. With so little time and so much to do, a coach has to find the right balance. There are 5,500 waking minutes, give or take a few, between now and kickoff, and Belichick doesn't plan on wasting a single one. A team can run maybe eight plays in five minutes. If we're on our game, that should be plenty.

## MONDAY: FIVE DAYS BEFORE KICKOFF

The decor of the Patriots' inner sanctum is constantly evolving and expanding. New framed action photos are added to the walls after each victory. The hallway leading to the team meeting room is decorated with portraits of the Patriot of the Week, an honor handpicked by Belichick and awarded after wins to the player who demonstrates selfless team-first behavior. These tributes hang throughout the season and are in this hallway for a reason: They are the last thing players pass as they head to the team meeting room each day.

Belichick welcomes the players back with the same spiel he laid out for the coaches the previous night: *Baltimore is a confident team that has won in Foxborough before. They will not be intimidated. Forget the win-loss record, forget September and October games, what matters is how they are playing now—and they are playing well.*

What is most interesting is what he doesn't mention: any of the previous games the two teams have played against each other. He stays in the moment, focusing on the task that lies ahead. Who cares what happened in the past? What's important, and you can hear it in Belichick's voice, is that he has great respect for this opponent. When he praises the Ravens' skill and toughness, he means it. In the regular season, Belichick has a habit of building up an opponent early in the week before systematically pointing out its myriad inadequacies as the days march on and kickoff approaches. The Ravens don't need any puffing up; their success speaks for itself.

The longest workday of the week (because it's when the game plan is installed and first run through) begins with the longest team meeting of the week (because of all there is to download). Like most team meetings, this one is not even five minutes old when Belichick brings up the importance of the kicking game. Again, special teams mean something different to Belichick. To him they set the physical and emotional tone of the team and the pace of our preparation. When Belichick mentions special teams so early in the meeting, what he's saying is, "We will focus on every detail, no matter how small or insignificant, because all of it matters and any of it can lead to victory."

The Ravens lead the NFL in hidden yards: yards that don't make the stat sheet but have an impact on the game. The Patriots are so thorough that we even focus on things you can't see. Stuff like a gunner on the punt team fighting through three blocks to down the ball at the 1 instead of letting it bounce into the end zone for a touchback. It won't show up on the stat sheet, but that guy just saved the Ravens 19 yards in a game that will be determined by inches. Hidden yards.

Similarly, the Ravens are the best net punting team in the AFC, which means that more often than not they control field position. They also lead the league in kickoff returns. Belichick warns that the Ravens are aggressive on the road and love trick plays in the kicking game, and then he tells the team what he told O'Brien the day before: We have to attack the long snapper. Next, Belichick puts on his weatherman's suit and directs the team to expect extreme cold, the slick heavy ball that comes with it, and the extra care in handling the football that will be required.

Turning to the section of the room where the defense is congregated, Belichick says the Ravens are under center almost 75 percent of the time and use a fullback more than any team in the NFL. Stopping the run will be key. He warns that they also like to call gadget plays and went for it on fourth down 18 times during the season. Belichick has great respect for Gary Kubiak, the Ravens offensive coordinator, and mentions the naked bootlegs that are a signature of his offense. Most important, when the Ravens need to make a play—in Belichickian terms, a "gotta have it" play—he expects them to try to get the ball to tight end Owen Daniels or wide receiver Steve Smith. Belichick is so certain about Daniels's key role in the Ravens attack that he will speak his name more than that of anyone on his own roster this week.

Belichick then addresses his quarterbacks, who are sitting in the middle of the front row like star students. His first point to them will become his primary message of the week: We must stand up to their defensive front. We need to win this game in the trenches. Our offensive line cannot be pushed around. Surprisingly, we are not overly concerned about Baltimore's outside pass rushers, Terrell Suggs and Elvis Dumervil, each of whom can get around the corner in a flash. Brady generally deals well with that type of rusher, getting rid of the ball quickly or stepping up into the pocket as the defenders race past. More problematic is the Ravens' inside rush, spearheaded by Tim Jernigan, Haloti Ngata, and Brandon Williams. If they can push our guards back, it will prevent Brady from stepping up. If he is trapped in the pocket, the Ravens can then tee off on him, and Brady, like any quarterback, is far less effective when he's taking a beating and fearing for his life. Suggs always plays his best against us. He's quick to let everyone know how much he hates us and never calls Brady by his name, instead referring to him as that "good-looking fellow from up north." Brady won't stay that way for long, though, if we don't play well up front.

Before each unit is sent off to be with its coaches and coordinators, Belichick closes the meeting by reading a few things the Ravens said after the Steelers game, including how much they're looking forward to coming to Foxborough. The Steelers are the

Ravens' main rival, but the Patriots are definitely a close second. Suggs: "We all know the matchup the NFL wants to see, New England–Seattle. We'll see if we can disrupt some people's plans."

Part of Belichick's game prep this week is to avoid overcomplicating things for the players. It's his job to decipher the avalanche of information that will flow through our staff over the next five days. As for the team, he wants them to focus on things such as special teams, converting third downs, covering Owen Daniels, protecting Brady, and practicing hard. So even his motivational approach—bulletin board quotes from the opponent—is the same thing you might see or hear in a high school locker room. It's familiar and effective, so why change it? We're not trying to reinvent the wheel this week; we're just trying to beat Baltimore.

Belichick ends the meeting by saying that word out of Baltimore is that we don't want to face the Ravens.

Obviously, we need to prove them wrong.

That means having our best week of practice, starting in a few hours.

## MONDAY PRACTICE:
## FOUR AND A HALF DAYS BEFORE KICKOFF

The practice conditions are much like the game will be: cold and getting colder. The field is frozen; the footing is not sound. But this team is used to navigating lousy weather. As the team strolls out into the elements, wide receiver Brandon LaFell is the only player not able to practice; he's been nursing a bad toe but should be ready for game day. This might be the most relevant fact of the week: In a violent game that is often dictated by injuries, we are completely healthy.

The team works hard. With pads on, the drills are physical, but they also serve as a moment of continuing education. My memo predicted that tackling will be a key this week, and we practice it accordingly. In football, proper pad level—knees bent, ready to strike, whether blocking or getting off a block—is everything. Broken down to its simplest terms, football is a game of leverage, and when pad level is too high, players lose that leverage. When pad level is at the correct height, though, the leverage it allows gives a player control at the point of contact. It might seem as if good pad level would be the price of entry in the NFL. Not so. Pad level is a fundamental that requires constant reemphasis and recalibration of muscle memory. The problem is that league rules governing practice permit one day of contact in pads a week, so most teams end up not reinforcing it as often as they should. Golfers work every club in their bag every day; football teams should work every part of their game each day as well. The winning ones do. We will emphasize pad level today and will continue to do so every day.

Brady is throwing well, and our receivers are catching the frozen balls without any trouble. During seven-on-seven passing drills, Belichick tasks the equipment men with waving tennis rackets to simulate the hands of defensive linemen trying to bat down balls. Brady hates this drill. It annoys him no end. But it's a necessary evil: Led by Baltimore defensive tackle Haloti Ngata, the Ravens have knocked down 17 passes this season.

The most crucial drill of the day—cut-block avoidance—also seems to be going well. Chandler Jones, our starting defensive end, who missed a significant portion of the season with a hip problem, is moving effortlessly around the low blocks. If the Ravens decide to start clearly declining Eugene Monroe at left tackle, the matchup will favor us. Another of our key players seems healed, too: starting corner Brandon Browner. He's a tone setter. He gets called for too many penalties and lacks speed, but more important for this time of year, his toughness is infectious. Our offensive line looks outstanding, too, especially tackles Sebastian Vollmer and Nate Solder. Just as we'd hoped, our scout team defense cannot penetrate our interior line, and Brady is able to step up in the pocket and cleanly deliver the ball downfield.

With a good first day under our belt, I join Belichick to watch the last part of practice, the one called the "Opportunity Period," in which development of our youngest and taxi squad players continues, even this late in the season. Only one of the guys working out in front of us will suit up on Saturday, but Belichick won't let them off easy regardless. He may be preparing for next Saturday, but that doesn't mean he can't also prepare for next season. And the one guy who may get called on is in many ways the most critical player outside of Tom Brady: backup quarterback Jimmy Garoppolo. Most teams don't even consider this contingency. In fact, as the season progresses, most teams increasingly give all meaningful practice reps to their starters. (That's what the Colts always did with Peyton Manning. When a TV announcer asked their offensive coordinator about it, he said if Manning ever went down, they were "fucked" and "we don't practice fucked.") An injury to a starting quarterback in the playoffs is a disaster in its own right, but it is compounded if the importance of the game means the backup has not gotten the practice reps he might normally get and surely needs. The Opportunity Period ensures that Garoppolo will be ready: maybe not Tom Brady–ready but more than ready enough.

After practice, the players sit through a brief review session and a meal. I have seen many organizations try to save money at mealtime, dishing out less than the best quality or selection. That is not the case in New England. The Patriots' cafeteria is impressive. The minute players enter the building, the blenders start whirring, cranking out protein shakes, and a hot meal awaits. The cafeteria sends a positive message to the players the same way companies such as Apple and Google pamper their employees with plush modern campuses. Some teams talk about being first-class; the Patriots are.

When the players head back to their meeting rooms to watch tape or to one of the sleep rooms Belichick had installed at the facility so that players can stay rested, the coaching staff sits down to rewatch practice. At the head of the table with remote in hand, Belichick admits that the practice field conditions are a problem. As much as he'd rather not give in to the elements in any way, he sees no choice. Tomorrow we will be on the turf inside Gillette Stadium.

The practice-review session is a glimpse into how the game might go, and Belichick operates in this meeting as he does on the sideline during a game: asking questions, making suggestions, letting the coaches know what is acceptable and what is not. (The only difference: no headsets.) Never raising his voice, he makes a point and lets the film continue to play. Just as with the tight end decision, there is no gray area; no one is confused, and by the end no one isn't 100 percent certain of his assignment.

We start, as always, with the kicking game. Coach O'Brien gives the calls for the returns and explains his thinking around each one. As we watch the units go through their paces, Belichick pays close attention not only to make sure the main team is performing as they should but to be certain the scout team is giving us a good look as well. As we watch the defense practice their first-and-10 calls, Belichick tells coordinator Matt Patricia to make sure we attack the quarterback from the get-go. Kubiak always comes out throwing against us, Belichick says.

The session takes an hour and a half, and Belichick makes notes throughout. That will come in handy tomorrow morning at the next team meeting, when he'll use clips of the prior day's practice as a teaching tool. Once the film is over, Belichick reminds the coaches that ball security and third downs are critical and urges them to keep the tempo high in practice. The meeting ends, and the coaches head back to their offices to prepare for tomorrow.

Most won't head home until well after midnight.

# TUESDAY: FOUR DAYS BEFORE KICKOFF

As the game approaches, the mood in the building never wavers. From one week to the next, the Patriots maintain the same demeanor. This is the case because Belichick never wavers either, always more concerned about preparation than about the magnitude of the game. He understands, of course, that the playoffs are not like other games, but he doesn't show it—not in his behavior or routine. Instead, he continually reminds his assistants not to change their methods or show a different look. "If the players sense we are tense, they will be tense," he reminds them. It's an approach that soon will be tested to the extreme.

At the 8 A.M. meeting today Belichick begins by complimenting the players for the previous day's effort. He lets them bask in that moment for about 10 whole seconds, then it's right back to work. Belichick shows clips of what Ravens quarterback Joe Flacco can do when he gets too much time on first down. As the video plays one "chunk" big-yardage play after another, Belichick's omniscient voice-over fills the room. "We must be aggressive on first down and get him to play fast," he says. The video shifts to short-yardage plays, and once again Belichick reminds us that the determining factor will be our ability to stay on the field on third and short while getting them off the field in the same situation. The messages this morning are no different, but the presentation is. There's an edge to his voice now. "Look at this moron; guy can't even make a tackle and get off the field," he says in a sarcastic, biting tone. Who the moron is hardly matters; he can be any of the zillions of players who fail at some point to perform up to Belichick's standards.

The players watch and listen as the video jumps to a montage of Jacoby Jones. The Ravens' return man and wide receiver is respected by our team and staff. He is big, powerful, and fast and breaks right through arm tackles. "Look, if we don't cover well and gang tackle, we won't control field position," Belichick explains bluntly as we watch Jones return a kick 108 yards for a touchdown during the season. Belichick's use of voice and video gets today's points across: Contain Flacco, win the third-down battle, swarm Jones.

Today's meeting is much shorter. Just before Belichick dismisses the players to their positional get-togethers, he informs them that practice will be in the stadium, adding unnecessarily that it will be bitter cold.

Then, so as not to disappoint his players or mess with our routine, he leaves them with his touching farewell: "Get your shit on and be ready."

As it turns out, the wind is a massive problem, whipping from every direction and making it that much more unbearable. It doesn't bother Brady, of course; he throws the ball the best he has thrown it all week. He's remarkable, really. I wish every fan could see him at work like this. Sometimes I think watching Brady every day is like living at the foot of Everest: The magnificence almost becomes routine. Julian Edelman, meanwhile, looks like the best player on the field, and Gronk is moving well. The only disappointment is that LeGarrette Blount, our power back, has the flu and is sent off the field to the training room.

After practice, as the team gathers around, Belichick reminds everyone to stay hydrated. No time for soft tissue injuries.

At the postpractice staff meeting, Belichick lists the latest inactives. The Ravens, he notes, are healthy, too. Jernigan and Monroe are banged up, but they should be ready. Then he reiterates for the defensive coaches their first priority. The certainty in his voice is unignorable. "When they need a fucking play," he snarls, "I'm telling you they are going to Daniels."

# WEDNESDAY: THREE DAYS BEFORE KICKOFF

Today the schedule begins to vary a bit from our regular-season routine. The next two days will run like a couple of usual Friday practices: no pads and an intense focus on situational football. That means red zone work, third-down situations, and Belichick's all-important "gotta have it" plays. But it also means no evening meetings, and so the coaches can go home, get away from the facility, and recharge with some family time.

At the full team meeting Belichick cues up the Ravens-Steelers game. Belichick will spread the viewing and real-time analysis over a couple of sessions. He takes his time for two reasons: (1) to adequately explain relevant game situations and (2) to drill down on the details of the few plays that cost the Steelers the chance to advance. You might think that once the lights go out, the players' wakefulness will soon follow, but that's not the case. Everyone is fully engaged, eyes on the screen, because they all know Belichick might call on them to answer some game-situation question. You don't want to be the snoring guy when he does, not if you want to stay a Patriot.

We watch the first half and listen to Belichick review all the game-changing moments. The Steelers dominated time of possession—almost 21 minutes to 9—yet trailed, 10–9. The reason: too many drive-killing negative plays, including three sacks. And though Ben Roethlisberger threw for 183 yards with only six incompletions, the offense couldn't find the end zone. Without the injured Le'Veon Bell, the Steelers had no running game, and as Belichick reminds everyone, you cannot expect to beat the Ravens throwing the ball 60 times. It all comes back to basics: We need to control the line of scrimmage. We need to run the ball. We need to convert on third downs, especially in the red zone. Meanwhile, the Ravens' first scoring drive was assisted by a personal foul penalty on Steelers safety Mike Mitchell, and Belichick jumps all over that. "These dumb fucking penalties are going to cost us," he says.

"We cannot have them. We have to stand up to these guys, but we cannot lose our composure."

The team watches as the Steelers answer the Ravens' drive with 12 plays of their own that end in a field goal. But the drive was slowed by a first-down sack that forced a second and 19, one more chance for Belichick to hammer home his no-negative-plays-especially-on-first-down mantra. As he puts it, "There are 70 plays in a game; we need to make them all count." The tape stops at halftime. The screen goes dark, and the team disperses.

Today's practice features the defensive backs working on long balls. Long balls are part of every Belichick practice, but this week they get even more attention because Flacco has drawn 15 pass interference penalties this season that eventually were converted into 56 points. We don't just practice covering the deep throws; we work on playing underthrows, too, reminding our defensive backs to get their heads turned around in time to play the ball while avoiding getting tangled up with a receiver. We are going to make the Ravens' offense earn its points.

## THURSDAY: TWO DAYS BEFORE KICKOFF

Today is Gotta Have It Day.

It begins with an 8 A.M. meeting featuring part 2 of Belichick's review of Steelers-Ravens. We settle in as Baltimore opens the second half with the ball, and right away it's the perfect storm for Professor Belichick. On third and two at their own 37, the Ravens take a shot down the field that, right on cue, results in a pass interference penalty because the Steeler in coverage, Antwon Blake, fails to find the ball in the air (the exact thing we worked on in yesterday's practice). It's a 32-yard gain. "Always be ready for the shots and play the ball," Belichick says.

During the next series, the Ravens take another shot. This one is a 40-yard completion on first down. "We cannot sit back and wait on first down," Belichick preaches. The score goes to 20–9, and Belichick fast-forwards, stopping only when Ravens running back Justin Forsett fumbles at the Steelers 47 with the game seemingly in Baltimore's control at the start of the fourth quarter. "This is how you lose games—not protecting the ball," Belichick says.

One play later, the Steelers score a quick touchdown. After their two-point conversion fails, Belichick fast-forwards again to a third and long on the Ravens' next possession. It's a critical moment, and Belichick doesn't let it pass. "The Ravens gotta have it, so who is getting the ball?" he asks. A few faint votes for Owen Daniels echo in the dark room, and Belichick confirms, "Right, when they need a play, it's going to be Daniels. We have to get him." This is how Belichick inserts his game plan into the team's collective subconscious one vital detail at a time. He plants the message—stopping Daniels is a key to winning—then he proves it and repeats it using several different media until it's ingrained in our brains. Then Belichick shows us what happens when we don't follow the plan. The tape rolls, Daniels gets free, and the Ravens convert on their way to another field goal that puts them up 23–15.

Roethlisberger throws an interception, and Belichick stops the tape.

"What's next?"

Again, a few unconvincing murmurs from the crowd. Almost before Belichick has a chance to agree—"Right, a shot"—Ravens backup tight end Crockett Gillmore catches a 21-yard touchdown pass that ices the game.

The Ravens beat the Steelers because they made all their "gotta have it" plays. It's a nice segue. Near the end of any preparation week, Belichick uses days like these to go over the plays and players he feels will be difference-makers in the game. First, he highlights Ravens wide receiver Michael Campanaro. God knows why; Campanaro is a seventh rounder who has been active for only four games and did not have a single catch against the Steelers. It seems like guesswork or secret intel, but it's actually Belichick's powers of deductive reasoning that have led him to Campanaro. He knows one of our weaknesses on defense also happens to be one of the Ravens' strengths: the middle of the field. Campanaro, meanwhile, is quick and strong and can separate in the slot and win in man coverage. It's a calculated prediction, not a wild guess. We will keep our eye on Campanaro on Saturday.

At practice, though, all eyes are on Alan Branch. The sun is out but the weather is brutal, yet the players seem to be inspired. Branch, a defensive tackle we signed late in the year to bolster our depth along the line, works so hard that sweat freezes on his body.

## FRIDAY: ONE DAY BEFORE KICKOFF

During the regular season, the day before a game is quick and easy. During the playoffs nothing is.

Belichick calls a last-second 7 A.M. coaches' meeting before the full team meeting to go over final details and a few future projects. All the coaches are in their seats at least 10 minutes early, meaning that for once Belichick is the last man in. This pleases him, and once seated at his spot at the table head, he looks at his notes and then up at his staff and announces that he wants everyone to review the previous four Patriots' postseasons to uncover anything we may have missed in our preparation. He wants them watching not through the lens of their particular unit or area of expertise but as a team of objective, independent observers. Of course, there is no assurance he will agree with their assessments or act on their recommendations, but no one doubts that he will process all the new information and won't hesitate to incorporate anything he deems worthwhile. More than anything, this is an exercise in staying focused on the big picture, leaving no stone unturned, and seeing the game through fresh eyes and with a different perspective.

Belichick then reiterates that he wants the team to play fast and aggressive but most of all poised. It's a fine line. *We cannot let the Ravens push us around, but we cannot lose our composure.* Finally, he demands a good start from our kicking game and precision in our two-minute drills. Belichick sends us off with this boiled-down report of the Ravens' mentality: "They think they can cover Gronk with [safety] Will Hill, dominate our offensive front, and win."

After the team meeting and walk-through, the players are free until they have to report to the hotel for the 7 P.M. special teams meeting. The coaches work on the playoff project, dutifully typing up pages and pages of notes for the boss before heading home for a few hours. They pass Belichick's car in the parking lot. He doesn't go home on nights before a game. He works out, watches more tape, shuts the world out, and locks in on the task at hand.

Belichick holds his evening coaches' meeting at the local hotel the team stays at the night before the game. This session has always been one of my favorites. In it, Belichick goes over how he sees the game playing out and doles out parting instructions to his coordinators. The first order of business, though, is to finalize the inactive list. Then it's on to the officials. Belichick reviews all the Patriots games that Bill Vinovich, the head official assigned to our game, has done. He informs the staff that he actually went over the trick plays we might run with Vinovich to make sure we don't catch his crew off guard. Fans, players, and coaches alike forget that the pace of the game is just as fast for officials as it is for the rest of us; forcing them to figure out a proper call on an unusual circumstance in the heat of the moment is asking a lot. When it benefits us, we try to make life a little easier for them. Belichick doesn't worry about Vinovich spilling our plans to the Ravens. He's not worried about the play's legality, either, because he's already had a chat with the league office about the rules. The man leaves nothing to chance.

Not that he doubted the legality of his play. It already had been confirmed by his own resident rules pundit, Ernie Adams. Many people have asked me what Adams actually does for Belichick. As far back as Cleveland, owner Art Modell would say, "I will pay

$10,000 to the person who can tell me what Ernie Adams does." Adams doesn't attend meetings, nor does he coach a position. He's a confidant of Belichick's, a trusted friend, a sounding board, another set of eyes and ears, and a legitimate rules expert. He knows the rule book as well as the head of officials, probably better. Add his great understanding of the history of the game, and Adams is an incredible resource and comfort for Belichick. The coach confers with him on replay challenges, and he's always nearby when Belichick is in a conversation with the refs.

Adams also brings me to the elephant in the room. Call me a Kool-Aid drinker if it makes you feel better, but here's the fact: The Patriots don't cheat. Okay, maybe they do a little. But only stuff that all teams in the NFL do to try to gain an advantage. And I'm not talking about unbalanced line play here; that's just knowing the rules, pushing things right up to the edge in an effort to gain every possible advantage. It's not cheating, although it's often portrayed that way. I'm talking about the biggie: filming another team's signals. It was wrong, and they paid a hefty price—draft picks, fines, and permanent damage to the franchise's reputation—but they were doing only what other teams have done and will continue to do.

How do I know? Because I have worked for some of the great signal stealers in the game. I am not going to dime anyone out; I'm no rat. But trust me, it happens all the time. In fact, it happens so often that everyone in the NFL knows who the signal stealers are and makes sure to hide their calls when they play them. And as much as it happens in the NFL, it happens much more in the college game, where the absence of radio communication means they have to call plays from the sideline.

My point is that the Patriots push the envelope and leave no stone unturned to a degree that is unmatched in football. Just don't confuse Belichick's obsession with all-out preparation for cheating. It ain't. And don't get me started on Deflategate. That was not some sinister conspiracy. I'm not sure it was anything at all. What I do know is that no one in the building that I talked to—Belichick included—had any idea about any of it.

Belichick ends his final meeting with directions for each and every coach. He starts with special teams, urging O'Brien and his assistant, Joe Judge, to make a play before getting in a little dig that he gleaned from my research: In our last nine postseason games, our special teams took 10 penalties. We cannot continue to beat ourselves, Belichick says. No one disagrees.

He turns to McDaniels to let him know that he wants the offense to put our best groups out there early so that we start fast and play with the lead. Most teams have an offensive script that doles out when each contributor gets involved, and that script depends on game situation and management. Because Belichick wants that early lead, he wants almost nothing held back—not formations, not players, not core plays. Playing with the lead, he says, is crucial against Kubiak, because it forces him into more drop-back formations, which are not a strong suit of his schemes. In this mode Belichick comes across as a chess grandmaster who is playing out both sides of the board in his head at all times, not just his moves but everything his opponent might do to counter them.

Belichick continues down his list: He wants to check from run to pass, not just pass to run; he wants to support Solder, our offensive tackle, early in the game against Suggs with a chip-blocking running back; he wants everyone to be sure where the yardage sticks are on crucial downs and to be aware that the Ravens will be all over Gronk on first and second downs. He wants to make first downs on all second and shorts—to stay out of third downs; he wants McDaniels to remember that once he sees their defensive game plan, he will know their game plan (the Ravens don't make many adjustments); he wants the offense to spread the Ravens out deep in our own territory.

Finally, he tells McDaniels the one play he does want to save for the second half: our unbalanced line play, or what has come in the last week to be known as the "Baltimore play." "I don't want them to have time to adjust," Belichick explains, thinking that using it in the first half would preclude his coming back to it in the second because the Ravens would have halftime to study it.

As for the defense, Belichick emphasizes keeping the line fresh for the fourth quarter because he senses the game will come down to the final minutes, as so many of the past battles with the Ravens have. Belichick tells Patricia he wants to start the game with calls we're familiar with to avoid early mistakes; he wants us playing clean, sharp, and fast. Plus, he'd rather get Kubiak to show his hand and then make the necessary adjustments before running more exotic calls. Belichick is still worried about cut blocks and wants to make sure the coaches in the skybox are paying close attention to how our defensive linemen are being handled. He reminds Patricia one more time to keep an eye on Campanaro and lets him know to expect more 11 personnel (one tight end, one back) from the Ravens on first down while warning about assuming they're going to run the ball out of 12 personnel (one tight end, two backs). Belichick is pretty confident they will come out throwing regardless of the formation.

After encouraging everyone to keep his poise and focus and to forget about bad plays as soon as they happen, there is nothing more to do or say.

The planning is over.

It's time to play.

## SATURDAY: PREGAME

The team—even Brady—spends the night at the hotel, and the next morning Belichick addresses them before everyone heads to the stadium. He is no rah-rah Rockne type; his well-worn monotone never rises or betrays emotion. Think *Dragnet*'s Joe "just the facts, ma'am" Friday. Still, the players don't know quite what to expect from this meeting, as Belichick never does the same thing twice. This time, Belichick shows the team a short tape of the season's positive plays to reinforce the fact that when we focus and do things correctly, we are tough to beat. Everyone is feeling pretty good as he stresses one more time what we need to do to win.

He finishes with a short discourse about sticking together, handling the inevitable ups and downs of the game, and never giving in—just as Chris Kyle never gave in.

It's not especially eloquent, but it's remarkably prescient.

Meeting over, Belichick drives directly to the office to start his final preparation. He goes over the practice video once more on the off chance that something has escaped his notice. He is not looking to have a conversation; he values this alone time. We all know better than to break his quiet focus. Even when he brings the video to the weight room to watch during his pregame workout, he is left alone, a prizefighter before a championship bout.

His weatherman's prediction is accurate; the shining sun is fighting a losing battle. Once night falls, it will be even worse, and that is bound to have an adverse effect on our home field advantage. It's not that fans won't show up—of course they will—it's that they will all be bundled up in scarves and gloves, and that will deaden the noise in the stands.

After watching the first half of the Seahawks-Panthers game in my office, I'm pretty convinced that Seattle will be the NFC's representative in the Super Bowl. The Seahawks lead at halftime 14–10, but I know from the scouting I did in the weeks leading up to the playoffs that they are a dominant fourth-quarter team, so an early deficit against them is hard to overcome. They just keep grinding until they wear you down. I see little hope for Carolina.

As I walk onto the field an hour and a half before kickoff, the stadium looks like a postcard. The sky is dark, but the moon is a lamppost. It's a perfect night for football.

# SATURDAY: GAME TIME

As is the norm when the Patriots win the coin toss, we defer, hoping for a dominant three and out to set the tone. But today, despite all the time, energy, and expertise we put into preparing for the Ravens, very little goes as planned. And that begins with the coin-toss tactic. Just as Belichick said they would, the Ravens come out firing. They throw on nearly every first down (another Belichick prediction) and score in just five plays. Before our fans have even settled into their seats, we're down 7–0. So much for starting fast. We certainly didn't game-plan for this.

To make matters worse, our offense starts slowly, too; after one first down, we're forced to punt. We've been preparing for this game around the clock for a week, and five minutes in, the team has done nothing Belichick asked of it. But just as he preached at our staff meeting on Tuesday morning, Belichick shows no signs of panic. He's as calm as can be on the headset. You'd think we were up three scores by the tenor of his voice. Maybe a little panic is in order, though, because on their next drive the Ravens march down the field again, in 11 plays this time, mixing the run and the pass, to go up 14–0. The stadium falls deathly silent.

Mike Tyson has a great line that he may or may not have borrowed from Joe Louis: "Everybody has a plan until they get punched in the mouth." That is exactly what has just happened to us. And that makes all the work we did to prepare exponentially more important. We have to stick with the plan. Our interior line holds the Ravens' pass rushers at bay, and with time and space, Brady begins to chip away. Getting the ball to Gronk and others, we answer quickly, scoring a touchdown from the 4-yard line with Brady running it in on third and short. Yes, Brady ran it in. Apparently, someone was listening to Belichick preach all week about the importance of converting on third downs in the red zone. (Gronk, by the way, will never come off the field and will end up with 108 yards receiving.) Later, after our defense steps up, Edelman has a 19-yard punt return that gives us good field position. (Our special teams play is tilting the field in our favor, and suddenly it makes sense that Belichick led off every meeting with that unit.) Now the game feels more like the one Belichick envisioned. Moving the ball down the field with his arm this time, Brady caps off the drive with a touchdown pass to Amendola to tie the score. With just under four minutes to go in the half, if we can stop the Ravens one more time, we can use the next two possessions—the last of this half and the first of the next half—to build a lead.

And then, wham! Another sock to the jaw.

Brady throws a rare interception, and you'll never guess who the Ravens go to when they need a touchdown at the end of the half. Right, Daniels. Or, as Belichick referred to him all week, "fucking Daniels." It's as if the entire team slept through our week of game prep. We squander our first possession of the second half, too, and Baltimore scores again to take a 28–14 lead. If there was no panic before, that's no longer the case. Now the headsets carry a definite urgency and maybe even a hint of fear.

From everybody but Belichick, that is. Instead, as the offense takes the field, the coach instructs McDaniels that it's time to break out the Baltimore play. Belichick has a keen sense of timing, rhythm, and momentum, especially in bigger games, and he realizes that we no longer have the luxury of holding anything back. Of course, the mere fact that he has such a play in his pocket— like one of the gadgets in Batman's utility belt or a "break glass in case of emergency" cabinet—is remarkable in and of itself. It's as if he knew we'd need something like this to rattle the Ravens and shake us out of our deep freeze. (If I didn't know better, I'd say Belichick enjoyed using our reputation for playing fast and loose with the rules to our advantage.) The unbalanced look completely baffles the Ravens, sending their staff into a wild frenzy. We gain 16 yards on the play—not bad, if less than we were looking for— but it delivers a secondary benefit: It sends the Ravens' bench into a tailspin. The cheating Pats are DOING IT AGAIN! That's how

I interpret their body language, anyway. Across the field, head coach John Harbaugh is apoplectic, screaming and ranting at Vinovich. Apparently, he doesn't know the NFL rule book and/or he missed the Alabama-LSU game.

Belichick sees how much the play has flustered Baltimore, so he decides to go for the jugular and double down. Run it again, he tells McDaniels. This time we flip the formation—this one's called "Raven"—and the play gains 14 yards. But the impact is much greater. Harbaugh looks as though he might stroke out before getting called for an unsportsmanlike conduct penalty that moves us inside their 5-yard line. I'm pretty sure that's what Belichick referred to during Wednesday's film study as a "dumb fucking penalty."

Two plays later, we score. It's 28–21. My intimations of panic have dissipated. The crowd is going nuts. The Ravens are rattled.

Game on.

With our defensive linemen fighting off the Ravens' cut blocks and our corners and safeties limiting Flacco's chunk plays downfield, we get the ball back at our own 30. Over the headsets, I hear Belichick remind McDaniels about the double pass play. It works perfectly as Edelman heaves it to Amendola to tie the score. The Ravens are on the ropes, but Harbaugh doesn't seem to get it. He's still bitching about those unbalanced formations. It almost makes you feel sorry for him. Almost.

As the fourth quarter begins, Baltimore goes on a 15-play drive that brings them to a third and seven at our 7. This is clearly a "gotta have it" play. Every Patriot knows where the ball is going. We prepared for this moment, and now all we have to do is operationalize Belichick's mantra. *Practice execution becomes game reality.* The coaches and Belichick are all yelling that we have to get Daniels. On cue, Flacco sends a pass toward his tight end—who is double covered. The ball sails over his head, and the Ravens have to settle for a field goal. Fun fact: The Ravens finish just

1 of 9 on third down while the Patriots convert on 6 of 11, and it proves to be the difference in the game.

Knowing we can take our first lead of the game, Brady marches us 74 yards, capping things off with a 23-yard touchdown pass to LaFell, bad toe and all. With the front of the pocket clean, Brady was repeatedly able to step up, avoid Suggs on the edge (he managed just half a sack in the game), and pass for 367 yards. Now, with slightly more than five minutes to play, Belichick and the staff urge the players to stay in the moment. Our defense is fresh, remembering Belichick's instructions this morning to keep something in the tank for a late, desperate surge by the Ravens.

The final minutes of a playoff game are a now-or-never war—football at its best. The Ravens' next drive involves all their receivers—including Campanaro, who makes a tough catch over the middle. Right before the two-minute warning, the Ravens are confronted with a fourth and three. When they break the huddle, Belichick "takes a Kodak"—a quick mental picture of the Ravens' formation—to try to predict what they will run. But on this, the ultimate "gotta have it" play, we know what's coming next: a pass to Daniels. We know it, but we just can't stop it; the Ravens convert. We know not to take stupid penalties, too, but we jump offside anyway, gift-wrapping a second and five for the Ravens. But we also know this: When you're in four-down territory, the best time to take a shot is on second down. And when Flacco does a poor job of looking off the safety, Duron Harmon intercepts the ball.

The pick seals the win. The Patriots become the first team in playoff history to overcome two 14-point deficits.

The game was a war. We took their best shots, stayed together, stuck to the plan, kept fighting, and turned my memo into memories.

# 8

# WHILE I HAVE YOU

## MY BIGGEST PET PEEVES

*I'm not looking to be consistent; I am looking to be correct.*

—AL DAVIS

D o you know what the most significant invention of the twenty-first century is? The mute button on the television remote. Bruce Springsteen was right when he sang that there were 57 channels and nothing on, because today I have my choice of more than 257 channels and, I swear, I'm still at a loss. Unless there's football, of course. Thank goodness for the gridiron. I don't care who's playing or whether it's college or pro, I just love to man my position as a professional armchair quarterback. When football is on the big screen, I'm constantly chirping to Millie—or, let's be honest, to no one at all—that whoever I'm watching should do this or call that or try the other thing. It can be annoying, I'll admit, but it keeps my instincts sharp. I watch some basketball, too, especially when former NBA coach Hubie Brown is the analyst. It's as if he's coaching both teams at all times. We're kindred spirits. He watches his game the way I like to think I watch mine.

But you don't have to sit with me long to realize that I get irritated quickly. Not with the game but with the way most commentators describe—or don't describe—what's happening on the field. That's where the mute button comes in. I'm not blaming the men doing the talking—I know that's a tough gig. It's just that my training in the sport allows me to see things they don't notice, and I can't just turn it off. Ask Millie.

One of the big problems is that the analysts are almost all former players who are blinkered by the perspective of the position they played. They don't see the whole field. It's not their fault; it's just their background and, to be fair, the nature of their sport. In baseball, players play offense and defense. In basketball, same thing. Football is way more specialized. You can go to positional meetings all week—heck, all year—and never have any idea of your team's overall game plan. When Hall of Fame Cleveland Browns tight end Ozzie Newsome retired and became a personnel man, he told me, "I have no idea what actually happens upstairs." Why would he? During his playing career, he was focused only on his position responsibilities. (Ozzie sure was a quick study, though; within a decade he was hoisting the Lombardi Trophy with the Ravens.)

Football strategy may not be rocket science, but there is more to it than meets the eye. Fans critique a particular play call or coverage breakdown without having any idea of the broader narrative. What seems obvious to them is almost never what's really taking place. What all you armchair quarterbacks need to do is turn the sound down and instead take your cues from the guys who may have a broader understanding of the game.

That's where I come in.

Here are some of my pet peeves, common strategy mistakes

that continue to spoil my weekends, along with an explanation of what's actually going on. Each is sick-making enough in its own right; the fact that they occur again and again with a stunning lack of on-air critique just compounds my dyspepsia. I'd like to think some of what follows, should it be read by those with influence, will cause changes in strategy—on the field or at least in the broadcast booth—but I have my doubts. I am, however, fairly confident that after you read it, I won't be the only one screaming at the TV as I stab at the mute button every Sunday.

## WHEN THEY CALL TIME WITH 2:05 ON THE CLOCK

At crunch time in the NFL, Andy Reid is one guy who can make me scream in agony as if I'm watching Santino heading toward the toll plaza in *The Godfather*. When his Chiefs are in the two-minute drill, my pleas of "Sonny, no! It's a trap!" become "Andy, no! It's a trap!" But Santino never listens, and Reid never learns.

Funny thing is, the current Kansas City coach is one of the game's best. In 19 seasons as an NFL head man, he has amassed 183 wins and has taken his teams to 24 playoff games, 5 conference championship games, and a Super Bowl, in 2004, when his Eagles lost to the Patriots. His résumé speaks for itself. But his playoff work comes up short. He's 11–13 overall in the postseason and 1–4 with the Chiefs. There are plenty of reasons for that, but one of the major problems is surely his shortcomings in late-game management. As good a coach as Reid is, he often leaves me scratching my head (or yelling at the TV) after making the same mistake again and again.

Here's what I'm talking about. The game is in the fourth quarter with two minutes and a few seconds on the clock, and Reid's team needs the ball back. On second and 10, the opponent calls a running play. The defense holds for a short gain, and Reid uses his last time-out to stop the clock once more before the two-minute warning. At that point I promptly lose my shit. Worse, no one with a microphone and access to millions of viewers bothers to point out what a huge blunder this is or suggest that it might be time for Reid to outsource his clock management.

Calling a time-out in this situation is a gift to the opponent, providing more options for the offense. Thanks to Andy's ill-timed time-out, the offense can throw on third down without worrying that an incompletion will help the Chiefs by stopping the clock. The two-minute warning is going to do that, anyway. If Reid lets the clock run to the two-minute warning, though, everyone in the stadium knows the offense will be running the ball on that crucial third down to keep the clock running.

Once it ticks past 2:06, the defense has to let it run down to the two-minute warning. Has to. When Reid calls that defensive time-out, he thinks he's saving seconds for his offense. He's not, but even if he is, he's missing the point. For a trailing offense at that stage of the game, the entire focus needs to be on the potential number of plays it still can run. As football math has it, each play takes about six seconds. So, if you want to think like a coach, don't look at the clock and think there are 54 seconds left in the game. Think: Best-case scenario, I have time to run nine more plays. When a team is down late and the game is on the line, offenses have to recalibrate to value plays more than time and yards more than first downs. The goal is to win. To win you need points. To get points you need yards. To get yards you need plays—but more than the three seconds Reid saved.

Defensive head coaches should be able to do the plays-to-time-left calculation in their heads, but the shrieks coming from my den every weekend are proof that they can't. If Reid were Al Davis's head coach, Davis might have watched him call that pre-two-minute-warning time-out—once. If he saw it again, Reid would be looking for a job. I'm not kidding. Davis understood game management theory. In fact, Bill Parcells, one of the best game managers ever, was schooled by Davis. Both Parcells and Belichick have been mocked for not celebrating after big late-game touchdowns, but it's not because they're joyless so much as because they're already deep in thought about calculating time scenarios to decide the next thing the team needs to do. You can celebrate after the game.

When Reid faced Belichick in Super Bowl XXXIX in 2005, his Eagles were down 24–14 with 5:40 to go. I guess having two time-outs left robbed Reid of the proper urgency because to the amazement of the entire Patriots coaching staff and a worldwide audience, the Eagles started their next drive as if the game were still in the first half. They scored, but it took them an eternity—almost four minutes—which left them no time to see whether the defense could get them the ball back. The Eagles were forced to try an onside kick, which they didn't recover. Almost 11 years later, Reid faced the Patriots again, this time with the Chiefs in the 2015 divisional round. Again his team was down by two touchdowns late, and again history—or should I say Reid?—repeated itself. With 6:29 to go and all three time-outs, the Chiefs took over with the same kind of non-urgency we saw in Philadelphia. They scored, but only after 16 plays that burned more than five minutes. Another desperation onside kick did not deliver.

Once again Andy Reid was left to suffer the same sad fate as Sonny.

## COROLLARY 1: WHEN THEY THROW CHECKDOWNS IN THE TWO-MINUTE DRILL

When I was in Cleveland, I sat in on a film session with our scouts after a day spent working on our two-minute drill. Watching one useless checkdown throw—you know, those safe tosses to a receiver, usually a running back, in the flat—after another got me more and more annoyed until I finally had to say something. Most of the scouts in the room turned and looked at me as if I were speaking in tongues. To them it seemed obvious: We needed to get first downs.

To me it was just as obvious: No, we didn't. (Unless it was fourth down, of course.) Last I checked, they don't give points for first downs. What we really needed was the maximum yards we could get in the smallest amount of time. I tried to explain to those scouts that throwing a checkdown in that situation is actually a big-time favor to the defense because you voluntarily burn what you need most (time on the clock) in exchange for what you need the least (first downs).

When you measure the risk/reward as it relates to that situation, throwing the ball downfield seems like the only smart choice. Even if it's down the middle of the field. Either you're going to get a big chunk of yards or the pass is going to be incomplete and stop the clock. But to do that you have to have coaches and a quarterback who think like a professional golfer teeing off in front of a lake. That guy isn't worried about hitting the ball into the water. He can't even see the water. If he's laying up with a short wedge to play it safe, he won't be on the tour very long. He focuses only on what's beyond the lake. Plunking one into the water never enters his mind.

That's the way a quarterback and his coaches need to handle a two-minute drill. To be fair, it goes against almost all our normal training. We talk about completion percentages and accuracy and read progressions all day long, but in a two-minute drill that all has to go out the window as the quarterback looks downfield because—as crazy as it sounds—a long incompletion is much better than a five-yard checkdown.

## COROLLARY 2: WHEN THEY DON'T CONSIDER ALL THE FACTORS

Let's check in on the Falcons-Eagles 2017 divisional playoff game. The Eagles are up 15–10 with just over six minutes to play, but the Falcons are starting a drive that will determine their entire season. Eventually, after running four-plus minutes off the clock, Atlanta finds itself first and goal at the Eagles' 9-yard line, on the doorstep of a second-straight NFC championship game.

The situation looks so dire for the Eagles that with 1:19 to play they call a time-out in an attempt to stockpile precious seconds for a last-ditch drive after the Falcons inevitably score.

Okay, time for a pop quiz: What should the Falcons call?

At this point in the game, they have two goals. Obviously, first and foremost, they want to score, but second and almost as important, they want to force the Eagles to burn their final time-out. Not for nothing: The Eagles' kicker made a 53-yarder at the end of the first half, so if the Eagles do get the ball back, having that time-out to stop the clock and set up a kick could be the difference in the game. Knowing this, the Falcons' first-down call has to be a run or an easily completable pass, right? Something that runs the clock and forces the Eagles to use their final time-out. Because once that happens, even a high school coach understands that Atlanta will have full control of the game. But what do the Falcons do? They throw a 50/50 pass into the end zone that falls incomplete. I'm sure there are many "experts" who would argue that this was smart, trying to get the ball to their best player, Julio Jones. Sorry fellas; right idea, wrong time.

On second down, the Falcons call a quick screen. Incomplete. The clock is now at 1:11. Forget for a moment that those two plays didn't move the ball an inch closer to the end zone. The real problem is that they used up only eight seconds and the Eagles still have their emergency time-out.

Talk about not understanding the whole situation. When a world-class pool player makes a shot, where she leaves the cue ball matters almost as much as pocketing the ball. An amateur at your local watering hole is thinking one shot at a time, but the pro is imagining the best way to run the entire table from the get-go. Falcons head coach Dan Quinn isn't thinking like a pool shark. His goal needed to be centered on the big picture. He needs to see the entire field, not just the next shot or the next play.

Now it's third down. A short completion. At least this causes the Eagles to burn their last time-out in order to set their defense and save clock. The clock now reads 1:05, but it almost doesn't matter. Atlanta has completely botched this series. Even if the Falcons score on fourth down, the Eagles have more than enough time to get in field-goal range and win the game. The Falcons don't score, of course. Quarterback Matt Ryan throws an end zone fade to Jones, who falls down and gets back up just in time for the ball to sail through his fingertips.

Before the ball even hit the ground, everyone was talking about how the Eagles' defense heroically held and saved the season. Nobody even mentioned the real story: how the Falcons' offense blew it. At least I don't think anyone was. I was screaming my objections too loud to hear them if they were.

## WHEN THEY TRY TO RUN IT BACK

Few things demonstrate a nearly total lack of understanding of even the simplest aspects of clock management than late-game kickoff returns. Here's the situation: Team B, down to its last time-out and trailing by four with less than a minute left, fields a kickoff three yards deep in the end zone and advances the ball to the 22-yard line as eight seconds tick off the clock. The announcers, of course, begin to talk about what the offense now has to do. They have nothing to say about what just happened.

Well, I do.

What the hell were they thinking?

The geniuses on Team B just gave up eight seconds—or one or two extra chances to win the game—in order to *lose* three yards on the kick return. Here's the math: The chances of breaking that return for a game-winning touchdown are virtually nonexistent. In 2017 only 4 of the 966 kickoffs were taken to the house. That's a success rate below one-half of 1 percent. Titans quarterback Marcus Mariota, who had five game-winning drives in 2017, beat those odds all by himself. Even more to the point, just four teams in 2017 had an average after-kickoff starting point beyond the 25-yard line. (The Ravens were best at 27.8.)

Trust me, this obvious miscalculation would never happen in New England or anywhere else where the head coach understands time management even a little. In fact, Bill Belichick figured out early on that it actually made sense to lure the not-so-smart teams into making this mistake. Instructing his kicker to leave the ball short of the goal line, he forced a return that burned precious seconds. Teams should be smarter than this, but you'd be surprised.

## WHEN THEY STRETCH FOR THE EXTRA YARD

What's the number one requirement of a ball carrier? To score? Nope. To gain yards? Nope. The first rule of ball carriers is to protect the rock. Yet more and more, it seems, runners near the goal line extend their ball-carrying arm to break the plane or touch the pylon to get a TD. Similarly, ball carriers have taken increasingly to cradling the ball as if it were a loaf of bread. The problem is that defenses have gotten better at playing the ball and knocking it loose. Most defenses, in fact, run daily drills in which they practice stripping the ball. It's time well spent when you consider that teams that win the turnover battle win the game nearly 80 percent of the time. (That's from a Harvard study, so you can trust it.) Think about that stat the next time you see a runner expose the ball to stretch for a measly extra yard. Even near the goal line, I'm telling you, the risk is not worth the reward.

In New England, players are reminded that carrying the ball is a privilege. If a player abuses that privilege with fumbles or by carrying the ball carelessly, he will lose that privilege until he earns it back. Belichick would never encourage extending the ball near the goal line; he means it when he says he never wants the ball to be unprotected. Of course, there will be times when an overzealous Patriot ignores the edict. But even if he scores, he can expect to get an earful from his coach. God help him if the ball comes loose.

## WHEN THEY SETTLE FOR THE LONG FIELD GOAL

Late in games, as soon as a team that's down by at least two points gets anywhere near midfield, television producers slap that virtual line onto the screen to indicate where the field-goal kicker's range begins. Now, you might think that it's a cool innovation (graphics!) or a helpful visual guide, and I might even agree—if not for the fact that it actually highlights the wrong target. Remember, the line represents the outer reaches of the kicker's range. Time constraints aside, why would that be any offense's goal? The point isn't to get into field-goal range. The point is to get into surefire field-goal range. This is no small difference. An offense that can move the ball just 11 more yards and decrease the length of the attempt from, say, 50 yards down to 39 has increased its odds of scoring points by more than 20 percent.

Too many teams grow significantly more conservative once they get the ball into field-goal range because they don't want to give up the chance to get three points. But they shouldn't just want a chance; they should want a real chance. Why pile more pressure on an already pressure-filled situation? Forcing a kicker to achieve at the edge of his capabilities in a must-make-it moment is not a winning formula. For a head coach, who needs to factor in weather changes, injuries, and his kicker's fluctuating mental state, field-goal range has to be a moving target, not a static line.

### COROLLARY: MISSED FIELD GOALS ARE ACTUALLY TURNOVERS

What has always bothered me about missed field goals is that they're filed away in the wrong statistical category. They're not missed field goals; they're turnovers. Think about it: After a miss, there's a change of possession and a loss of yardage as the ball placement is seven yards behind the original line of scrimmage. In 2017, kickers converted 69 percent (107 of 154) of field goal attempts from beyond 50 yards. That means that in a game of inches, an offense handed the ball over to the defense near mid-field 47 times.

Sure sounds like turnovers to me. Why do we continue to pretend otherwise?

## WHEN THEY DON'T GIVE THEMSELVES A CHANCE

There's a moment in the fourth quarter of every close-ish game in which it transforms into an "onside kick game." You know what I mean: A team is up two scores, and the only way an opponent can come back and win is if it manages to secure an extra possession with a successful onside kick. What's funny, though, is how few of those games actually ever end that way. Teams are so focused on scoring a touchdown first that they fail to leave themselves enough time to kick a field goal even if they can get the ball back. I know the traditional thinking on this is that you want to hang on to the chance to win the game as long as possible (even if that chance is contingent on a miracle turnover or broken play), which means you don't want to go for a field goal first because if you miss, the game's over right then. But I've always thought such thinking is too rigid. You need two scores; it makes no difference to anyone but the gamblers what order you get them in. Doesn't it actually make more sense to move the ball into makeable field-goal range as fast as possible to give yourself the most time to get that touchdown?

I learned this by watching Parcells when he was coaching the Patriots. Whenever he found himself in an onside kick game, he'd factor in intangibles such as time-outs left, weather, the kicker's confidence and range, and the moment a drive feels like it has stalled. But he was never afraid to follow his gut and attempt a field goal first even if it meant facing the wrath of the media and all the other armchair quarterbacks out there. You know why? Because it was the right move.

## WHEN THE GOAL IS
## A THIRD AND MANAGEABLE

On first down the offense doesn't gain any yardage, which prompts the announcers to proclaim that it now needs to spend second down getting into a third and manageable situation, which then prompts me to proclaim that nobody knows anything. I'm sorry, but isn't the goal to score? Who designs plays to gain three or four yards? Shouldn't you call every play with the idea that it could break for a big gain? Look, I understand that sometimes you have to manage a situation and make keeping a drive alive your priority. But more often than not this is not the case. I might feel differently if third and manageable solved an offense's scoring problems. It doesn't.

The truth is, most NFL play callers don't even understand what third down and manageable actually means. Most will define it as third and six. In the last few years, however, the average conversion rate for this down and distance has been about 26 percent. Getting in third and manageable might sound like a solid plan, but shouldn't a solid plan have a success rate better than one in four? Third down in general is a tough position to be in. The game buckles down on third down. Defenses are designed for just such situations. Even the best teams convert third downs at only about a 45 percent rate. (The league average in 2017 was 38 percent.)

In the end, the best third-down strategy is to avoid third downs altogether.

Instead of teams trying to get into third and manageable situations, I propose that they'd be better off taking their cues from the Canadian Football League. I'm serious. The CFL gives offenses three downs, not four, so they never have to concern themselves with third and manageable because they have only two chances to make a first down. In the CFL, every play call needs to be aggressive.

A part of me thinks this CFL style is where offensive philosophy is headed. Why wait until third down to fight to keep the drive going? Sweetening the pot, most defenses are still in their basic schemes on second down, and so their best pass rushers aren't even on the field. Why not take a shot when you have the advantage? Sooner or later defenses will adjust and begin using nickel (passing) packages on second downs. And that will be just fine, too, because then every down will be an equal fight for a first down, and third and manageable situations will be history, which they should be.

## WHEN THEY DON'T TELL US WHO IS IN THE GAME

NFL football today is about one thing above all else: matchups. In basketball, analysts highlight changes in the lineup all the time, announcing stuff such as "Team A has gone small to cause problems for the much slower Team B." Why don't football analysts do this more often? Even well-informed fans can get lost in the different formations and personnel disguises, missing the significance of the constantly rotating matchups that are now the key to most NFL games.

It wouldn't be that hard to communicate this before every snap. Every personnel group is described with two digits, the first indicating the number of running backs and the second the number of tight ends. If the Patriots come out in 11 personnel, they have one back and one tight end on the field and thus probably three wide-outs. The defense would more than likely counter with its nickel package (three defensive backs). The play-by-play guy could just mention this quickly or the networks could just add "11p/nickel" to the "bug," the on-screen graphic that displays score, time and down, and distance.

Some announcers do a good job of mentioning a two-tight-end set that suggests a running play or an empty backfield that foretells a pass. But it would be nice if they did this on every down. That way we'd know that if Belichick stays in 11 personnel, we should focus on the depth in the defensive backfield. And then if the Pats gain 150 yards rushing from that package, we can rightfully expect the media to ask about the nickel defense's porous run support. Too often, though, fans watching at home have no idea what personnel group is in the game, and if they don't know this, how can they understand the point-counterpoint drama going on at field level? Plus, imagine the second-guessing that would occur if fans actually had the information necessary to second-guess.

## WHEN THE EIGHT-MAN FRONT GETS WAY TOO MUCH CREDIT

Another thing that drives me nuts: when a commentator offers a simple solution to a complex problem, such as when a team is running the ball well and he suggests that the defense needs to jump into an eight-man front. Yes, the vaunted eight-man front. They mention it as if it were the antidote to every potent ground game. But if the eight-man front always stopped the run, there wouldn't be any 1,000-yard rushers, right?

In the same way that third and manageable is a misnomer, eight-man run-stuffing fronts aren't actually made up of eight run-stuffers. Rather, they include a member of the secondary, usually a safety, who has to move up into the box. He's not a typical run stopper, yet his responsibility is the same as that of those who are much bigger and much better at it. Furthermore, there are eight gaps that need to be defended on any run play, and if the defense isn't properly aligned at all times to man all those ever-moving, ever-changing gaps, it won't help if you have an 18-man front stacked in the box.

Al Davis never learned. He loved eight-man fronts. But all Denver had to do to beat the Raiders was stretch their offense with a series of simple bootleg plays, because as soon as the eight-man front lost gap control, it became more like a six-man front. Then the Broncos could run the ball up and down the field. The Raiders never budged: Davis was the only coach who believed in eight-man fronts more than TV's talking heads do.

## WHEN THEY MAKE IT MORE COMPLICATED THAN IT IS

All a quarterback cares about is this: Is the middle of the field open or closed? That's it. If the middle of the field is open, it means the safeties are playing a Cover 2 shell, and that in turn means that the front will be a seven-man defense. If the middle of the field is closed, however, it means that a safety is covering the middle third of the field and therefore the front will be an eight-man attack. When a quarterback comes to the line of scrimmage, one of his primary presnap reads is to determine where the safeties are. Yours should be, too. Because once you and he pin down that placement, the wheel of possible plays in everyone's heads can begin to spin. If the read is "open," that means the middle seam may be vulnerable, and you can think play-action pass to a tight end who releases straight down the field and sneaks behind a slower linebacker. If the read is "closed," start looking for routes that head toward the sideline.

Once you make that middle-of-the-field read, you can continue to think like a quarterback by determining whether the defense is playing zone or man to man. This one's even less complicated. Before the snap, take a look: If the wideout or tight end comes in motion, is anyone on the defense following him? If the answer is yes, that's man. If it's no, it's zone. How simple is that?

## WHEN THE RECEIVER GETS TOO MUCH CREDIT

On December 13, 2009, Broncos wideout Brandon Marshall set an NFL record by catching 21 passes in a game. I recently rewatched that performance to put that accomplishment in perspective. A couple of things stood out: First, Marshall was targeted a whopping 28 times, and second, his team had just 29 completions total. To say he was the go-to guy is an understatement.

Still, I wondered how many of his catches could be credited to Marshall's talent and how many were the result of the play design. My conservative breakdown was that 17 catches could have been made by any professional receiver. This is no knock on Marshall; I respect his game, his hands, and his skill in getting in and out of cuts smoothly. But although great hands, speed, or leaping ability sometimes can overcome suffocating double teams or an inaccurate quarterback, more often than not it's the scheme that gets a receiver open and makes the difference.

Some version of the following happens all the time in the college game: A receiver runs 10 yards down the field, breaks outside, and makes a catch. There's little man-to-man press coverage in college, so more than likely he'll have run the route against a soft zone, essentially with no one near him. It might as well be a practice drill. Yet the announcer goes all Dick Vitale, screaming about how talented the receiver is to have gotten so open. Stop. The design of the play got him open.

Or think of a well-designed catch this way: At the end of an NBA blowout, when a player snags an uncontested rebound off a missed free throw, it still counts on the stat sheet even though he didn't have to work nearly as hard for it as he did for a similar board in the second quarter. The stats don't make a distinction, but spectators know.

Likewise, when a receiver gets free access downfield and the quarterback hits him right in the hands (running against air is what we call it), credit the scheme, not the receiver.

## WHEN THEY SAY SNOW FAVORS THE RUN

Nothing conjures up gridiron nostalgia quite like a frozen field blanketed in white powder. I mean, that's old-time football right there. Unfortunately, it also means that old-time, outdated football clichés can't be far behind. Here's the worst one: *If it's snowing, the running game will have to take over.* Nope. For a number of reasons it's actually just the opposite. On a snow-covered field the passing game has the advantage.

As long as pass catchers can handle the slick, hard balls, the slippery field conditions favor the player who knows where he's going, not the one who is reacting and trying to keep up. Snow games are like target practice for a quarterback. Running the ball, in contrast, requires dependable footing first and foremost—

not least for the blockers, who need a firm base to drive defenders off the ball.

Sure, the ball is harder to catch. But it's also harder to keep hold of, especially in tight quarters with everyone tugging at it. In the open field it's much easier to maintain a handle when you only have to worry about one or two tacklers who are preoccupied with maintaining their footing. It helps if the receiver has perfected the fundamentals of his position and has the key cuts for all his routes locked into his muscle memory so that he can run them in his sleep—or on a sheet of ice. That feel for a pass route lessens the chance of a fall. Of course, that's the first thing the Patriots practice every spring, with Belichick or one of his coaches standing right in the middle of the defensive backfield ready to pounce and loudly correct a player if he cuts off the wrong foot.

Belichick, as I mentioned before, dabbles in meteorology maybe more than any other coach. He knows what the conditions will be wherever the next game is because he wants to make sure to prepare his team properly. He wants them to have the right shoes. He wants them to have a feel for frozen or wet footballs, so he introduces greased-down or frozen footballs into practice. Sometimes, when the forecast is for rain, he justs dunks the ball in a jug of water before every snap.

So, as with most variables, snow and rain, not to mention sleet and hail, favor the Patriots.

## WHEN THEY PLAY BATTLESHIP FOOTBALL

Do you know the game Battleship? Two people deploy their fleet behind a screen and then take turns calling out coordinates for "bomb" strikes in hopes of hitting the opponent's ships. F-5? Miss. H-5? Miss. G-3? Hit! Followed by G-4, G-5, and G-6 until the ship is sunk. That's how some football play callers work all the time.

They randomly probe for a play that might work, and when they find one, they repeat it again and again, sometimes disguising it with a different formation or look. Needless to say, smart play callers avoid Battleship syndrome.

Probing or guessing from play to play doesn't allow a team to gain control of the game. Of course, game plans inevitably require adjustments on Sunday. But those adjustments shouldn't be haphazard attempts to fix what isn't working or find an opponent's weaknesses. Teams need to have backup plans long before kickoff. Successful in-game tweaks are born of a clear understanding of what the other side is doing to keep you from accomplishing your goals.

Teams that play the Patriots, for example, know that Brady likes to control the middle of the field with the passing game, so they crowd that area with defenders and challenge him to throw the ball outside the numbers. But the Patriots don't counter by blindly probing for weak spots with any old out-breaking route. Whatever they do fits into a master plan—say, two throws to the sidelines to open the middle of the field, followed by a draw play.

That's gamesmanship.

Anything else is Battleship.

## WHEN COACHES DON'T GET ENOUGH CREDIT

In 1966, when Robert Evans was appointed the head of production at Paramount Pictures, most people in the industry shook their heads in disbelief. How could a man with so little experience run a major motion picture studio? At that time Paramount was a financial mess, headed toward bankruptcy, and the studio's new owner, Charles Bluhdorn, believed that only a unique approach that countered the conventional wisdom of his competitors would save the day. That made Evans the right man for the job. Paramount had to evolve or it would perish.

Evans had a simple but revolutionary idea: to move away from the long-standing tradition of blowing most of a film's budget on A-list actors and instead invest in the talent behind the camera. Evans put his money into directors, screenwriters, and great stories (mostly from books) that could be turned into screenplays so strong that they'd transform solid but less-expensive actors into Oscar winners. During his eight-year stint as studio head, Paramount reemerged as a dominant force in Hollywood behind critically acclaimed hits such as *The Godfather, Rosemary's Baby, The Odd Couple,* and *Love Story.*

Talent "behind the camera" is just as important in the NFL. Some fans assume the level of coaching on every staff is equal—and equally high—essentially canceling the other staff out and leaving the most talented team to win. But the truth is that when the salary cap brought parity to the NFL, it also created an Evans-like shift that put a premium on the talent behind the talent. Just like in Hollywood, it took a while for the paychecks to catch up with the philosophy. I still remember sitting with Belichick in Cleveland going over salaries for the upcoming season. When we came to a left tackle, Paul Farren, who was due to make nearly $500,000, Belichick looked at me and said, "I have a hard time with Farren making more than I make." Of course he was right.

Ever since then I've thought that coaching salaries should at least be in line with the minimum salaries for players. Al Davis loved to hire young offensive coordinators or position coaches he could develop into head coaches, partly because it meant he could keep running the defense but also because it saved him a lot of money. He never thought twice about paying players. But coaches? That was another matter. Davis would not have approved of the way the Raiders are paying their new coach, Jon Gruden. But if $100 million, give or take, over 10 years would give Davis a stroke, it is a clear indication of how much top-level coaching is valued in today's NFL.

The problem isn't paying for coaches who can have a huge impact on the success of your team. The problem is paying lots of money for mediocre guys whose impact is negligible at best. Bill Walsh told me—and I told you in Chapter 2—that not all coaches have the same potential impact on the game. A great running back coach might be a player favorite, but he's not going to have much effect on wins and losses. Some coaches are there to execute a plan, not create one. But there are six staff spots—call them rainmakers—that are in a position to make a significant difference one way or another and should be paid accordingly.

Obviously, head coach is one of them. All three coordinators, too. And the offensive and defensive line coaches. Offensive line coaches are often well paid, and deservedly so, because if they can mold one post-third-round draft choice into a capable NFL starter each year, they have more than earned that salary. The defensive line coach, by contrast, is much like a lion tamer—he might as well be wearing a top hat and coat—because his players come from a pool of what is traditionally the most high-strung and hardest-to-control players. Those giant divas on the d-line need a demanding taskmaster. At least that's been my experience. The best teams I've been with featured that kind of lineman—and that kind of coach.

Despite their importance, many coaches remain undervalued simply because it's so hard to quantify what they're worth to a team's success. To help remedy that, I've always wondered whether it would be possible to rank coaches and staffs, to determine what kind of difference they made on a team. I asked some statistics whizzes at the University of California to help me with this idea, and they suggested that I cluster coaches into groups ranked like golf scores (lowest is best). The system we came up with has the top four at each position worth 2.5 points, the next four worth 5 points, and so on. Adding the results gives you a staff total that allows head-to-head comparisons. Obviously, this is not a scientific research project. My coach values are at best only as accurate as my draft grades, but they still can offer some insight.

For instance, let's say the Patriots, with a Hall of Fame head coach and at least three potential head-coaching candidates on the sideline, have a staff total of 37 points and are playing a staff that graded at 80. (Remember, the lower the score, the better.) That opponent would need to have a pretty significant talent advantage to cover its coaching deficit. Can a team's roster be talented enough to overcome a 43-point coaching discrepancy? Probably not. That's why coaching matters, and that's why in a few years a $100 million NFL coach will be considered a bargain.

If you're still not convinced, play the "Belichick game" with me. Think of a team, any team, and ask what its record would be if Belichick coached it. If he left New England tomorrow for Miami, would the Dolphins win the AFC East? It's plausible, right? So don't kid yourself; a top coach is worth as much as a top quarterback.

Now, I might be old, but I don't want to be that geezer who rants and raves about how experience matters. It really does, though, especially on the sidelines. In fact, sometimes Super Bowls are determined by it. Walsh once said to me, "I am a much better coach at 52 than I was at 42; I've got a better grasp." And experience helps the most when game preparation meets game management.

In Super Bowl LI, Belichick felt confident that his team would score a lot of points against the Falcons. It's not that he didn't respect Atlanta's defense; it's just that after careful review he saw how his team would be able to move the ball, especially late in the game. He was so convinced that it was going to be a high-scoring game, in fact, that he began to think about ways to extend a lead from, say, a 20-point advantage to 21. Being up by 20 is nice, but being up by 21 is way better, especially in a high-flying game, since it means your opponent will have to score three touchdowns to beat you. Belichick's solution was to devote two five-minute periods in practice before the Super Bowl to work on the Patriots' collection of two-point conversions.

As it turns out, those plays won the Super Bowl. Entering the fourth quarter, the Pats were down 28–9. After kicking a field goal, they cut the lead to 16 with less than 10 minutes to play. It was still a seemingly impossible deficit for most teams. But not the Patriots. Because they had so much confidence in their two-point conversions, it felt like only a two-score game to them. They ended up using all three of the two-point plays Belichick had them practice—the final one to score the touchdown that won the game in overtime.

Some might call it luck.

The best minds in sports would call it something else.

Branch Rickey, the legendary, visionary baseball man, had a saying that perfectly defines the often misunderstood value of NFL coaching. "Luck," Rickey used to say, "is often the residue of design."

That's why the best coaches get lucky a lot. It's also why when I watch the best coaches on Sunday, my house is blessedly quiet.

# 9

# WWBD

## WHAT WOULD BELICHICK DO?

*The only sign we have in the locker room is a quote from*
The Art of War: *"Every battle is won before it is fought."*

—BILL BELICHICK

**W**hat would Belichick do?" is a popular question made famous by Bill Simmons, the Sports Guy, Boston's most obsessed fan. While observing and commentating on (and, okay, cheering for) the Patriots' dynasty during the last two decades, Simmons formulated his WWBD framework and applied it across the sports landscape, especially as a lens through which to examine the NBA. Here's an example: Are you wondering if the Celtics should show loyalty to a highly paid and beloved veteran once his production and skills diminish? Well, ask yourself: What would Belichick do? Answer: Send the guy packing like

Drew Bledsoe, replace him with someone younger and cheaper, and deflect the public-relations fallout with a playoff run. See? "What would Belichick do?" is easy, insightful, and kind of fun, too.

Bill also happens to be my boss at the website The Ringer, so I hope he won't mind that I've borrowed his premise for this chapter. Throughout this book I've shown you many examples of what Belichick does. Now I want to go deeper and explain how and why he does what he does. I've placed an examination of the following guiding principles into their own chapter because I strongly believe that not only are they the root of Belichick's success but they also can foster success in other leaders, team builders, decision makers, and innovators.

Go to Amazon and search for books that talk about Warren Buffett, chairman and CEO of Berkshire Hathaway, who is generally considered the most successful investor of our time. More than 1,000 titles await your purchase. Why? Because everyone wants to read about how he has amassed his unfathomable fortune. To investors, WWBD stands for something a little different: What would Buffett do? To my mind, Belichick is the Buffett of coaching; his rate of winning is far above the competition's. People who want to know what Buffett's secret formula is should want to know about Belichick's, too. (And no, it's not as simple as "draft Tom Brady.")

Look, I get it; Belichick is not a fan favorite if you live in Buffalo or Pittsburgh or Manhattan or Cleveland or, really, just about anywhere that isn't flying the Patriots flag. But if you can put aside your rooting interest long enough to see how the guy accomplishes his goals, it may do some good. You don't have to root for the Patriots to take away some specific action points from the team's two decades of accomplishment. A deeper understanding of the WWBD concept can guide us all.

The first time I met Belichick was in Mobile, Alabama, in 1989, the original home of Mardi Gras in the States. (Look it up.) In 1951, Mobile began hosting another weeklong celebration of a secular religion: the Senior Bowl. Long before the draft went high tech and the Combine was created and analytics became deciding factors in the NFL draft, the Senior Bowl was the pro game's annual convention, as scouts and coaches from every team flocked to it to get their best look at all the top prospects. If you were a college kid and were invited to play in the game, that was what you did: You showed up, no questions asked. The same thing went for anyone in the business of football. For decades Mobile served as the NFL's de facto annual industry convention, and the old Hilton on Government Avenue was its headquarters. This was long before and even after the Super Bowl became an industry event unto itself. The Super Bowl has never been the nuts-and-bolts working week that the Senior Bowl was.

It was in the Hilton's coffee shop that I had my first encounter with Belichick. The Browns were looking for a coach, and their general manager, Ernie Accorsi, was handling the search. As Accorsi and Belichick chatted, I walked over to their table to say hello. Little did I know then that many of my best days in the game would be by the side of the guy sipping a Coke.

Belichick was just 37 at the time, and so that spring the Browns job went to veteran coach Bud Carson, who didn't last even two seasons in Cleveland. The next time around, though, Art Modell hired the right guy, thanks in large part to a fervent endorsement from one lifelong Browns fan, the college basketball coaching icon Bobby Knight. Within minutes of Belichick getting the Cleveland job and arriving at the team's offices in Berea, Ohio, I had my first assignment—and my first glimpse into his unique methodology. With barely a hello, he handed me a three-holed sheet of notebook paper on which he'd outlined in his meticulous handwriting an evaluation he wanted me to perform on every player on the roster: strong points, weak points, summary, injury history, playing time, special teams role, contract information, production in every phase the player participated in, and general prediction for his role the next year and the year after. No small talk accompanied the delegation of the task—not even a real explanation, to be honest—just "here's what I need." And I loved it.

Almost immediately everyone in the organization had a specific task like this and a new focus to move the franchise forward and make the team better. From the beginning, he was a genius at focusing everyone on the primary objective. No less of a control freak than Nick Saban once said of his former boss, "He expertly defines what everybody in the organization is supposed to do." That description sounds simple and mundane, but it is not often the way things work when guys become head coaches for the first time. Thus, it was clear from the beginning of Belichick's tenure in Cleveland that he wasn't quite like anyone else who has coached the game.

Most first-time head coaches take a few days to acclimate, regroup, and, if we're being honest, celebrate after getting their shot. But after his introductory press conference in Cleveland, Belichick took only about five minutes to let it soak in. Want to guess what he did next?

See, this is how Simmons's WWBD premise works. If you're ever wondering what to do after landing your dream job, ask yourself this question: What would Belichick do?

Answer: Take charge and get to work.

Because this technique provides such good insight into Belichick's distinct way of thinking and problem solving, I've decided to apply the WWBD lens to several different scenarios, starting with the process of book writing. So I now ask myself, "WWBD next?"

My guess is cut the pleasantries and get to the meat of the chapter.

So that's what I'll do.

# COMBATING COMPLACENCY: WWBD?

Most people focus on Belichick's five Super Bowl rings as his ultimate achievement, but I think that in light of the parity in today's
NFL, guiding seven straight teams to the AFC championship
game will go down beside Joe DiMaggio's 56-game hitting streak
as one of the unbreakable records in sports. With that much
success—whether in football or in the business world—sooner or
later the challenge is how to maintain your drive and intensity.

By now, I think my admiration for Bruce Springsteen is abun-
dantly clear. I love the songs, but I admire the singer more, because he works so hard at what he does. I've seen him play "Born
to Run" in concert dozens of times, yet at each concert it is as if
he is playing it for the first time. It's what informs my Born to Run
Theory, a corollary of the 10,000-hour rule that Malcolm Gladwell
popularized. The idea is that to master anything you need at least
10,000 hours of practice. What Gladwell left out of the theory he
documented so well in his book *Outliers* was that once mastery oc-
curs, boredom can set in and undermine that mastery. It's hard to
do the same thing day after day; it's human nature to fall prey to
the grind. But Springsteen has played "Born to Run" almost every
night—night after night after night—since 1975, and it's always
with real enthusiasm and passion. He never seems tired of playing
the song and therefore never cheats anyone in the audience who
might be hearing it live for the first time.

In the same way, Belichick never allows himself to get bored,
which means he never cuts a corner or underestimates an opponent. He never thinks he knows it all even if he's played a team a
dozen times. If he were a high school teacher, he wouldn't just dust
off the lessons from last year to teach the next class. (How many
of you aced exams in high school after looking over your older sib-
ling's tests because the teacher didn't change questions from one
year to the next? Okay, don't answer, but you get my point.) The

fact that you've been right for a while doesn't mean you will always be right. Buffett admits to spending several hours of his day just reading (mostly company annual reports). He's pushing 90 years and $90 billion, yet he still strives to be better by trying to learn a bit more each and every day. Reading and research is the best remedy for boredom. But it also guarantees that your thinking will continue to evolve.

Self-motivation for a successful coach can be a challenge. We tend to worry that a huge new contract will cause a player to lose his edge, but no one ever considers that with a coach, even though, unlike players' contracts, theirs are fully guaranteed. Worse, it's those with the most experience who know which corners to cut and how to spend a little less time preparing. But none of that has ever been a problem for Belichick. He still treats every season, every game—heck, every possession—as if it were the only one that matters.

Whether the Patriots have just won the Super Bowl or not, the first thing Belichick does is wipe the slate clean. One of his favorite sayings is "To live in the past is to die in the present." It's why you see no Super Bowl trophies as you walk through the players' entrance and why all the photos from the previous season are removed as soon as the season is over. That clean slate demands a trip back to basic principles and fundamentals after a detailed examination of the current process. Each spring feels almost as if it were Belichick's first day on the job in Cleveland all over again. He explains to coaches and staff that the team cannot be the same as it was before charging them with figuring out how to improve its every aspect.

After the 2015 season, Belichick asked me to break down the successful teams in the NFL; after playing in six Super Bowls he still wanted to know what other teams did well, how their front offices and coaching staffs operated, and what lessons we could learn from them. My report was both a disappointment and a relief. It turned out that none of the teams I studied had much to tell us that we didn't already know. Dig deeper into college free agents? Keep working the bottom of the roster? We did all that.

It is no surprise that a guy who is on an eternal quest to learn more is also a persistent teacher. Whenever there is a holiday— Martin Luther King Day or Labor Day or Arbor Day—Belichick uses it as an opportunity to educate his team. He might ask players to explain the difference between Memorial Day and Veterans Day. (Do you know?) Guys who have been around for a long while know that these questions are coming and tell the newbies to prepare. That is exactly what Belichick wants. It's his way of opening up the lines of communication off the field so that they will remain open on it. He wants to push the connection between curiosity and improvement.

Bill Walsh, too, was forever talking about world leaders and bringing in speakers to address the team. (I suppose I could have called this chapter "What Would Bill Do?" to cover all my bases.) Walsh forged a deep friendship with Harry Edwards, a sociologist from the University of California, who over the years assisted the coach in many endeavors that made the team better—from interviewing prospects to understanding the challenges facing players from disadvantaged backgrounds. Edwards might have had the title of consultant, but he was more than that. He was a team builder, a culture builder, a unifier.

What has impressed me the most about Belichick and Walsh is their self-awareness. With the same kind of success in the NFL many lesser men have become close-minded, authoritarian, and lazy. Instead of hiding or denying their shortcomings, the Bills embraced them and tried to correct them.

In Walsh's case, he saw the locker room changing and understood that he didn't have all the tools needed to relate to younger players. Edwards helped Walsh understand where modern players were coming from and how they were likely to react and behave because of their background. Walsh actually changed the way he addressed the team and the language he used to present his schemes on the basis of what he learned from Edwards.

He could have just said, "I'm the boss. Look at these Super Bowl rings; they'll have to learn to relate to me." But he knew that if his organization was to avoid complacency and continue to thrive, everyone needed to learn, develop, and grow, including the head coach.

## MAKING DIFFICULT DECISIONS: WWBD?

When it comes to the art of making tough choices, something every great leader must master, I always come back to two anecdotes regarding the office of the president. In a 1954 speech to the Second Assembly of the World Council of Churches, President Dwight D. Eisenhower, quoting J. Roscoe Miller, the president of Northwestern University, said: "I have two kinds of problems: the urgent and the important. The urgent are not important, and the important are never urgent." It is said that he ran the country by organizing his workload with this "Eisenhower principle," attacking the important issues, not what the press thought needed his attention at that moment. I also love the story of Attorney General Robert F. Kennedy bringing a significant problem into the Oval Office and his brother, the president, asking why everyone walked in only with the hard stuff, to which Bobby replied that it was because they could handle the easy stuff themselves.

Now, obviously, running a team is nothing like running a country, but still, each day a head coach has to make tough, hard choices and has to do it under extremely tight deadlines and incredible pressure and sometimes with the whole world watching.

Just as Bobby Kennedy pointed out, the art of decision making begins with knowing what to concern yourself with. George Allen, the former Rams and Redskins coach, was legendary for his obsessive and sometimes destructive attention to what the Kennedys would have called the easy stuff. As the story goes, Allen wanted to save time during lunch by making the players' cafeteria more efficient, so he devised a method that split the soup line into one for players who wanted crackers and one for those who didn't. Yes, crackers. Urgent? Well, to the hungry guys at the end of the line, maybe. But important? Come on. I mean, it didn't help the team win more football games, although it may well have made it heavy favorites in the Souper Bowl.

In all seriousness, though, one of the consistent themes throughout Belichick's illustrious career and one of the things that differentiate him from nearly all his peers is his grasp of the art of tough decision making. It started in Cleveland, when Belichick made the wildly unpopular but absolutely correct decision to bench a hometown hero, quarterback Bernie Kosar. Similarly, in 2002 in New England, Belichick's decision to trade another very popular, loyal player, Drew Bledsoe, to a divisional rival was met with serious blowback. Why give Bledsoe the chance to come back and haunt you? Al Davis never would have entertained such a move. (And it's an incessant fear or superstition among most fans, too.) His steadfast mandate was that the Raiders not only would never trade a player—no matter his talent level—to any team in their division, they would never trade him to any team on the next season's schedule. He just wouldn't take the risk. Belichick, though, will do business with any team. He doesn't worry about a traded player taking his revenge because he is confident that he knows the player well enough to neutralize him on the field. Bledsoe started six games against the Patriots after the trade and won one of them while throwing 11 interceptions. (For the answer to why fans and a lot of football professionals continue to believe it's dumb to trade players to rivals, you can look to the field of behavioral economics, the study of human biases in judgment and decision making. People tend to view the world through the most "available" information, and in the case of trades between two rivals, the rare examples when they bite the trading team tend to stand out in most people's minds.)

Though Belichick has made other moves that have looked impetuous or counterproductive to the outside world, I can assure you they were not. He is nothing if not patient, reviewing all the relevant information first. He listens and reads and analyzes before collating it all to determine his own idea of a player's worth. Take Danny Amendola, for instance. When he's healthy, he's a coach's dream, but the wide receiver's injury history makes him a player primed for release every season. Belichick weighs Amendola's leadership value so highly that he always saved a spot on the roster for him even as some assistants argued strongly against it. Belichick's patience—some might call it stubbornness—was rewarded time and again. Amendola was Mr. Clutch in his tenure with the Patriots, making important catches at the most crucial times.

Belichick is a master at measuring the risk/reward of any potential transaction. He also is the rare football mind who can lead players on the field with a deep personal connection as a coach and then, when acting as a general manager, instantly and ruthlessly set aside those feelings to calculate a player's true economic worth. He never lets the emotions of one role interfere with his calculations in another.

A year after the Bledsoe trade, Belichick lost another team leader, Pro Bowl safety Lawyer Milloy, just days before opening weekend. When Milloy wouldn't agree to a pay cut, Belichick released him, leaving him to sign with the Bills, New England's opening-day opponent. After the Bills crushed the Patriots 31–0, longtime ESPN analyst Tom Jackson suggested that the Patriots must hate their coach. Talking directly into the camera, he unloaded on Belichick. You think maybe Jackson overreacted? Belichick was only doing what he had decided was best for the team. He made a call and didn't turn back.

Milloy, by the way, never made another Pro Bowl.

The Patriots ended the season as Super Bowl champs.

Belichick has repeated this formula—unceremoniously cutting ties with beloved vets before their trade value significantly drops—so many times that I've lost track. But the list includes Deion Branch, Mike Vrabel, Richard Seymour, Adam Vinatieri, Vince Wilfork, Logan Mankins, and Jamie Collins, to name a few.

In San Francisco, Walsh made decisions the same way, often meeting with the same kind of blowback, which he handled in the exact same manner—by not caring at all. In 1985, for instance, he made the tough—and unpopular—choice to push wide receiver Freddie Solomon into retirement to make room for Jerry Rice. As much as Walsh loved his players, the team always came first. In Walsh's mind, thinking of his players as human beings first meant only that he was obligated to not let them twist in the wind until he came to a resolution.

Walsh called this the three F's of decision making: firmness, fairness, fast.

Having all the necessary information, Walsh said, allows the decision maker to be firm and unmoved by outside influences. That's why guys like Walsh and Belichick weigh each move, understanding every consequence, before acting. Knowledge breeds conviction. And with all three Fs working in unison, the team has the best chance of coming out ahead.

In 1986 I added my own F to Walsh's list: fibbing. That year we took a third-round chance on a talented but raw receiver and return man named John Taylor out of tiny Delaware State. I had seen Taylor in action and loved what I saw, so I pushed hard for him. But in rookie camp and then in the preseason, it was clear that he was not ready to play on Sundays. His talent was NFL-ready, but he couldn't handle the volume of the offense or lock down all the skills needed for the pro game. Walsh saw his talent, too, but the roster numbers weren't adding up. John McVay, our general manager, would torture me by whispering that my guy wasn't going to make it. He wasn't being mean; he was just reading the signs. He told me to call other teams to gauge interest in Taylor. I almost got a bite from my friend Gary Horton, a pro scout with Tampa Bay, but in the end the Bucs passed. Horton's superiors figured that if Walsh was willing to get rid of Taylor, he couldn't be any good.

Back then, I was the Turk, the guy who got the names from McVay on cutdown day before fetching doomed players for the meeting they did not want to have. In those days there was no practice squad, and so a player either made the roster or was out of a job. The only leeway was provided by the injured reserve list, which allowed teams to keep a rehabbing player under contract until he was healthy. Teams often took advantage of that loophole, stashing a player on the IR to keep him around for the next season. Well, I knew Taylor was on the cut list, so I pulled him over in the hallway and advised him to see our head trainer, Lindsy McLean. "You need to tell him you hurt your lower back and that you're in significant pain," I advised. Taylor stared at me a little confused but then nodded and ran off to the training room. The next thing I saw was McLean running down the hall toward the steps to find McVay to let him know we didn't need to cut Taylor because he wasn't healthy.

With Taylor safely stockpiled, we were soon on the road again to scout the next batch of college talent. By the time I got back to the office later in the season, Taylor was the talk of the team. His back had, ahem, healed, and with just a few more weeks of reps and study he looked like a completely different player. Walsh was impressed. So was McVay. Taylor went on to catch 393 passes and score 49 touchdowns in the regular season and playoffs, and he won three Super Bowls in San Francisco, including one in which he made a last-minute game-winning catch.

One way or the other, we got the Taylor decision right, and almost 30 years later it still feels good. I bet Belichick feels the same way with 99 percent of the personnel moves he made over the years. Of course, there is at least one with which he may never be at peace: trading Jimmy Garoppolo. As I described earlier in the book, Belichick loves Garoppolo; we drafted him because we were as sure as we could be that he would be the heir apparent to Brady. He already had shown that he could fill those shoes—I don't need to tell you just how big those shoes are—whenever he was asked to. During Brady's suspension at the start of the 2016 season, Garoppolo ran the team flawlessly. The kid was the real deal.

And the rest of the league knew it. During the 2017 off-season, lots of GMs came calling for the young star in waiting, but Belichick had no intention of giving him up. Brady was 40, for heaven's sake. His days had to be numbered, right? The Patriots looked to lock up Garoppolo with an extension. The only problem was that Brady is a beloved idol who shares an agent—Don Yee—with Garoppolo. That meant Yee held all the cards and for once Belichick wouldn't be dealing from strength. To keep Garoppolo, the Patriots probably were going to have to franchise him, pay him like a starting QB (which would blow up their salary cap), or watch him walk in free agency.

There was a fourth option: He could have made an impossibly tough call and cut Brady—risking being run out of New England for the reward of handing the job to Garoppolo. With his track record of calculated, unemotional personnel judgments informed only by the long-term needs of the team, that's what you would expect Belichick to do.

If the call was his alone to make anyway—which, the word is, it was not. Because when Belichick passed on those off-season offers, it was clear that he had no intention of losing Garoppolo, and the assumption had to be that he was preparing to franchise him. Otherwise, it meant Belichick was just keeping his fingers crossed in the hope that Brady would opt to retire on his own. And Belichick does not depend on fate.

But for whatever reason—Belichick has been as closed-lipped about this as he is about everything—the option to tag Garoppolo was dropped. And once it was, Belichick had to act fast, before he lost all his leverage and a franchise quarterback with nothing to show for it. So he did the next most clear-eyed thing. He traded Garoppolo to the 49ers.

It may well be that this trade—a franchise QB for a second-round pick—goes down as the worst deal of Belichick's career. And the question will be hard to ignore: In the ultimate WWBD moment, did Belichick, of all people, stray from the tenets of his own philosophy?

## DEVELOPING A WINNING TEMPERAMENT: WWBD?

When Belichick and I were together in Cleveland, Bill Parcells would call me to ask, "How's Doom doing?" At first I had no earthly idea who "Doom" was. But after Parcells explained his favorite nickname for Belichick, it made perfect sense. Belichick does not present as the most positive, fun-loving person in the world, and Parcells, who is one of those guys who always know exactly what buttons to push, enjoyed needling Belichick about his dour reputation.

But I can promise you this: Belichick's world is not nearly as dire as he makes it out to be. In fact, away from the media, he is caring and kind, and he actually has a dry, wicked sense of humor. The human side of Belichick is different from the one most people see on Sunday: less intense and incredibly generous. During our time in Cleveland he gave money he earned from his radio show to the coaching staff as a bonus at the end of the year. When we beat a team in our division, he passed out hundred-dollar bills as thank-yous. Trust me, if he calls you a friend, he will give you whatever you need. Most people never see that side of him. They see only a gruff media-unfriendly cipher, and that's too bad. Of course, Belichick couldn't care less that only a few select people know his warmer, more upbeat side.

In season Belichick is actually at his most positive at the start of his Wednesday team meeting as he convincingly details the strengths of the next opponent. In this role he's a spin doctor extraordinaire, making even the lamest quarterback seem like Peyton Manning. But in his own way, Belichick means it. He points out worst-case scenarios because that helps him sell the message that each game has to be taken seriously. What makes his players listen is that they know that every complimentary thing he says about the opponent is plausibly true, because it's all backed up by facts. He never cries wolf about a wolf that isn't there. Doom always has the tracks in the snow to prove the wolf exists.

I hate to contradict Parcells, but a better description of Belichick's temperament is a term I coined called *realistic optimism*. (Which, I'll grant you, isn't great for nickname purposes.) Walsh was the same way. He saw himself as a teacher and therefore believed in being positive with his pupils, building them up rather than breaking them down. Still, he was too well informed not to understand that trouble always lurked. But it's unfair to call either Belichick or Walsh a pessimist, let alone an agent of doom. A pessimist leads an unhappy life, waiting for the next bad thing, never trusting the emotional highs. A realistic optimist may seem a crank to casual observers, but in actuality he's quite content.

That's the case because he sees the world as it is and knows he has the means to conquer whatever challenges await. Realistic optimism is the offspring of confidence and self-assurance, something that both Walsh and Belichick had in abundance. These two coaches achieved spectacularly because at their core they knew exactly who they were, and they knew those traits were unique and extremely valuable in a copycat league such as the NFL.

When one team has success, another wants to duplicate its path to good fortune. It's what I call the "Texas snake problem." Texas is home to two species—the Texas coral snake and the Mexican milk snake—which look very much alike. The Texas coral snake

is almost black-mamba-level dangerous; its venom can kill. The
Mexican milk snake can't hurt you; it's an impostor. It thrives
only as long as it can dupe predators into thinking it is dangerous.
Teams try to get away with this kind of lazy copycatting all the
time. They try to succeed by hiring a coach who has all the same
markings and temperaments as Belichick or Walsh without really
understanding what makes both men killers: drive, decision making, and realistic optimism.

But mimicking success rarely earns success. Even in New England. Every once in a while a Patriots coach will watch tape on
the treadmill because Belichick does or tailor his clothes with a
pair of scissors. But when that's as deep as the imitation goes, the
players and the rest of the staff see right through it. A guy like
that is inevitably a short-timer.

What wouldn't Belichick do? Fake it.

# 10

# FEARLESS FORECAST

## THE FUTURE OF FOOTBALL

*If you don't like change, you are going to like irrelevance even less.*
—ERIC SHINSEKI, US ARMY GENERAL (RET.)

One of my first memories of color television (yes, I am old) was watching *Batman* on ABC every Tuesday and Wednesday night in the 1960s; the program featured Adam West in the title role and Burt Ward as Robin, his trusted companion in tights. I loved how the dynamic duo always managed to catch the arch-villains by the end of each two-episode story arc even though I secretly wondered why the Joker or King Tut never pulled out a revolver and, you know, just shot the unarmed Caped Crusaders. I have to say that my all-time-favorite scenes were the ones that took place down in the Batcave. I just loved that Batcave. All those crime-fighting gadgets seemed so far-fetched and impossible. I mean, the Batcomputer solving one of the Riddler's riddles? How'd it do that? Of course, if you watch the show today—and I'm not too proud to admit that I do—one of the first things you notice is that most of those crazy make-believe contraptions down in the Batcave are now part of our daily lives. Batcomputers, Batmaps, Batphones, Batcircuit streaming TV; as crazy as it sounds, the show was actually a fairly accurate peek into tomorrow. It reminds me (of course) of a lyric from a Springsteen song that says we're all "Livin' in the future . . . And none of this has happened yet."

Except now it has.

So . . . what's next? I'm often asked what the game will look like 10 years from now—or 20. Some worry—and more than a few hope—that there won't even be football down the line. It's safe to say that the game I love is at a crossroads. Unfortunately, those inside that world just aren't conditioned to think that way. The nineteenth-century philosopher Thomas Carlyle said: "Our main business is not to see what lies dimly at a distance, but to do what lies clearly at hand." That is the essence of football. Inside the game, what matters most is the next opponent, the next series, the next play. However, from my current perspective I can see that change will be necessary to keep football alive. I'm convinced that it can actually be a good thing, because the changes most needed—adjustments to safety regimens, improvements in technology—will spark an evolution in strategies and the game itself. The futuristic elements of football that we can only dream about today will come to fruition one day, and if you love this sport the way I do, that's an exciting and uplifting thought to consider.

As we come to the end of this book, I thought it would be fun and maybe even helpful to spend a few pages imagining what comes next for my favorite game.

———

P layer health is the top agenda item for owners, players, and fans alike. At least that's what they all claim. And whether they're being truthful or just mouthing platitudes, it needs to be—today, tomorrow, next week, next year, and for as long as football is played.

Trying to make what is a brutal game less dangerous has always been a challenge, and that isn't about to change. Modern football was actually launched—in 1906—with rules that made the forward pass explicitly legal to make the game safer. The technique had been "invented" a few years earlier by Native American players at what were then called Indian schools, who used it to great effect when playing against larger white players. Most high school and college coaches—there was no professional game to speak of then—disliked forward passing, which they thought of as a gimmick. But in 1905, around 20 prep and college players died as a result of injuries sustained on the gridiron. (In that era, most organized football was a "mass momentum" rushing game in which all 22 guys on the field went headfirst at one another.) Spurred on by President Theodore Roosevelt, a football fan who was being pressured to ban the game, college rule makers hoped that by encouraging forward passing—and later by lengthening the distance needed for a first down from 5 to 10 yards and increasing the number of downs from three to four—they would open up the game, making it more exciting even as they made it less hazardous.

And it worked—until it didn't. Some people blame larger and faster athletes. Others blame improved equipment that gives players a false sense of invulnerability. Still others blame poor tackling techniques. I think it's a combination of all three, but whatever the root causes, no one wants to see what happened to Steelers linebacker Ryan Shazier on a *Monday Night Football* broadcast late in the 2017 season. Defending a short crossing route, Shazier lowered his head to make a tackle—as players do hundreds of times a game—and immediately grabbed at his back before going limp.

As he was taken off the field, immobilized on a stretcher, everyone watching could only hope he would be all right. (Although he continues to improve, his return to football is highly unlikely.) There's no getting around the fact that horrific injuries stemming from routine plays are increasingly common on NFL fields.

Can we prevent it from happening?

No.

I'm sorry, but that's the unvarnished truth. That said, in the last few years there has been a concerted effort to make the game safe—or as safe as it can be—and it has begun to influence the way things are done on the field.

When I was with the 49ers in the 1980s, we had Ronnie Lott, one of the greatest cornerbacks ever to grace the field. Did he lead with his head? Sometimes. Did he hit harder than just about anyone else? Always. Did he use those two parts of his game to physically intimidate opponents and take over games? Absolutely. In fact, when we faced the Los Angeles Rams and their Hall of Fame running back Eric Dickerson, we swapped our free safety Dwight Hicks with Lott so that Lott could patrol the middle of the field and use his power—and his sheer presence—to wear down Dickerson. A few years later, Belichick, looking for his own Ronnie Lott, drafted Eric Turner, a big guy with a love for contact, at the top of the 1991 draft for the Browns. In Lott and Turner's day, receivers weren't eager to range across the middle for fear of being demolished as they laid out to make a catch. The rib-crushing reputations of Lott and Turner were like a twelfth defender.

That said, I'm not so sure we'd take Turner or Lott so high in the draft today.

Recent safety-first changes make me think that guys like that, even when they tackle with the proper technique, can't have the same impact. In fact, when the Jets made LSU's Jamal Adams a high pick in 2017, my initial reaction was, "Sure, the guy is a great player, but the rules will prevent him from dominating in the league." Nowadays, why would you spend a high draft pick or pay a lot of money to protect the middle of the field or intimidate receivers when both tactics have been legislated out of the game? Cutting across the middle is a less fraught proposition now that "defenseless" receivers are protected by the prospect of unnecessary roughness penalties on overly aggressive defensive backs, who also face huge fines and even suspensions. To be fair, such protections go only so far: Eagles safety Malcolm Jenkins knocked Patriots wide receiver Brandin Cooks out of Super Bowl LII with a crushing blow that was completely legal; a lot of good those rules did Cooks. Still, a player's ability to intimidate definitely has been curtailed by those "defenseless player" rules and the crackdown on helmet-to-helmet collisions. Thus, using a top-10 pick on a guy whose game features intimidation feels like a bit of a waste.

I still think Adams will be an excellent pro, but will he be a force, a presence? I don't believe so. And going forward, this will be an issue in front offices. Talent executives will have to understand how increased safety initiatives change certain players' value. More and more, defending the pass is about coverage, not collision. The game is a skill and space game now. No matter how hard he hits, if a defensive back cannot hit in space or make plays in the passing game—bat down balls or intercept them—it won't matter. Unless a player can have an impact on the game on all three downs, he will lose value. I sympathize with players now being punished for playing the game in the physical style they were taught when they were young, but the rules have turned bangers into more of a liability than an asset.

When I think about making the game safer, my mind wanders to that robot featured in Fox's graphics. In a perfect world all the players in the league would be dressed in a protective shell like that guy. But it's not so easy. Players don't like to feel constricted or weighed down. They want to be able to play fast and without hindrance. Many of them won't wear large shoulder pads, and even though NFL rules mandate knee and thigh pads, which help reduce injuries, players hate wearing them. Until the guys on the field learn to value safety more than performance, they are never going to lobby for safer equipment if they think it will limit them in any way. Given the chance, I bet some of them would go without a helmet if they thought it would make them faster. (I'm exaggerating—but only a little.) It's not talked about nearly enough, but every stakeholder in the game must make a concerted effort to educate players on the risks they face and how to mitigate them. That includes schools, conferences, leagues, teams, coaches, suits, and the players' union.

While we're on the subject of helmets, there are smart people who think that if you removed face masks from them right now, players might be less inclined to lead with their heads. I don't buy it. Football skills are based on muscle memory and therefore are to a large degree instinctive. Unless players grow up tackling without a face mask—and good luck getting parents to agree to that—at some point they will unconsciously revert to their old ways. And if the game was on the line and it felt like a headfirst tackle was the best way to stop the ball carrier, every player in the NFL would go helmet-first, face mask or not.

Instead, I have to believe there is some next-generation head protection just waiting to be created. For that matter, you'd think someone could invent body protection that allows for full range of motion. I mean, today there are bulletproof vests that look like something Mr. Rogers wore every afternoon. Surely, with $14 billion in revenues, the NFL can afford to research and develop some appropriate armor for the players. I am not a headgear engineer or a neuroscientist, but I know that if my game is to survive, those roles will be as important as those of players and coaches.

Of course, rules, equipment, and fundamentals can solve only so much of the problem. At the core of the issue is the fact that the players keep getting faster and stronger, and that means more impact-related injuries. I remember being in Cleveland at a reunion honoring the great Jim Brown, the storied running back, and noticing that Brown seemed like he was nearly twice the size of his left tackle, Dick Schafrath. Linemen then were not the giants they are today. That growth will just continue, which means collisions, even legal ones, will be more violent.

In addition, careers now last longer on average, and that can only increase the cumulative damage that players will incur. There were no 40-year-olds playing at Tom Brady's level 40 years ago. Maybe he's a once-in-a-generation freak, but it's just as likely that his fanatical conditioning program—from nutrition to workouts to next-gen recovery techniques—are what's keeping him revving at such a high level. I would expect that we'll see even more research into and focus on nutrition and conditioning in football.

It's no exaggeration to say that Brady's body truly is his temple. In the old days, players treated their bodies more like carnival tents. Before the 1980s, most guys didn't waste the off-season staying fit. That's what training camp was for. In my time, though, I never spoke to a player who didn't say he was either heading to a workout or just getting back from one. Never.

Potential wide receivers or defensive backs eligible for the draft are just as predictable. When I ask them what they'll run in the 40, the answer is always the same: 4.44. Twenty years ago that time was extremely rare. Trust me, I kept track of all the sub-4.50 timers at the Combine and recorded no more than a handful of players that fast out of the 250 invited each year. Today I no longer bother. I'd run out of ink. A sub-4.5 is the standard, not the exception, and with that increase in speed comes an increase in impact velocity. No rule change can fix or reverse that, not unless you can change the fundamentals of physics or take tackling out of the game. And football without tackling isn't football. I mean, how would you like to watch the Pro Bowl every Sunday? Ending tackling ends the sport. Although I do not suggest messing with the basic premise of the game, I can recommend a few healthy changes.

Most important, we need to develop better ways to teach young players the fundamentals of tackling. As it is, every responsible coach in the country now teaches players to "see what they hit." It's the first lesson of tackling. In fact, there's a giant sign on every locker room door in the NFL reminding players to keep their heads up. The problem is that until very recently tacklers were taught to lead with their helmets, and that will take a while, perhaps even a generation, to unlearn.

From the earliest age kids need to learn to play the game "the right way." I am a big fan of Pop Warner football, but I agree with all the recent studies that say that the bodies (and brains) of kids that age are just not ready to hit. The rush to introduce tackling leads to lifelong bad—and dangerous—habits. Another negative of Pop Warner is that too many young kids have yet to find their niche on the field. For example, a fat kid (like I was) is automatically assigned to play offensive line, when in a few years it's perfectly possible he will lean out and become a dynamite wide receiver. Problem is, if he has had a bad experience in the trenches, he'll never stick around long enough to find his fit at a skill position. More than likely he'll move on to another sport, and that's not good for football, a sport in which youth participation numbers have been in steady decline.

To counter that, we need to develop passion for the game as well as the fundamentals to play it. A recent study advocated keeping kids away from tackle football until high school, and I agree. Youth football should be primarily a skill camp, teaching kids how to play a variety of positions properly. It will keep players healthy and interested until they are better able to deal with the rigors of tackle football.

Bill Walsh in his own way was ahead of the curve on this. He pretty much invented the concept of keeping professional players fresh for Sundays by cutting down on padded practices during the week. He was no finesse coach; he definitely understood the importance of physicality. But he knew that going all out all the time was counterproductive. In Cleveland, though, Belichick noticed that whenever his players didn't wear pads, practice was slow and sloppy. As a result, he actually spent time teaching our guys how to get the most out of practicing without pads: how to take the right steps, use the proper footwork, make the necessary moves. It led to more high-intensity practices that were truer simulations of a game with a much lower risk of injury or fatigue.

Now, because of rules limiting padded practices during the season, it is more important than ever for teams to figure out how to re-create game intensity while practicing in shorts during the week. How do you improve technique without contact? I'm not certain, but I know that coaches will have to find a way to address this catch-22: instilling the proper fundamentals of tackling while limiting the amount of contact in practice. Today teams use moving, motorized tackling dummies to help perfect technique. I'm curious to see what the next generation of computer-enhanced and robotic tackling equipment will look like.

Another simple way to keep players healthy is to give them the proper time to heal by increasing game-day rosters from 46 to the full 53. More eligible players means teams wouldn't have to pressure guys to return to the field (often through the use of painkilling injections) before they are 100 percent ready.

Now, I know this next suggestion is bold and perhaps drastic, but bear with me: I think making the games shorter would solve many of football's biggest problems. Sixty minutes is a long time. How about playing 48, 12 minutes a quarter, with maybe an 8-minute overtime? (Calm down. I understand any changes to the official game time would screw up comparisons to all the historic stats. But the height of the pitcher's mound keeps changing and the DH blew up American League ERAs, and everybody in baseball somehow survived.) It's just simple math, really: Fewer minutes means fewer impacts, which means fewer injuries. Also, all those injuries caused by late-game fatigue and poor technique could be avoided. And with the game's current emphasis on playing with tempo, cutting game time by 12 minutes wouldn't affect scoring or the drama all that much; in fact, it might enhance it.

With each possession being that much more vital, coaches would have to utilize a different strategy. Instead of today's average of 12 possessions a game, teams would get maybe 9. Each series of offensive downs that didn't end in a score could cost the team the win. The whole game would become one desperate two-minute drill after another.

Did you see Super Bowl LII? It would be like that, only shorter. I rest my case.

And yes, I know, taking 12 minutes out of the game reduces the commercial space networks could sell. So make the halftimes longer. It will have the added benefit of offering teams extra time to get their adjustments down and medical issues dealt with. Make the time between quarters slightly longer, too. Better that the commercials run then anyway, as it means fewer in-game interruptions to mess with the flow of the game. Would paying fans feel cheated? I don't think so. The games would be more exciting. Less would be much more.

Along with reducing the game from 60 minutes to 48, my futuristic league would reduce time-outs from three to one in each half (the two-minute warning would stay). Coaches still will need to manage the clock correctly, but that strategy would change a bit. In the fourth quarter, a trailing team would be reluctant to punt the ball away, as fewer time-outs would have them rightfully concerned that they might not get it back. Coaches will need to find a different way to gain control of the clock. Don't worry; it can be done. Think back to Super Bowl LI. The Pats came back from 28–3 and still had two time-outs remaining when the game entered overtime. Sure, the Falcons' questionable play calling helped, but as crazy as it sounds, the Patriots were prepared for this extreme hurry-up contingency.

Removing time-outs from the game would place greater importance on practicing real-time clock control. Doesn't it seem weird to you that basketball coaches have to call a time-out to set up the final play of the game? Shouldn't the team have been trained in such a situation already? No team in the NFL spends more time preparing for those moments than the Patriots. From the first day of off-season training to the last weekend, Belichick has his team working on end-of-game situations, and never is a time-out part of the scenario. He wants his team to believe that time-outs are unnecessary. So yes, in my future, the Patriots already have an advantage.

One thing won't ever change: Athletes will never stop getting bigger, stronger, and faster. Jim Hines, an Olympic sprinter in 1998, was the first human to break 10 seconds in the 100 meters. Fifty years ago his 9.95 was considered the limit of human performance. Today he'd finish almost 11 feet behind Usain Bolt. That's a huge gap; he might not even be on the TV screen at the tape.

Athletic evolution, coupled with today's more advanced training methods, has altered expectations and performance. There's no reason to believe that continuing advances in training and technology won't extend human limits even further. So the question becomes: How will tomorrow's superhero-style athletes change the way football is played?

Well, player size won't change the way linemen do their job on either side of the ball. Big and strong is what their game is all about, so bigger and stronger won't rearrange the dynamic much. Maybe the left tackle isn't the marquee line position it once was now that there are athletic defenders rushing the quarterback from so many different angles, but for the most part these agile hulks will keep on fighting for territory in the trenches as they always have. But skill players? They're a totally different story. As they get more athletic and even better at what they do, offensive schemes will evolve to maximize their talents. When that happens, football will react the way it always does: by looking into the past to see its future.

Most of you reading this will be too young to remember the single wing's heyday. That formation featured an unbalanced line and three skill players in the backfield. Sometimes the quarterback would line up behind a tackle or guard, and the tailback would line up behind the center and take the direct snap. Think of that crucial fourth-down call in Super Bowl LII when tight end Trey Burton passed the ball to quarterback Nick Foles, who had shifted out of the normal quarterback spot. It looked like a backyard play or something from the football future, but it was actually just a variation of the century-old single wing.

Carl Snavely, the college Hall of Fame coach who had a 180–96–16 record in his years at Bucknell, North Carolina, Cornell, and Washington University in St. Louis, once said about the formation first invented by Glenn "Pop" Warner: "There is no way to improve on football beyond the unbalanced line single-wing." Well, sorry, Carl, but Bill Walsh would like to disagree. That said, with so many talented athletes these days, offensive position designations may become something for the history books, filed next to Hines's 100-meter time. Futuristic football will simply designate all nonlinemen on offense as interchangeable "skilled players," all of them capable of throwing, catching, or running with the ball. And guess what the best system is for such a scheme? Yup, the single wing. For more than 50 years football has been slowly evolving back to its roots in rugby, and I for one can't wait to see what happens next.

Basketball is evolving in a similar fashion. Ben Simmons, the Philadelphia 76ers point guard prodigy, is still an outlier at 6'10", but he's a lot less of one than he would have been just a few years ago. These days on the hardwood, more and more players can play anywhere. We watch center-size point guards pass to small-forward-size centers. Someday all of football will look the same way. In some places, it's already started. Programs identify both the Eagles' Zach Ertz and the Chiefs' Travis Kelce as tight ends on the basis of their size, but they're really much more like wide receivers, lining up all over the field. Tight end has evolved from a glorified extra tackle to a unique skill position. It's a trend that will continue. Eventually, there will be a similar positional response on defense—smaller, faster linebackers or bigger, stronger cornerbacks—to cover those massive receivers disguised as tight ends. If you push this theory a little more, who knows, we might eventually see Ben Simmons types at wideout being covered by 6'10" corners. Hey, I can remember when 6'5" was too tall to be fast. Give the giraffes a little more time, and they'll be up to speed and running the West Coast offense, and our game will be one step closer to basketball on grass.

How about this: Imagine if the Texans had a pair of Deshaun Watsons—two highly and equally skilled quarterbacks who were equally dangerous with the ball in their hands. Think of the stress you could put on the defense with both of those players on the field at the same time. Defensive coordinators would have no idea what to do. On one down, Watson 1 might be a passer throwing to Watson 2. On the next, Watson 2 might line up as a running back who fakes a sweep, pulls up, and throws an 80-yard bomb to Watson 1, who originally was lined up behind center.

This, of course, would force the defense to attack differently. They'd have to defend players instead of plays. There would be a ton of man coverage and a need for the same kind of multidimensional players on defense, because you'd never really know who was going to control the ball or where it might be going. Meanwhile, I bet owners would like a game populated with such human Swiss Army knives because the high cost of quarterbacks would sink when all but the most versatile skill position guys would have the same value. Instead of one quarterback making $10 million, you'd have 10 quasi-QBs making $1 million each. Which plan seems more sustainable?

Today's teams won't platoon quarterbacks because most coaches—and schemes—are heavily dependent on a reliable consistency under center and in the passing game. But as Al Davis once said to me, "I'd rather be right than consistent," and the future will agree with Al: Consistency will take a backseat to scoring points. Classic drop-back passers are already getting harder and harder to find. Quarterback launch points are becoming more varied—not just behind the center but behind the tackle or the guard or even outside the pocket near the sideline. And so eventually there will be much more movement in the backfield. First down will look like a Harlem Globetrotters weave drill: players sprinting in every direction, handing the ball off from one player to the next before Watson 1 launches a bomb to Watson 2.

Come on, how much fun would that be to watch—even for only 48 minutes?!

n 1985, Feng-hsiung Hsu was a graduate student at Carnegie Mellon, developing a computer that could play chess well enough to compete against a grand master. The project, first called "chip test," eventually got Hsu hired by IBM, and in 1996 the fruits of his team's labor, Deep Blue, faced off against Garry Kasparov, arguably the greatest (human) chess player ever. Kasparov won that match, but a year later Deep Blue won the rematch. Artificial intelligence had proved itself more potent than the human brain, at least in chess.

I can't help wondering when that will happen in football. Computers have revolutionized just about every aspect of our lives—from phones to music to maps—and there are times when it seems like football is the last holdout against technology. That's just not sustainable.

In my vision of football's future, artificial intelligence will help coaches not only on Sunday but through the week. After all, I think chess and football have much in common, starting with the constant moves and countermoves that are the trademark of both. Deep Blue can simulate 200 million possible positions at a time.

That kind of computer power sure would be useful on Sundays in the NFL. (I can promise you Deep Blue would not call a time-out with 2:05 left in the game.)

There's definitely potential here even if the comparison is not exact. Chess is one move at a time; football has 22 moving parts. Chess has no weather concerns, no injury reports, and no field position issues, either. Still, think about it: Our kids hold tiny devices in their hands with almost as much computing power as Deep Blue, yet coaches still rely on a hand-drawn chart to decide when to attempt a two-point conversion. Seems practically medieval, right? (Like, say, using two sticks and a link of chain for the most important measurement in the game.) Computers already have infiltrated football to some degree, but mostly for predictive stuff: win probabilities, fourth-down charts, and such. I don't think we are far away at all from a time when computers call plays, not coaches. Deep Blue analyzed billions of games in seconds to come up with the best possible moves for each particular situation presented by Kasparov. Surely it could match wits with the likes of Rex Ryan.

Okay, the teams would need NFL approval to access their AI, on game day at least. During the week, though, there would be no limitations on computer use, not for helping with the game plan, not for devising new ways to attack. Make no mistake, play callers would benefit from midweek data crunching and game simulations. Lots of offensive play callers in the NFL watch a college game on Saturday night with their own call sheet in front of them to respond to game situations and help get their minds right for Sunday. It's a good enough mental workout, but doesn't it make way more sense to use the unlimited power of a computer-generated game simulation to prepare?

Advancements in computer science and technology may begin to pop up in other areas of football first, such as game and practice film. Some team will be the first to put cameras on every player in practice, so instead of watching one video of all 22 players on the field, coaches will be able to home in on each individual player. The more detailed practice film gets, the more assistant coaches will be able to improve their teaching skills with things such as safer tackling technique. Imagine this: During a break, a player takes off his helmet and downloads the video of his last series to a screen on his wristband so that he can review it, study it, and learn from it. Because it is instantaneous, he can immediately put what he's discovered into action on the very next play instead of waiting until Monday to figure out what went wrong.

Are you skeptical about these ideas? That's okay. I was skeptical that Batman's map could pinpoint the exact location of Catwoman's secret lair. Now we have maps on our phones that talk to us, show us satellite images from space of the restaurant we trying to find, and warn us when there's a guy with a flat tire up ahead. I'm just saying.

In any case, tune in tomorrow, same Bat Time, same Bat Channel.

Al Davis always liked to remind me that working in football is a lifelong commitment, not just a profession. Now I see how right he was. As long as you're involved in the game, you need to keep pushing. From the moment I turned on the engine in Bill Walsh's Porsche, I was given a firsthand look at the advantages of curiosity, continued study, and constant growth. Turns out that those car-ride classrooms were as much about life lessons as they were about football instruction.

I hope I have been at least somewhat effective at passing those lessons on to you. I wrote this book because I wanted to show fans of the game I love what it really takes to build a championship team—to build a successful enterprise of any kind, for that matter. Belichick always tells his players that they need to take the classroom to the field. The rest of us do, too. To my mind, the most important lessons boil down to a handful of ideas that are as powerful as they are simple.

CULTURE COMES FIRST. You can have the best game plan (or strategy or tactics), the best team (or product or service), and the best players (or engineers or salespeople), and you may achieve short-term success. But if you haven't created an underlying ecosystem of excellence, short-term success is all it will ever be.

PRESS EVERY EDGE ALL THE TIME, BECAUSE ANY EDGE MAY MATTER ANYTIME. The great ones understand that a focus on details is crucial not because they know what will matter when but because they don't.

SYSTEMS OVER STARS. Obviously, I have seen some super-stars up close in my day: Jerry Rice, Joe Montana, Tom Brady. But superstar is the second way I'd describe each. The first is "superb system guy." Talent matters, but willingness to buy into the program matters more.

LEADERSHIP IS A LONG-TERM PROPOSITION. Devotion to the process has to matter more than chasing the score. True leaders always value sustainable success over quick fixes. Much as empire builders such as Warren Buffet and Jeff Bezos have ignored the quarter-to-quarter earnings game, dynastic coaches ignore all distractions—fan pressure, media scrutiny, player grumbling—once they are convinced that a decision is right for their team.

YOU'RE NEVER DONE GETTING BETTER. Greatness over time is in direct correlation to growth over time, and growth over time requires finding new ways to do the same old things. Real leaders, real achievers, real champions are never done learning.

Real front-office guys, too. I may no longer be employed by the league, but the game is still an important part of me, and it always will be. These days, I am teaching my two grandsons, Dominic and Leo, all about this great game. And to do that I have to keep learning, especially from my mistakes. That's one reason I have a category of people I call "change-my-mind guys." At first glance, this group of players and coaches didn't impress me all that much. But over time they forced me to reevaluate them. It can be a humbling exercise. And at this stage of my career, I can tell you, these change-my-mind guys often end up leaving the biggest impressions.

Malcolm Butler is one of my all-time favorite change-my-mind guys. When I was with the Patriots, we originally signed Butler on little more than a "look-see" deal. And the next time I looked, I saw a guy who had won us a Super Bowl. After more than 30 years in the business, Butler finally changed my mind about scouting talent from smaller schools.

My latest change-my-mind guy might be the greatest one of them all: Eagles head coach Doug Pederson. I freely admit that after he got the job in Philadelphia I considered him one of the worst hires ever. I mean, he was an offensive coordinator who had never even been a full-time play caller in the league. There was nothing to suggest he was worthy of or ready for a head coaching job. Honestly, nothing he did in his first season in Philadelphia—where he basically just copied the Chiefs' attack—caused me to rethink my assessment. But in the 2017 season, the originality of his offense and the leadership, teaching skills, and game planning he showed while winning the Super Bowl with a backup QB were nothing short of masterly. I want to say one more time to him and the football world: Man, was I wrong.

But that's the thing: After it's all said and done, football is really a game of surprises.

I'll be sure to let Dominic and Leo know that.

It will be lesson number one in our first car-ride classroom.

# ACKNOWLEDGMENTS

Sophocles wrote: "One must wait until the evening to see how splendid the day has been." In the evening of my incredibly fortunate career in the NFL, I can now say the days have been splendid, mostly because of the many people who helped along the way. If I'm honest, the following printed thank-yous don't begin to represent how strongly I feel them in my heart. But here goes.

First and foremost, I want to extend my sincerest thanks and most profound love to my wife, Millie; my two sons, Mick and Matthew, and their beautiful wives, Michelle and Julie; and my two remarkable grandsons, Dominic Anthony and Leo Stanley. Without Millie, there would be no family and no book. Through the years, she has made so many sacrifices for the good of our family with love and incredible support; I could not have found a better life-loving partner. And I am blessed to call my two boys my best friends. I cannot wait to watch them as they fill out their football careers.

Because she was the first person to encourage me to read and write, I want to thank my mother, Jane, who would have been beyond excited to open this book. Writing it reminded me of my childhood, of the way she pushed me to chase my dreams. For that, I will be forever grateful. Also, thanks to my 91-year-old father, Mike, who still cuts hair every day, continuing to demonstrate the incredible work ethic I can only try to duplicate; to my in-laws who have since passed away, Big Stosh and Lucille, as they always made me feel like their son and supported my every move (of which there were plenty); and to my brothers-in-law Mike Kluzinski (with his wife, Yeimy, and my niece Michelle), and the late Stanley Kluzinski, who always cheered loudly.

To my sisters, Marie and Annette; Marie's husband, Tom; Annette's daughter, Brianna: thank you. Thanks to my uncle Mike Palermo, who passed away this year, as well as his wife, Betty, for being guiding influences throughout my life. So, too, to my cousin Vince Lombardi, his deceased wife, Nina, and their children, Alyssa, Nick, and Joe, as well as Susan. They've always been my most loyal fans. And to the self-proclaimed mayor of the boardwalk in Ocean City, New Jersey, Sal Deldeo, and his wife, Barbara, who passed away last year, I owe sincere thank-yous and appreciation for their never-ending support, as well as to my aunt Gloria.

Speaking of great support, the entire Nolan family has given me much-needed help in many ways: Pat, Bernadette, Justin, Melissa, Katie, Mike, Patrick, Michael, Vincent, and Lilly have become my extended family. The Barry family—my second mother, Marie; her deceased husband, Gerry; and their entire family—have been a real source of encouragement and support. As have the Bradys, from Paul to Susan to Leah to Shane to Jake, as well as the Galantes: Tony, Janet, Joey, and Michael. The Lindquist family: Kurt, Mary, Jeff, Emily, and Cadan; the Greene family: Bobby, Genny, and James; and finally the Baxters: Rick, Debbie, Chelsea, Kyle, Lindsay, and Courtney—a heartfelt thank-you to all.

Some thanks need to be extended to others who passed away

before this book became a reality. Their impact on my life has been everlasting: Mike Salveski and Roger Sicoli, my high school coaches; Bob Karmelowicz and Bob Owens at UNLV, my first coaching mentors; Ernie Plank, the former 49ers scout who treated me like a son and shared his wisdom; Tony Razzano, the man who hired me in San Francisco, as well as the Niners scouts Neil Schmidt, Bob Whitman, and Billy Wilson, all of whom were so very generous with their knowledge; Allen Webb, the 49ers pro personnel director, who was forever answering my annoying questions and helped me learn how to study football; Bobb McKittrick, the team's offensive line coach, whose lessons about pass protection schemes I still remember; Norb Hecker, a Packers assistant under Vince Lombardi, who was as kind and helpful as his movie hero John Wayne was manly; Robert Albo, Raiders team doctor, one of the most caring men with one of the hardest handshakes; Browns owner Art Modell, who was funny and generous and always called me "kid," which I loved; and Dom Anile, head coach at C. W. Post and director of personnel for the Colts and Panthers, who helped us develop Cleveland's grading and player procurement systems. Joel Buchsbaum was the first draftnik to become my friend and a source of valuable information. I still miss him and often reach for the phone to call his 718 exchange during draft time.

It goes without saying, but I'll type it nonetheless, that this book would not have been possible without Bill Walsh, who let me inside what is arguably the most important organization in the modern football era and taught me so much about so many aspects of the game and leadership. I am likewise indebted to Al Davis, for bringing me into his vaunted organization. Both men affected my life substantially, and their impact is manifest on every page of this book.

My career changed on February 5, 1991, when Bill Belichick was named the head coach of the Browns. Our professional partnership and our personal friendship over the past 25 years have been as enriching as they have been rewarding, which is saying something. Imagine the good fortune at being able to call the greatest coach of all time my friend.

I want to acknowledge some other coaches I played for along the way—for their patience, passion, and willingness to teach the game: Ed Woolley, Bill Leete, Micky Kwiatkowski, Frank Guthridge, Jim Burner, and John Cervino. All my teammates at Ocean City High School, Valley Forge Military Academy, and Hofstra University deserve thanks as well, but in particular: Glen Wagner, Carmen Costanza, Johnny Cervino, Al Burch, Rick Moretti, Jim Chadwick, Joe Tyrell, Mike Ricketts, Fred Serino, Joe Buontempo, Dennis Pezzolesi, Peter Barcia, Frank Bianchini, Rich Petillo, Bud Rinck, and Ira Smith.

I wrote so many letters to college head coaches from my dorm room at Hofstra that I must have been annoying to many. But each letter I sent to then Florida State head coach Bobby Bowden was always returned with a kind word. I never worked for Bowden, but I will always remember his encouragement. And another person I have tried to meet and thank personally for his words and inspirations is "The Boss," Bruce Springsteen. I have been backstage numerous times to thank him, and each time I've come up short. Therefore, since it may never happen, I must thank him on these pages, because without his musical advice I might never have had that meeting across the river, or ever crossed Highway Nine.

In Las Vegas, Harvey Hyde at UNLV was like a second father to me, and not just because he gave me my first paying job in football. Others at UNLV who deserve my gratitude are Ron Mims, Barry Lamb, Pat Hill, Scott O'Brien, Al Tanara, Randy Whitsitt, Tim Wilson, Tim Grugrich, and Mark Warkentein.

In San Francisco, as you might imagine, the list of those who lent me a hand in one way or another is long. It starts with Hall of Fame owner Edward J. DeBartolo Jr. At my first-ever Super Bowl, he saw that my parents were with me at the game, ripped my tickets out of my hand, and replaced them with three much-improved seats. His generosity is legendary, with good reason. Others deserving thanks are John McVay, Carmen Policy, John Galetka, Paul Hackett, George Seifert, Bill McPherson, Ray Rhodes, Neal Dahlan, Fred von Appen, Mike Holmgren, Sherman Lewis, Jerry Walker, Rodney Knox, Bronco Hinek, and Tommy Hart.

Many players on the Niners were also patient with a kid trying to become a scout: Joe Montana, Matt Cavanaugh, Dwight Clark, Roger Craig, Mike Wilson, Randy Cross, Guy McIntyre, Keith Fahnhorst, Dwaine Board, Manu Tuiasosopo, Michael Carter, Ronnie Lott, Eric Wright, Keena Turner, and the great Charles Haley, to name a few.

In Cleveland, general manager Ernie Accorsi taught me the inner workings of a front office. Marty Schottenheimer, head coach at the time, made every team he guided better. Other Cleveland-era shout-outs go to Bill Cowher, Howard Mudd, Joe Pendry, Kurt Schottenheimer, Kirk Ferentz, Mike Sheppard, Richard Mann, Gary Tranquill, Steve Crosby, Ernie Adams, Kevin Spencer, Jim Bates, Al Groh, Jacob Burney, Woody Widenhofer, Jerry Simmons, Jim Schwartz, Eric Mangini, Ozzie Newsome, Scott Pioli, Tom Dimitroff, Thomas Dimitroff, Gary Horton, John Lombardi, Ellis Rainsberger, Phil Savage, Pat Moore, Sam Deluca, Dan Sagney, and George Kokinis. My one year working for the Haslam family was too short, and I wished things would have been different, but the Haslams were kind, were generous to my family, and deserve my recognition, starting with Big Jim Haslam, Jimmy, Dee, Steve, and Ann Bailey. Thank you.

My time with the Browns was also the beginning of my invaluable relationship with Nick Saban, from whom I've learned so much, and Rick Venturi, who helped me as I wrote this book when my memory failed. Venturi knows football as well as any human on the planet, and I cherish our conversations. And my friendship with Jerry Angelo gave me many scouting tips and helped me learn about life on the road.

In Philadelphia, Eagles owner Jeffrey Lurie entrusted me to run his 1998 draft with help from Bryan Broaddus, a dear friend, as well as Bobby Depaul, Dan Shonka, Sean Payton, David Shaw, Danny Smith, Mike Trgovac, John Harbaugh, and Emmitt Thomas—what a privilege. Joe Banner, who hired me in Philadelphia and Cleveland, is one of the smartest men I have worked with during my time in the NFL.

In Oakland, Al Davis was far from the only person who made a difference. I enjoyed working with Amy Trask, Dan Ventrelle, Rod Martin, Scotty Toucet, Ed Dodds, Jack Barhite, Sherratt Reicher, Pete Caracciolo, Mark Artega, Paul Kelly, Chet Franklin, Jim and John Otten, Mike Ornstein, Dave Nash, Tom Delaney, and the late great George "Run Run" Jones, who made every day in Raiderland a treat. Also, Bill Callahan (still one of my favorite coaches to watch work), Jon Gruden, Mike Waufle, Ron Lynn, Chuck Pagano, Don Martindale, Rob Ryan, Norv Turner, John Morton, Aaron Kromer, Jim Harbaugh, Skip Peete, Willie Brown, Jeff Fish, Garrett Giemont, Chuck Bresnahan, Bob Casullo, Fred Pagac, Gary Stephans, Fred Biletnikoff, Marc Trestman, Jim McElwain, Bill Romanowski, John Shoop, and, of course, my dear friend and summertime partner, Rich Gannon. But the most profound impact came from my friendship with Marc Badain, the current Raiders president. Badain has always been smart and funny, and like the little brother I never had.

In New England, there are so many to recognize, starting with owner Robert Kraft, and his sons, Jonathan and Dan. Then there's Josh McDaniels, Chad O'Shea, Ivan Fears, Dave "Guge" DeGugliemimo, Brian Daboll, Matt Patricia, Pat Graham, Steven Belichick, Brian Flores, Josh Boyer, Brandan Daly, Dante Scarnecchia, Joe Judge, Jack Easterby, Nick Cesario, Harold Nash, Moses Cabera, Jerry Schuplinski, Nick Caley, Nancy Meier, Monti Ossenfort, Matt Groh, Brian Smith, Bob Quinn, James Lipfert, Dujuan Daniels, Tim Heffelfinger, Jonathan Howard, Frank Ross, David Ziegler, Patrick Stewart, Ronnie McGill, Steve Cargile, Berj Najarian, Jim Whalen, Joe Van Allen, Ted Harper, Brandon Murphy and his grandfather Murph, Jimmy Dee, Fernando Neto, Jared Rita, Teddy Ciopper, and Brandon Yeargan.

I owe thanks to all the players representing the Patriots during my time in New England, starting with the hardest-working and most dedicated athlete I have ever watched work, Tom Brady. Brady is a megastar with a humble manner, and I appreciate his friendship, as well as that of Julian Edelman, who was always asking how he could become a better receiver. Each member of those teams during my two-plus-year-stay in New England are worthy of my sincere and humble thank-you. A fantastic group of men.

For their encouragement and support throughout the dangerous process of writing, I'd like to thank Gary Belsky and Neil Fine; they were terrific. Jim Nantz has been a cherished friend, adviser, and supporter, for which I am eternally grateful. I often say, as nice as Nantz appears on television, he is even nicer in person, if that is even possible. Thanks also to Shane Parrish, Tom Crean, Bob Boland, Ken Scigulinsky, Jay Kelleher, Will Hill, Jimmy Sexton, Greg Schiano, Earl Myers, Mike Gottfried, Sean Sweeney, Fran Frascella, Eric Musselman, Gil Brandt, Rick Gosselin, Dr. Anthony, Dr. Steven, Ryan Holiday, and Peter Abate for their friendship and wisdom. My editor, Mary Reynics, has been a great resource and helping hand, but she wouldn't have had anything to do if my agent, David Larabell, hadn't first made this book happen. I owe much to Bill Simmons for his guidance, and to my podcast partner, Tate Frazier, video producer Joel Solomon, and all the others at The Ringer. I genuinely appreciate their support. And this section would not be complete without my many thanks and love to Bella and Lana, who were with me each step of the writing process—albeit with a few cookies and walking breaks.

I reserve final thanks to Peter Kaufman, whose magnanimous generosity, kind spirit, and enthusiasm for knowledge allowed me to write this book. Peter, who spends his life helping others, has helped me more than I can express.

# INDEX

Adams, Ernie, x, 193–194
Adams, Jamal, 244–245
Allen, George, 232–233
Amendola, Danny, 130, 174, 199, 200, 234
announcers, pet peeves committed by, 212–215, 217–218
Arizona Cardinals, 29–30, 78
assessing players. *See* evaluating and drafting players

Baltimore Ravens, Patriots planning for. *See* game planning, playoffs (2014 bye week)
Barnett, Gary, 45, 48
Bates, Jim, 8, 152
Battleship football, 219–220
Becker, John, 31
Belichick, Bill. *See also* game planning, playoffs; special teams; What would Belichick do? (WWBD)
    ability to spot QBs, 112
    author, this book and, 8, 226–228
    blaming self for losses, 168

Brady and. *See* Belichick, Bill, Brady and
Cleveland vs. New England, 40–41, 42
coaches not getting enough credit and, 220–224
coaching style, 3–4
command of opportunity and, 40–41, 42
command of self and, 38
on commitment, 35–36
culture importance, 26
decision-making of, 3, 73, 83, 85, 178, 186, 232–238
defense and, 138–144, 145–147, 149–150, 151–153, 154, 158, 160, 161, 162–165, 166
demanding truth, 174
dream dinner with Saban and, 138–142
father's influence on, 94–95
five-tool leadership points, 4
"game show" interaction style, 14–15

Belichick, Bill (*cont.*)
  goal-line defense makeover
    (3-corner defense), 2–5
  greatness legacy, 229
  interactions with, purpose of, 174
  moving forward, living in the
    present, 230
  moving on from veterans, 233–235,
    236–238
  offense and, 112, 117–118, 135–136
  overview of author's career with, 2
  "padding" games, 146–147
  postseason success, 167, 168
  practices without pads, 248–249
  quizzing staff and players, 14–15,
    168–169
  Rams coach recommendation, 45,
    48, 49
  Randy Moss and, 77–78
  Saban and, 8, 24, 49, 97, 138–143,
    152, 154, 228
  scouting, assessing, and drafting
    players, 73, 74–75, 77–78, 79–80,
    81–86, 89, 136
  in search of answers/solutions,
    83–85
  season-end autopsy and player
    evaluations, 81–86
  seeking, developing toughness,
    96, 97
  self-awareness of, 231
  self-motivation of, 230
  Super Bowl XLIX win background,
    1, 2–5, 36
  as teacher, 82–83, 147, 231
  truth importance to, 174
  value of, the "Belichick game" and,
    223
  virtues and work habits, 229–231
  as Warren Buffett of coaching,
    226
Belichick, Bill, Brady and, 40–41. *See
  also* Brady, Tom
  Belichick's rules and, 43, 196
  finding Brady's replacement,
    85–86, 134–135, 136–137
  Garoppolo and, 85–86, 135–137,
    185, 236–238
  signature scouting sessions,
    176–177
  trick plays and, 174–175, 181, 193,
    199–200
Belichick, Steve, 94–95

Bell, Nick, 108–109
biases, NFL draft and, 70–74
Bidwill, Bill, 29–30
Bledsoe, Drew, 135, 226, 233–234
Bortles, Blake, 72, 135
Brace, Ron, 73
Brady, Paul, 87
Brady, Tom. *See also* Belichick, Bill,
    Brady and
  age and caring for body, 247
  beating, 131
  bye week practices (2014 playoffs),
    184, 188
  football intelligence and, 130–131
  innate ability of, 132
  vs. Ravens (2014 playoffs), 199, 201
  relating to younger teammates, 84
  rushers and, 182
  thick skin, quarterbacks and, 128
  throwing in wind, 188
  trust between receivers and, 178
  watching tape and, 130–131
Brandt, Gil, 134
Brooks, Herb, 101–102
Brooks, Rich, 31, 34, 48–49
Brown, Eddie, 67, 87
Brown, Mike, 80
Brown, Paul, 10, 156–157
Browner, Brandon, 165–166, 184
Butler, Malcolm, 5, 82, 258

Caldwell, David, 72
Cameron, Cam, 45
Campanaro, Michael, 191–192, 196,
    201
"card players," 71–72
Carpool Karaoke, of Walsh, 8, 13–14,
    15, 23, 256
carriage/body language, of QBs, 133
Carroll, Pete, 1, 5, 45, 48
Carson, Bud, 106, 227
Carter, Virgil, 116–117, 118, 119–120,
    121
"the Catch," 122
change-my-mind guys, 258–259
checkdowns, in two-minute drill,
    206–207
Cincinnati Bengals, West Coast
    offense and, 116–126
Clark, Dwight, 122
clock management and time-outs,
    future of, 250–251
clock management irritants

calling time-out with 2:05 on clock,
    204–206
not considering all factors, 208–209
not giving themselves a chance,
    212–213
throwing checkdowns in two-
    minute drill, 206–207
trying to run back kick from end
    zone, 209–210
coaching staff
    hiring head coach. *See* leadership,
        coaching and
    not getting enough credit, 220–224
    Walsh approach to hiring, 20–23
Collins, La'el, 78–79
command, of coaches. *See* leadership,
    coaching and
complacency, combating (WWBD),
    229–232
Cousins, Kirk, 126–127
Cowher, Bill, 44
Craig, Jim, 101–102
culture, importance of, 16–17, 23–26,
    257. *See also* Standard of
    Performance
cut-blocks, 179, 184, 196

Daniels, Owen, 182, 183, 188, 191, 199,
    200, 201
Davis, Al
    author, this book and, 8
    author's career and relationship
        with, 2, 8, 28–29
    on being right rather than
        consistent, 253–254
    blitzing perspective, 156
    feud with Modell, 29
    "game show" interaction style, 14
    "scholarship players" and, 72–73
    scouting, assessing, and drafting
        players, 66–68, 69, 70, 72,
        76–77
    special teams philosophy, 98–100
    trying to change work ethic, 129
    Walsh learning from, 28
    Walsh with draft picks to beat,
        90, 91
    West Coast offense origins and,
        123
Davis, Butch, 45
DeBartolo, Eddie, Jr., 17–18, 64, 115
decisions, Belichick making. *See*
    Belichick, Bill

defense, 138–166
    Belichick and, 138–144, 145–147,
        149–150, 151–153, 154, 158, 160,
        161, 162–165, 166
    dream dinner about, 138–142
    knowledge of, for successful
        offense, 117–118
    Mike backer location and, 158
    quarterback movement on third
        down and, 160–162
    Red 2, 141, 148–149
    run-pass option and, 140
    Walsh and, 138, 147, 159
    West Coast offense messing with,
        123–124
defense, essential rules of, 142–166
    defuse explosive plays, 153–154
    disguise importance, 142–144
    disrupt timing of opponents,
        151–153
    eliminate four-point plays, 159–162
    games won/lost in final four
        minutes, 162–165
    make offense play left-handed,
        149–150
    remember Newton's second law (of
        motion), 154–155
    study the offense, 144–147
    talking, adjusting as requirement,
        165–166
    teach defense, not coach it, 147–149
    think pressure first, sacks second,
        155–159
Dillman, Bradford, 92
disguises, 142–144, 253
disguising defense, 142–144
Ditka, Mike, 44
drafting players. *See* evaluating and
    drafting players

Edelman, Julian, 174, 188, 198–199,
    200
edge, pressing, 257
eight-man front, getting too much
    credit, 215–216
Eisenhower, Dwight D., 232
"Emeril Lagasse Theory," 25–26
evaluating and drafting players, 63–93
    Belichick and, 73, 74–75, 77–78,
        79–80, 81–86, 89, 136
    biases and, 70–74
    "card player" practice squaders,
        71–72

evaluating and drafting players (*cont.*)
  character assessment and, 74–81
  Davis and, 66–68, 69, 70, 72, 76–77
  first rule of scouting and, 70
  football intelligence and, 70–71
  49ers' epic draft (1986), 63–66,
    87–93
  future of skill players and, 251–253
  importance before free agency, 64
  locker room and quality of
    players, 73
  moving on from mistakes, 73–74
  pedigree and prep play importance,
    66–67
  preparation and approaches, 65–70.
    *See also* biases and; character
    assessment and
  salary cap and, 64
  scouting blinders and, 72–73
  season-end autopsy and off-season
    evaluations, 81–86
  Senior Bowl and, 69–70, 227
  success rates and screw-ups, 73–74.
    *See also* quarterbacks, predicting
    success of
  team chemistry and, 73
  track and field experience and,
    67–69
  trading down and, 88–90
  Troutwine's TAP profile and,
    79–80
  Walsh and, 64–65, 66, 67–69, 86,
    87–93

Fangio, Vic, 45, 48
Favre, Brett, 129–130
Ferentz, Kirk, 8, 35
field goals, pet-peeve decisions on,
  211–212
Flacco, Joe, 187, 188, 190, 200, 201
Flores, Brian, 5
four-point plays, eliminating, 159–162
French, Roger, 21, 22
Frey, Glenn, 42
future of football, 241–259. *See also*
    player health
  *Batman* analogy, 241–242
  computer science and, 254–256
  keeping football alive, 242
  platooning QBs, 253–254
  player size and athleticism, 251
  shorter game, longer half, 249–250
  single wing and, 252

skill player interchangeability,
  251–253
time-outs and clock management,
  250–251

Gailey, Chan, 45, 48
game planning, playoffs (2014 bye
    week), 167–201. *See also specific
    player names*
  about: preparatory phase of,
    167–176
  adapting during game and,
    198–199
  *American Sniper*, Chris Kyle and,
    175–176, 187
  analysis of Patriots' previous
    playoff performances, 170–174
  avoiding complacency, 169
  bye week balance and, 168
  coaches' meetings, 177–180,
    185–186, 188, 192–193, 195–196
  concern about Ravens, 170, 179
  cut-block avoidance and, 179, 184,
    196
  day six before kickoff, 176–180
  day five before kickoff, 180–183
  day four-and-a-half before kickoff,
    183–186
  day four before kickoff, 187–188
  day three before kickoff, 189–190
  day two before kickoff, 190–192
  day one before kickoff, 192–196
  day of game (pregame), 196–197
  day of game (game time), 198–201
  evenness and focus of Belichick,
    187
  experience vs. preparation,
    169–170
  field/playing conditions and, 183,
    184, 186
  "gotta have it" plays, 182, 189,
    190–191, 200, 201
  hidden yards and, 181
  inactives and, 177, 188
  keeping things simple, 183
  kicking game and, 178–179, 181
  long-ball defense, 190
  not knowing opponent, 170
  "Opportunity Period," 185
  penalty alert, 189–190
  practice-review session, 186
  rushers of the Ravens and, 182–183,
    195

signature skull session with Brady,
176–177
stopping the run, 181–182
summary and recommendations
for, 170–174
tennis racket defense drills, 172,
184
three things Belichick always
includes, 170
time management importance,
170–172
trick plays, 174–175, 181, 193,
199–200
truth importance to Belichick,
174
"game show" interaction styles,
14–15
Gannon, Rich, 37, 113–114
Garoppolo, Jimmy, 85–86, 135–137,
185, 236–238
Gibbs, Joe, 143–144
Gottfried, Mike, 106
greatness, lesson about, 257–258
Green, Denny, 44
Griffin, Don, 91–92
Groh, Al, 152
Gronkowski, Rob, 169, 177, 188, 193,
195, 198
Gruden, Jon, 36–37, 45, 114, 221–222

Hackett, Paul, 20–21
Haley, Charles, 19–20
Hallman, Harold, 92–93
Harbaugh, Jim, 39
Harbaugh, John, 39, 200
Harmon, Ronnie, 87, 88
head coach, hiring. See also leadership,
coaching and
finding, recommending coaching
candidates for Rams, 34–35,
43–50
report recommending coach for
Rams, 44–49
"Vienna problem," 45–46
head coach, hiring, questions to ask
candidates, 51–62
about: overview of, 51
on coaches, support staff, 58–61
on off-season, 52–53
on organization, 61–62
on philosophy (general), 52
on regular season, 55–57
on training camp/preseason, 53–54

health. See player health
Hernandez, Aaron, 79
hidden yards, 181
high school (prep) play, 66–67
Hill, Pat, 8
Hock, Dee, 23
Holmgren, Mike, 21–22, 23, 44, 47,
113–114
Hoomanawanui, Michael, 177–178

Infante, Lindy, 23
innate ability, of QBs, 132–133
intelligence, football, 70–71, 118,
130–132
Irvin, Michael, 103, 153

Johnson, Bill, 123
Johnson, Jimmy, 44
Jones, Jacoby, 187–188
Jones, James, 105, 109, 110
Jones, Julio, 150

Kennedy, Robert F., 232
kickoffs, running out of end zone,
209–210
Kubiak, Gary, 45, 182, 186, 195

LaFell, Brandon, 174, 183, 201
Lagasse, Emeril, 25–26
LaMonte, Bob, 47
leadership, coaching and
Belichick and, 4, 40–41, 42. See also
Belichick, Bill
as long-term proposition, 257
Patton movie and, 43
St. Louis Rams and, 27–28,
30–32
Walsh and. See Walsh, Bill
leadership, pillars of, 35–43
command of opportunity, 40–42
command of self, 38–39
command of the message, 37
command of the process, 42–43
command of the room, 35–37
leadership, quarterbacks and,
134–137
lessons learned, this book, 8, 256–259
Levy, Marv, 35, 41–42, 44
Lewis, Marvin, 80–81
Lewis, Michael, 70
Lewis, Ray, 75–76
Lewis, Sherman, 45
Lockette, Ricardo, 5

Lombardi, Michael
  background and perspective on
    Belichick, 8, 226–228
  job search following 1995 season,
    28–33
  lessons learned, this book and, 8,
    256–259
  Modell-Davis feud and, 29
  youth and football calling, 5–7
Lombardi, Vince, 6, 126, 155
Lott, Ronnie, 15, 90, 244

Mallett, Ryan, 134–135
Manning, Peyton, 128, 131, 149–150,
    152, 162–163, 185
Manziel, Johnny, 86, 129, 135,
    136
Mariota, Marcus, 126–127, 210
Mariucci, Steve, 45
Mathieu, Tyrann, 78, 79
McCourty, Devin, 3
McDaniels, Josh, 26, 135, 136, 146, 177,
    195–196, 199, 200
McDonough, Will, 87, 89, 90
McKyer, Tim, 90
McVay, John, 23, 88–90, 235–236
message, command of, 37
Metcalf, Eric, punt return anecdote,
    94–95, 96–98, 104–105, 110
middle-of-the-field reads, 216–217
Mike backer, 158
Miller, Patrick, 91, 92
Mixon, Joe, 81
Modell, Art, 29, 30, 41, 42, 81,
    193–194, 227
Montana, Joe, 13, 112–113, 122
Moore, Stevon, 98, 104, 105, 107–108
Mora, Jim, 42–43, 44
Mornhinweg, Marty, 24, 46, 47
Morton, John, 39
Moss, Randy, 76–78, 136
Mueller, Vance, 90

Nehemiah, Renaldo, 68
New England Patriots. See Belichick,
    Bill; game planning, playoffs
    (2014 bye week); special teams;
    specific players and coaches
Newsome, Ozzie, 8, 203
NFL draft. See evaluating and drafting
    players
NFL Films, 32–33
Ninkovich, Rob, 82, 168–169

Oakland Raiders. See Davis, Al;
    Gruden, Jon
O'Brien, Scott, ix, 81, 97–98, 105,
    106–108, 178–179, 186, 195
offense. See also quarterbacks references
  Belichick and, 112, 117–118,
    135–136
  defense knowledge for success of,
    117–118
  defense studying to stop, 144–147
  Walsh and, 111–126, 132, 133
opportunity, command of, 40–42
"Opportunity Period," 185
organization. See Walsh, Bill,
    organization and
Ortmayer, Steve, 27–28, 30–32
Owens, James, 112

"padding" games, 146
Parcells, Bill, 6, 37, 44, 47–48, 126, 151,
    206, 213, 238, 239
pet peeves of author, 202–224. See also
    clock management irritants
  about: perspective to observe
    strategy and, 203–204; watching
    TV sports and, 202–203
  announcer not telling us who is in
    game, 214–215
  coaches not getting enough credit,
    220–224
  eight-man front getting too much
    credit, 215–216
  making it more complicated than it
    is, 216–217
  playing Battleship football, 219–220
  receiver getting too much credit,
    217–218
  saying snow favors the run, 218–219
  settling for long field goal, 211–212
  stretching for the extra yard,
    210–211
  third and manageable as stated
    goal by announcer, 213–214
Peters, Tom, 11–12, 23, 35
Phillips, Lawrence, 75–76
player health
  equipment and, 245–246
  forward pass origin/evolution and,
    243
  healing time from injuries, 249
  injury causes and, 243–244
  longer careers and, 247
  practice routines and, 248–249

roster size and, 249
safety-first changes for, 244–245
shorter game, longer half and,
    249–250
stronger, faster players and,
    246–247
teaching fundamentals for,
    247–248
players, future and. *See* future of
    football
playoffs, preparing for. *See* game
    planning, playoffs (2014 bye
    week)
Plunkett, Jim, 10–11
Polian, Bill, 41, 152
prep (high school) play, 66–67
Prescott, Dak, 69–70
pressure, as defense priority,
    155–159
process, command of, 42–43

quarterbacks. *See also* West Coast
    offense
    backup being ready, 185
    Belichick's ability to spot, 112
    changing offense to match skill set,
        116
    importance of fitting systems, 125
    platooning, future of, 253–254
    Walsh's ability to spot, sign,
        112–116
quarterbacks, predicting success of,
    126–137
    about: overview of qualities for,
        126
    carriage/body language and, 133
    football smarts and, 118,
        130–132
    innate ability and, 132–133
    leadership and, 134–137
    success ratios, 73–74, 131–132
    thick skin and, 128
    winning habit/way and, 126–128
    work ethic and, 129–130
Quinn, Bob, 14
Quinn, Dan, 209

Rathman, Tom, 90
Razzano, David, 30–31, 32
Razzano, Tony, 91
receivers, getting too much credit,
    217–218
Reeves, Dan, 44

Reid, Andy, 47, 204–206
Revis, Darrelle, 85, 165–166
Reynolds, Danny, 5–6
Reynolds, Jack "Hacksaw," 15
Rhodes, Ray, 23–24, 39, 158–159
Rice, Jerry, 67, 87, 235
Rickey, Branch, 7, 224
Roberts, Larry, 89, 90
Robinson, Gerald, 87, 88
room, command of, 35–37
Ross, Bobby, 44
running, pet peeves related to,
    209–211, 218–219
Ryan, Matt, 150, 209
Ryan, Rex, 46

Saban, Nick, 8, 24–25, 45, 48–49, 97,
    138–143, 142, 152, 154, 175, 228
Sabol, Steve, 32
salary cap, 40, 61, 64, 157, 221
San Francisco 49ers. *See* DeBartolo,
    Eddie, Jr.; Walsh, Bill; *specific
    players and coaches*
Sapp, Warren, 81
Scales, Patrick, 178–179
Schottenheimer, Marty, 44, 103
Schwartz, Jim, ix, x, 80
scouting, first rule of, 70. *See*
    evaluating and drafting players
*In Search of Excellence* (Peters and
    Waterman), 11–12
Seger, Bob, 42
Seifert, George, 24, 25, 44, 148
self, command of, 38–39
Senior Bowl, 69–70, 227
Shaw, John, 27, 30–31, 33–34, 40, 42,
    44, 45–46, 47–49
Shazier, Ryan, 243–244
Shell, Art, 77
Silver, Nate, 73–74
Simmons, Ben, 252–253
Simmons, Bill, 225, 228
Simpson, O. J., 11
snow, saying it favors the run, 218–219
Solder, Nate, 184, 195
special teams, 94–110
    "all-in" tough-minded culture for,
        96, 97, 99, 100–104
    Belichick and, 95–98, 100, 101–102,
        104, 106, 108–109, 178–179
    Belichick-engineered punt return
        anecdote, 94–95, 96–98,
        104–105, 110

special teams (*cont.*)
  Davis and, 98–99
  game planning for 2014 playoffs
      and, 178–179, 181
  left-footed punters and, 99–100
  Scott O'Brien and, ix, 81, 97–98,
      105, 106–108, 178–179, 186, 195
  T-shirt motivation incentives,
      103–104
  U.S. Olympic hockey team
      comparison, 101–102
speed, acceleration, and impact,
    154–155
St. Louis Rams. *See also* Shaw, John
  author's *Godfather* moment with,
      27–28, 30–32
  finding, recommending coaching
      candidates for, 34–35, 43–50
  pillars of leadership and, 34–43
  report recommending coach for,
      44–49
Standard of Performance, 11–13,
    15–17, 18, 23, 26
Strat-O-Matic, 5–6
strategy, questionable. *See* clock
    management irritants; pet
    peeves of author
Suggs, Terrell, 182, 183, 195, 201
Super Bowl XLIX, 1, 2–5, 36, 81,
    161–162
systems over stars, 257

Talib, Aqib, 85
Tannehill, Ryan, 132–133
TAP (Troutwine Athletic Profile), 80
Taylor, John, 91, 235–236
Taylor, Lawrence, 169–170
teaching vs. coaching, 147–149
thick skin, QBs and, 128
Thomas, Emmitt, 45
Thomas, Joe, 10–11, 17
Thornton, John, 71–72
time management, of playoff prep,
    170–172
time-outs, future of clock management
    and, 250–251. *See also* clock
    management irritants
timing of opponent, disrupting,
    151–153
Toon, Al, 67, 87
track and field experience, 67–69
trick plays, 174–175, 181, 193, 199–200
Troutwine, Bob, 79–80

Trubisky, Mitch, 127–128
Trumpy, Bob, 123
Turner, Eric, 97, 98, 102, 104, 244

Venturi, Rick, 148–149
Vermeil, Dick, 49
"Vienna problem," 45–46
von Appen, Fred, 22

Walsh, Bill. *See also* West Coast
    offense
  ability to spot QBs, 112–116
  author, this book and, 8
  author's career and relationship
      with, 1–2, 8, 9–10, 11–12
  "beat Al Davis" draft choices, 90,
      91
  "Bill wants," 111–112
  Carpool Karaoke and, 8, 13–14, 15,
      23, 256
  changing offense to match
      quarterback, 116
  command of self and, 38
  curiosity of, 11
  decision making of, 235
  early coaching career, 10
  footwork focus of, 118–119
  on general managers of losing
      teams, 33
  genius of, 16–17
  keeping players fresh for games,
      248
  learning from Al Davis, 28
  philosophy of, 11–13
  schooling everyone, 17–18
  *The Score Takes Care of Itself* by, 16,
      116
  scouting, assessing, and drafting
      players, 64–65, 66, 67–69, 86,
      87–93
  self-awareness of, 231
  as teacher, 231–232, 239
Walsh, Bill, organization and
  attention to detail, 13, 15
  authority and hierarchy, 17–18
  avoiding "Civil War," 18
  concern for everyone, 13
  copycats and, 23–26
  culture importance, 16–17, 23–26
  "disrupting" football, 11
  excellence/perfection obsession,
      11–13
  guiding principles, 15–17

hiring/building coaching staff,
    20–23
legacy of, 13
loyalty and obedience, 20–21
owner DeBartolo and, 17–18
pass rusher draft example, 18–20
scouting and player evaluation,
    18–20
Standard of Performance, 11–13,
    15–17, 18, 23, 26
turning 49ers around, 10–11, 17
Watson, Deshaun, 127–128, 132, 139,
    253, 254
Weis, Charlie, 26
West Coast offense
    "the Catch" and, 122
    copycat failures, 23–26
    expansion of, 119–120
    features of, 119–126
    football intelligence and, 118
    footwork importance, 118–119
    inspiration and development,
        116–119
    messing with the defense,
        123–124
    passing accuracy importance, 121
    precursor to, 123
    the run as weapon of, 124–125
    T formation and, 122

timing/synchrony importance, 118,
    119
transforming NFL, 119, 121
as triangle offense, 120–121
What would Belichick do? (WWBD),
    225–240
    about: background/origin of
        concept, 225–228
    author's background and
        perspective on Belichick and, 8,
        226–228
    combating complacency, 229–232
    developing winning temperament,
        238–240
    making difficult decisions, 232–238
White, Mike, 24
Wilfork, Vince, 82, 150, 179, 235
Williams, John L., 87, 88
winning temperament, developing
    (WWBD), 238–240
winning way, 126–128
Winston, Jameis, 126–127, 128
work ethic, QBs and, 129–130
WWBD. *See* What would Belichick do?
    (WWBD)

Young, Steve, 112, 114–115

Zygmunt, Jay, 33, 44

# ABOUT THE AUTHOR

Michael Lombardi was most recently on the New England Patriots coaching staff for Bill Belichick after thirty years working in the front offices of the San Francisco 49ers, the Philadelphia Eagles, the Oakland Raiders, and the Cleveland Browns (where he was general manager). He writes for Bill Simmons's The Ringer, where he also hosts his top-ten sports podcast, *GM Street*.